Gelina Harlaftis is Associate Professor of Maritime History,
Department of History, Ionian University, Corfu

Nikos Karapidakis is Professor of Medieval History,
Department of History, Ionian University, Corfu

Kostas Sbonias is Assistant Professor of Prehistorical Archaeology,
Department of History, Ionian University, Corfu

Vaios Vaiopoulos is Assistant Professor of Latin Language and Literature,
Department of History, Ionian University, Corfu

INTERNATIONAL LIBRARY OF HISTORICAL STUDIES

Series ISBN: 978 1 84885 222 8

See www.ibtauris.com/ILHS for a full list of titles

52. *Feeding the Nation: Nutrition and Health in Britain before World War One*
Yuriko Akiyama
978 1 84511 682 8

53. *Islam in the Baltic: Europe's Early Muslim Community*
Harry Norris
978 1 84511 587 6

54. *East India Patronage and the British State: The Scottish Elite and Politics in the Eighteenth Century*
George McGilvary
978 1 84511 661 3

55. *Communism in Rural France: French Agricultural Workers and the Popular Front*
John Bulaitis
978 1 84511 708 5

56. *The Ages of Faith: Popular Religion in Late Medieval England and Western Europe*
Norman Tanner
978 1 84511 760 3

57. *An Introduction to Medieval Jewish Philosophy*
Daniel Rynhold
978 1 84511 747 4

58. *Radical Religion in Cromwell's England: A Concise History from the English Civil War to the End of the Commonwealth*
Andrew Bradstock
978 1 84511 764 1

60. *The Female Mystic: Great Women Thinkers of the Middle Ages*
Andrea Janelle Dickens
978 1 84511 640 8

61. *Holy War, Just War: Early Modern Christianity, Religious Ethics and the Rhetoric of Empire*
Patrick Provost-Smith
978 1 84511 675 0

63. *Coleridge and Liberal Religious Thought: Romanticism, Science and Theological Tradition*
Graham Neville
978 1 84885 089 7

64. *The New Ways of History: Developments in Historiography*
Gelina Harlaftis, Nikos Karapidakis, Kostas Sbonias and Vaios Vaipoulos (eds)
978 1 84885 1 269

65. *Naval Shipbuilding in the Age of Sail: An Industrial History 1100–1800*
Philip MacDougall
978 1 84885 119 1

66. *Spatial Conceptions of the Nation: Modernizing Geographies in Greece and Turkey*
Nikiforos Diamandouros, Thalia Dragonas and Çaglar Keyder (eds)
978 1 84885 131 3

67. *Trade and Cultural Exchange in the Early Modern Mediterranean: Braudel's Maritime Legacy*
Maria Fusaro, Colin Heywood and Mohamed-Salah Omri (eds)
978 1 84885 163 4

68. *Britain, Portugal and South America in the Napoleonic Wars: Alliances and Diplomacy in Economic Maritime Conflict*
Martin Robson
978 1 84885 196 2

69. *Demetrius, the Military Saint of Byzantium: Cult and Worship in the Middle Ages*
Eugenia Russell
978 1 84885 367 6

70. *A Concise History of Early Christian Heresy*
Alastair Logan
978 1 84885 406 2

THE NEW WAYS OF HISTORY

Developments in Historiography

Edited by

Gelina Harlaftis
Nikos Karapidakis
Kostas Sbonias
Vaios Vaiopoulos

BLOOMSBURY
NEW DELHI • LONDON • OXFORD • NEW YORK • SYDNEY

BLOOMSBURY INDIA
Bloomsbury Publishing India Pvt. Ltd
Second Floor, LSC Building No. 4, DDA Complex, Pocket C–6&7,
Vasant Kunj, New Delhi 110070

BLOOMSBURY, Bloomsbury Academic India and the Diana
logo are trademarks of Bloomsbury Publishing Plc

First published in India 2022
Published in 2010 by I.B.Tauris & Co Ltd
Distributed in the United States and Canada exclusively by Palgrave Macmillan

A catalog record for this book is available from the Library of Congress.
A catalogue record for this book is available from the British Library.

ISBN: 978-93-56400-78-8
For sale in the Indian subcontinent only

Exclusively distributed in the Indian subcontinent by
Manohar Publishers & Distributors
4753/23, Ansari Road
Darya Ganj, New Delhi 110002
Tel.: 23284848, 23289100
Email: sales@manoharbooks.com, manoharbooks@gmail.com

Printed and bound in India by Replika Press Pvt. Ltd.

Celebrating twenty (and five) years
of the Department of History
of the Ionian University

Contents

Figures

Acknowledgements

We would like to thank the Ionian University for making possible the conference 'Twenty Years of Historiography' in October 2005 in order to celebrate the twenty years of the Department of History. We would also like to thank our colleagues in the Department of History for their direct and indirect involvement in the above effort. Without the assistance of the Ionian University, the publication of this volume would not have been possible. Our warm thanks to Alex Dumas who edited this volume and who, once again, proved to be a valuable collaborator. We would also like to thank Helena Taylor for her excellent translations.

Introduction

New Ways of History?

History!
What trivial information it retained
What erroneous rumours it transmitted to us!
How many disasters and how many plots!
Ah! Kleio! But of course
She noted down whatever she heard:
It seems she took very little pain
To realize
What was true
And what was not!
A whole life of study and attention and research
Today allows us
To reveal – to say –
That everything about Pandora
And her box
Are fairytales unworthy of comment.[1]

The above poem on history and the cover of the book were penned and painted respectively by Nikos Engonopoulos (1907–1985), a professor in the Advanced School of Fine Arts of the Technical University of Athens. Engonopoulos was part of the movement of Surrealism, which appeared in Athens in the 1930s, introducing new, liberating and controversial manners of expression that provoked much opposition and sarcasm at the time. One of the first critics of his art wrote that 'he produces strange examples of an art which is at once traditional and modern'.[2] Engonopoulos painted ancient Greeks in a Byzantine technique and with the eye of a Modern Greek. As the editors of this book are all Greek, they could think of nothing more appropriate than to introduce it with images of our past and present: the baggage of 'our glorious' heritage of the ancient world, breaking through with an element of surprise, humour and unexpected juxtapositions.

The aim of the book is to trigger reflection on old and new ways of history in both teaching and research, by attempting to 'decompartmantalize' the various fields and periods of history, which 'too often [have] a diet of rich synchronic detail but too little overview'.[2] Historians have been thinking increasingly of new ways in which to deal with the past. They have sought the best ways to research the past, have tried new modes of historical narrative, have cut history into pieces, have come back to grand long-term interpretations, have doubted their own ability to learn about the past. The various historical fields, the new ways of history and the theoretical trends are not usually combined or examined in one single volume. Specialization in history is such that historians tend to read, publish and communicate only with historians of their own field, area or period of study. One of the main strengths of this volume of collected essays is that it gives an overview of developments during the last 20 years and the changing agenda of questions in several historical fields, chronological, thematic and regional. And this is done not so much by specialists in historiography as by historians practising in a particular field of history. The discussion is enhanced by the perennial question of how to treat time in history. In this way, the comparative perspective is highlighted and further insight is given into the different historical trends and periods under consideration.

Nevertheless, the structure of the book does not always indicate new ways. Half the book is devoted to the old, familiar, three-fold division of history into ancient, medieval and modern, and half is on thematic and regional/area history, covering history and archaeology, history and the social sciences, economic and business history, maritime history, diaspora history, Ottoman history. The book opens and closes with chapters on historiography, which deal with the main questionnaire of historians. But why only these histories? Why are so many others missing, such as social, gender or cultural history, which were so much *en vogue* in the previous decade? These are valid questions, but, even so, the selection of subjects is not just 'cheerfully eclectic', to use an expression of Penelope Corfield; there is a reason for this choice.

All the editors of this volume come from the Department of History of the Ionian University, based in Corfu, and most of the contributors had met back in 2005, at a conference held to celebrate the 20 years (1985–2005) of this department. Our intention then was to discuss the history that was taught in the department, in a diachronic perspective that spanned from prehistory to the present. So, the 'histories' found in the chapters of the book are all drawn from the curriculum of the Department of History of the Ionian University.

What might be interesting to academics in countries carrying a long historical tradition, such as England, France, Germany or the United States, is how cosmopolitan a small Department of History in a small university, on a small island in a small European country, can be. In the Department of History of the Ionian University, the historical traditions of Europe and North America blend. Different national historiographical traditions meet and mix, whereas in the countries from which they originate these can be hermetically sealed. The historians who are teaching or have taught in the department, have studied, apart from Greece, in France, Germany, Italy, Britain, the United States of America and Canada, and they have brought back with them experience of the educational systems in which they were trained. New ways can emerge from 'polyphony', provided those who engage in discussion can harmonize in a common melody.

It is appropriate that this volume to celebrate the 20 (and five) years of the Department of History of the Ionian University carries the title *New Ways of History*. The formation of the department was conceived as 'new ways' in history by the Greek historian Spyros Asdrachas (a son of the Ionian island of Lefkas), who taught economic history for many years in the famous IVe Section of the École Pratique des Hautes Études, Paris. Asdrachas, along with Vassilis Panayotopoulos, Ilias Iliou and other scholars who came back to Greece, mainly from France, after the fall of the dictatorship in 1974, are among those considered the founders of the 'new Greek history' of the 1970s and 1980s; an interdisciplinary history that became the axis not only of the humanities but also of the social sciences.[4] As recently as the 1980s, history in Greece was a discipline led by scholars educated in classics and literature; the generic term used in the country is philologists. In fact, no independent Department of History existed until the 1980s; if one wanted to become a historian, one had to get admitted to a Department of Literature (Philology). This is, of course, the result of the weight attached to ancient history and archaeology in Greek universities; similarly, however, in Britain and North America, ancient history is studied in classics departments not in history departments (see Chapter 2). The wave of the 'new Greek history' in the 1980s connected history with the social sciences and in this way new subjects, archival material and interpretations became part of the new trend in Greek historiography, which was accompanied by an upsurge of historical publications; the other wave of 'new history', of the 1990s, connected with cultural studies and postmodernism, barely touched academic institutions in Greece, with the exception of the University of Thessaly.

The 'new ways' were implemented in the new Department of History, established in 1985, the first department of the new Ionian University, which was founded that same year; the Ionian University was part of a new policy of the then socialist government of Greece, which brought massive reforms in the Greek university system and set up new academic institutions in the provinces, in order to decentralize higher education. 'New' historical fields, for the Greek university *status quo*, were introduced in the new department in Corfu, in the late 1980s and 1990s. For example, 'Medieval History', that is, Western European Medieval history, was not taught in the main universities of Athens or Thessaloniki; the Middle Ages were regarded only from a Hellenocentric viewpoint and their study meant, in effect, 'Byzantine' history. Medieval history was introduced and is still taught in the Department of History of the Ionian University. The same is true of the 'new' field, for Greece, of 'Ottoman History'; one has to remember that the history of Greeks in southeastern Europe and/or the East Mediterranean was conceived as a history of 'conquests', so in most departments of history in Greece the periods of foreign rule – 'Latin Occupation', Frankish Occupation', Venetian Occupation', 'Ottoman Occupation', 'British Occupation' – are taught. The teaching of 'Ottoman History' as a separate field of study from a non-Greek angle was a 'new way' that was adopted by the new departments of history in the new universities, such as the University of Crete and the Ionian University. Meeting the social sciences was another pioneering trend in history and economic history which was introduced in the Ionian University. History of Demography was introduced too, a new subject at the time. Anthropology in the British and American tradition, linked with prehistory, was also introduced for the first time, with Professor August Sordinas; the department still teaches anthropology and ethnology. In the first decade of the twenty-first century, new fields kept appearing in the curriculum, such as Landscape History, Maritime History, North and Latin American History. Even so, despite the 'new ways', the Department of History of the Ionian University has not always managed to keep up with new ways and new themes as much as it could have done; it has not fully combated historicism or the complacency and isolation of Greek academic historiography, and it has had to balance in a symbiosis old and new traditions of historiography. It could be that this volume is indicative of the department's slow but steady progress in the 'new ways'.

The Ionian University likes to think that it continues the long intellectual tradition of the Ionian Islands, which belonged to Venice for nigh on five hundred years. A significant historiographical production from the Ionian Islands, described as 'The Historical School of the Seven Islands', seems to have been generated since at least the seventeenth and into the nineteenth century.[5] When the Ionian Islands became part of the British Empire (1815–1864), as a British protectorate, the British took the lead in continuing this tradition. A British philhellene, Frederic North, Count of Guilford, who had visited Corfu in 1791, when it still belonged to Venice, established in 1824 the Ionian Academy, the first modern Greek University; the University of Athens was not founded until 1837. The Ionian Academy functioned for forty years, until 1864, when the Ionian Islands were united with Greece. Moreover, a number of renowned historians and intellectuals who taught in the Athens University hailed from the Ionian Islands: Spyridon Zambelios (1815–1881) from Lefkas, Spyridon Lambros (1851–1919) from Corfu, Dionyssios Zakynthinos (1905–1993) from Cephalonia, Andreas Andreades (1876–1935) from Corfu.

Diachrony, periodization and continuity are part of the historian's agenda. Continuity has never ceased to be a hot topic in modern Greek historiography. Greece's most famous nineteenth-century historian, Konstantinos Paparrigopoulos, wrote his unprecedented grand narrative of fifteen volumes in the middle years of the century to prove it. The first chapter of the present book, by Penelope J. Corfield, is on this subject and considers three linked themes. Firstly, she considers the flight from big long-term interpretations of history during the past half-century, citing as reasons *inter alia* not only the intellectual collapse of traditional 'grand narratives' of Progress and/or of inexorable Marxist economic stages, but also the more mundane process of the academic institutionalization of period divisions and sectoral specialisms within history teaching and research. Secondly, she discusses the ways in which a return to diachronic, through-time interpretations can take place, within both history teaching and research. And thirdly, she suggests her own analysis, as presented in her last book, of an integral, threefold patterning within history: of continuity, micro-change and macro-change (alternatively defined as persistence, momentum and turbulence).

The next three chapters present some of the key developments in the study of antiquity, in the fields of ancient history and archaeology. In Chapter 2 Robin Osborne investigates the changing priorities of the academy. He argues that ancient history is changed by a changing agenda of questions, rather than by changes in the body of evidence available. In ancient history, political history was dominant until the 1970s and non-political history was something of a newcomer. Osborne identifies the major changes that have occurred in the way that ancient historians have adapted and incorporated the trends and changes of all history in ancient history.

In Chapter 3, John Bintliff presents some of the key developments in Archaeology over the last generation of research, summarizing new discoveries, new methods and new ways of interpretation. His review is diachronic and, as he states, this extension of archaeological research to include all periods from prehistory to the early modern times is one of the most significant innovations in Greek archaeology. Bintliff first summarizes the results of the most recent research concerning the Palaeolithic, the Mesolithic, the Neolithic and the Bronze Age. He then goes on to show that in the field of Classical Archaeology one of the most powerful changes has been the application of anthropological and analytical approaches to ordinary material culture, as opposed to fine art and public architecture. The development of Landscape Archaeology and the spread of intensive, field-by-field surface survey, as well as the combination of archival research with regional surface survey and recording standing buildings, have opened new ways for reconstructing changing life in city and countryside in Classical Greece, as well as for the development of the new landscape history of Roman, Crusader, Ottoman and Early Modern Greece, through the study of settlement history, daily life, population, economy, landholding and domestic architecture.

The three chapters that follow are devoted to the Middle Ages in Western and Eastern Europe. In Chapter 4, Anita Guerreau-Jalabert gives a comparative approach to Medieval Studies in France. She stresses the abandonment of the large themes of social and economic history, which the *Annales* School had brought to the fore. In the last 20 years, new themes have been researched, re-defining political history as the history of power, institutions and regulations; emphasis is also given to cultural history and history of representations, which has replaced the history of mentalities. Medievalists have to 'fight' the growing interest in modern history and find themselves in a period of reconsideration of the foundations of this field.

In Chapter 5, Cecile Morrisson, on a more optimistic note, reflects on the progress of Byzantine History, which found itself with an ambivalent identity, somewhere between Medievalism, Classics and Orientalism. She finds that, after a long path, in the last 30 years Byzantinists have reinserted Byzantium into general history and have indicated that 'the theatre of European history did not stop at the borders of the Carolingian Empire and its marches, nor at the outposts of the Latin Orient'. Byzantine Studies, which for too long were restricted to political and diplomatic history, have benefitted from the turn towards an interdisciplinary approach, which brought a new agenda of questions asked, re-interpretation of resources and new syntheses. Collaboration with other disciplines, such as archaeology, geography, numismatics, economics, climatology, art, have provided a new evidentiary base for new approaches. Compilation, translation, publication and digitalization of archives have made access to resources easier.

In Chapter 6, Nikos Karapidakis, occasioned by a lecture by Averil Cameron, published in English and Greek, in the periodical *Nea Hestia*, as well as the texts published in response, in the same periodical, deliberates perceptively on Byzantine Studies and on studies in medieval history in general.

In Chapter 7, Benjamin Arbel gives an evaluation of Renaissance studies for the period 1985–2005. The Renaissance, a historical phenomenon of Western Europe, has acquired also a chronological definition. Arbel provides a quantified approach to three leading journals: the Italian *Rinascimento*, the French *Bibliothèque d'Humanisme et Rennaissance* and the American *Renaissance Quartely*. Some of the results of this bibliographical survey of the articles in these journals reveal the lack of the grand works of synthesis, which has been stressed already in the first chapter, the predominance of works on the Church, literature and sources, but also the introduction of interdisciplinary approaches, such as social and economic history, gender, science and magic, philosophy, music, etc.

The encounter of history with the social sciences preoccupies the next three chapters. In Chapter 8, Peter Mathias deals with economic history and its progress in living with its neighbours, in the Anglo-Saxon context. This is the story after the peak that economic history, known as 'economic and social history', reached in Britain in the mid-1970s. Since then, economic history has been a declining subject in British universities and internationally, until the beginning of the twenty-first century, when it has gathered again momentum. The main reason for its decline was the impact of what was called 'new economic history', better known as cliometrics, which flourished mainly on the other side of the Atlantic. History students, who in economic history had to deal increasingly with sophisticated quantification and elaborate statistical methods, opted for the 'softer' socio-cultural history that prospered in the 1990s and brought the shrinkage of 'hard' economic history. However, economic history did not disappear. On the contrary, it has come back in what Mathias describes as 'mega-economic' history, connected with the rise of interest in global history and globalization, and the return of core-periphery relationships and world-system discourse. Offshoots of economic history have sprouted and grown as independent fields, such as business history, transport history, financial and banking history, urban history, etc. What is more, economic and social dimensions of change have now penetrated all other aspects of history, as we have seen in ancient, Byzantine, maritime, diaspora, Ottoman history, etc. Mathias concludes that 'even if economic history was in danger of losing its own battle, it has now recovered and, on the wider scene, has been winning a war'.

In Chapter 9, Walter A. Friedman discusses business history, which, like economic history, lives a life between economists and historians. Business has been ignored by mainstream historians for too long, and up until the 1970s business history was a semi-neglected 'sub-species of economic history' (see Chapter 8) that attracted no real interest from theorists or economic historians themselves. Its path has been linked with Harvard Business School, where a chair was founded in the field in 1927; the man who held this chair in the post-war period was Alfred Chandler, a historian by training, who really invented the history of the big corporation internationally and provided a comparative methodology in firm-centred studies in both the United States and Europe. His work was the base from where business history took off after the 1990s. It is true that business history was partially hit in the 'decade of post-modernism', but it was also enriched by new approaches, new ways of examining business, focusing not only on big but also on small firms in all countries and continents of the world, networks, family, ethnicity, class, gender, popular culture, race, and other aspects of society. Some business history has reached out to the social sciences and relates to psychology, economics, sociology and business management. It also relates to 'mega-economic' history, with studies in multinational enterprises and international business, and takes part in the discourse on global history and globalization. Thus, by following new ways, business history has succeeded in becoming a field of history in its own right, part of mainstream history.

In Chapter 10, Paschalis Kitromilides gives us a glance at the encounter of history with the social sciences, stressing once more the influence of the *Annales* School in twentieth-century intellectual history. He discusses in particular the encounter of history with sociology, anthropology and political theory, and emphasizes the need for social scientists to work with archival material and not secondary sources. He gives an overview of historical writing on Modern Greece along these lines. Economic history, as has been mentioned already, gave impetus to the 'new history' of the 1970s and 1980s, and produced a whole new generation of prominent historians. It shook the foundations of traditional political history and its ideologically preordained character, geared to nationalism and following the method of an array of events. Anthropology gave another impetus but, according to Kitromilides, it ended in 'catastrophic results', not least when it took 'the strange and convoluted ways of postmodernism, producing work marked by arbitrariness and subjectivism'. The encounter of political science and history has suffered in the last decades, due to its total autocracy in the decades before, but still continues in a limited way through diplomatic history. Kitromilides concludes that Greek history writing has been transformed and enriched by a continuing dialogue with the social sciences. The danger to history in Greece is its great popular appeal and the superficial way it is used in the mass media as part of political and power games.

Thematic and area/regional history follows. In Chapter 11, Donald Quataert examines trends in history writing regarding the Late Ottoman Empire, a flourishing field. Partly due to the growing availability of Ottoman and non-Ottoman sources, of state and private archives, and partly due to the fact that Ottoman history is no longer identified only with Turkey but is also understood increasingly as the histories of the Balkan and the Arab provinces, a new breeze has been blowing from the Levant. A new generation of historians has emerged, which writes about Ottoman history from the Ottoman archives, in Ottoman Turkish, Greek, Bulgarian, Serbian and other languages. Ottoman history is now the largest sub-field of the highly important regional history of the Middle East. It has flourished as an economic and social history, while it has profited also from other histories, such as women's history and labour history.

In Chapter 12, Ina Baghdiantz McCabe discusses Diaspora Studies – only recently recognized as an academic field – as new ways of history. The study of diasporas stands in stark contrast to national historiographical traditions, as it transcends the nation-state. In a globalized world, global diaspora communities are increasingly important actors in international conflict and cooperation. McCabe discusses how and where the term can be used; does it include just migration or forcible displacement? How has confusion been created between ethnic groups and diasporas? The three classical historical diasporas, the Armenians, the Greeks and the Jews, epitomize the resilience of older traditional forms of certain peoples that for centuries trespassed boundaries to nation-states. Over 30 new groups have now joined them under the umbrella term 'diaspora'. This is a multi-disciplinary field, drawing from the history of mentalities, histories of daily life, theoretical schools of feminism, postmodernism, global history, economic history, history of material culture, etc. What is so interesting in diaspora studies is that this is not a traditional field, it is a field with no national boundaries and it transcends chronologies. Historians have focused on merchant diasporas, in the networks of ethnic and religious minorities dispersed from their original homeland but united among themselves by strong ties of culture, religion, language and ethnicity. In a way, national historiographies have masked the significance of trade diasporas and their entrepreneurial networks. Over the last 500 years, a succession of regional and long-distance trading networks, initially in Asia and Europe, from the Mediterranean to the northern European seas, the Indian Ocean and the southeast Asian seas, but subsequently stretching across the Atlantic and Pacific oceans, lay at the heart of the gradual integration of the world into one global system.

In Chapter 13, Gelina Harlaftis examines the development of Maritime History or the history of *thalassa* (sea in Greek) as an independent field of history. Maritime history has grown since the 1970s, mainly as an economic and social history of the modern period. However, the history of the seas has become very much *en vogue* in the last decade and the new ways of history have been sought through the 'rediscovery' of the sea by historians of the ancient, medieval and early modern periods. So, in the pursuit of 'new ways', historians have made maritime history/sea history/history of *thalassa* mainstream history. The new wave called 'new thalassology' has 'sailed' together with the upsurge of global history in the twenty-first century, including colonial/imperial history. As always when discovering something 'new' one neglects the 'old', and 'new thalassology' scholars, particularly geographers, have neglected maritime history, a history that has flourished as a distinct field of history in the last 20 years 'aboard the ship' of an international organization called the International Maritime Economic History Association. The chapter points out the rich produce of maritime historians worldwide, who have been working for years at sea before the neophytes discovered it. Maritime history as a field of history could not but follow the prototype history of *thalassa,* Braudel's *La Mediterranée*, and is a synthesis of history with the social sciences, including economics, sociology, anthropology, linguistics and geography, combining the French and British historiographical traditions. The new boost of history of *thalassa*, which relates so well to global history, a history of contacts and interactions between different civilizations, has increased historians' interest in the diachronic dimension, from ancient to present times.

The last chapter, written by François Hartog, is on historiography and reflects on the concept of 'the present' and its relation to the historian. Such reflection is prompted by the practice of the historians, society's demands of them and the difficulties to which they have to respond. The main concepts around which these demands revolve are inheritance, memory, celebration of anniversaries, 'the present', identity, crimes against humanity, globalization. The historian has to deal with the media, or various pressure groups, which implement strategies of 'history' that explain 'who we are' or give an identity. Moreover, the concept of globalization and its influence on historiography or the so-called global history elicits relevant answers of post-modernism. Is this a transitional stage or the domination of 'the present' in historical thought?

The following essays provide plenty of food for thought in answer to that and the other pertinent questions raised throughout this volume. All authors reflect on the different views of history in their own sub-disciplines, on existing traditions, limitations and ways to go ahead. In this way from the juxtaposition of various approaches of different historical fields one gets a clearer picture of the recent trends in history as a whole. After all, history is always renewing itself, in both old and new directions.

Notes

1 Translation by Alexandra Dumas. Engonopoulos, Nikos, *Στην κοιλάδα με τους ροδώνες (Stin koilada me tous rodones)* (Athens, 1978).

2 Prevelakis, Pandelis, 'The art of modern Greece', *The Studio* CXV, 541, (April 1938), in Katerina Perpinioti-Agazir, *Νίκος Εγγονόπουλος. Ο ζωγραφικός του κόσμος* (*Nikos Engonopoulos. His painting world* (Athens, 2007)), p. 20.

3 See Chapter 1.

4 See 'The New Trends in the Historiography of New Hellenism', *Synchrona Themata* (December 1988), pp. 35–7.

5 Lambrou, Spyr. P., 'Η ιστορική σχολή της Επτανήσου' (The historical school of the Seven Islands), *Neos Ellinomnimon* 12 (1915), pp. 319–47; Karapidakis, Nikos, 'Η ιστορία των δυτικών κυριαρχιών: η παρέκκλιση από την κοινωνική ιστορία στην εθνική. Η διάσταση μεταξύ των στοχαστών και των ιστοριογράφων της κατάκτησης' (The history of the Western conquests: the diversion from social history to the national. The breach between intellectuals and the historiographers of conquest) in P.M. Kitromilides and T. Sklavenitis (eds), *The Historiography of Modern and Contemporary Greece* (Athens, 2004), vols I–II.

Bibliography

Engonopoulos, Nikos, *Στην κοιλάδα με τους ροδώνες (Stin koilada me tous rodones)* (Athens, Ikaros Publications, 1978) (translation by Alexandra Dumas).

Karapidakis, Nikos, 'Η ιστορία των δυτικών κυριαρχιών: η παρέκκλιση από την κοινωνική ιστορία στην εθνική. Η διάσταση μεταξύ των στοχαστών και των ιστοριογράφων της κατάκτησης' (The history of the Western conquests: the diversion from social history to the national. The breach between intellectuals and the historiographers of conquest) in Paschalis M. Kitromilides and Triandafylos Sklavenitis (eds), *The Historiography of Modern and Contemporary Greece* (Athens, 2004) vols I–II.

Lambrou, Spyridon P., 'Η ιστορική σχολή της Επτανήσου' (The historical school of the Seven Islands), *Neos Ellinomnimon* 12 (1915), pp. 319–47.

Prevelakis, Pandelis, 'The art of modern Greece', *The Studio* CXV, 541, (April 1938), in Katerina Perpinioti-Agazir, *Νίκος Εγγονόπουλος. Ο ζωγραφικός του κόσμος* (*Nikos Engonopoulos. His painting world*) (Athens, Benaki Museum, 2007).

1

Historians and the Return to the Diachronic[1]

Penelope J. Corfield

A conscious 'temporal turn' is long overdue.[2] Many subjects seem now to be returning to investigate time; and the historians, whose subject-matter explicitly invites them to 'think long', should be leading a return to big-picture analysis, in innovative ways.

This chapter investigates three related questions. Firstly, why has there been such a prolonged flight from Grand Narratives, with their big, sweeping tales about the trajectory of history through the millennia? Secondly, and more immediately, what issues need to be confronted in order to return to debating through-time interpretations in both research and teaching? And, thirdly, is there a new multi-dimensional way of approaching the diachronic, to avoid the pitfalls into which the classic Grand Narratives fell? A coda ends by considering the implications for better understanding the future, in the light of better understanding the past. That last point is timely, in view of the recent failure of mathematicalized risk assessments, as made by the global financial service sector in the years leading to the 2008/9 credit crisis.[3] These calculations invited hubris, by believing that the future can be calibrated with total precision. Yet there is a countervailing nemesis, which is triggered by refusing to take action to forestall pending problems. History offers advice on the balance between calculable trends and incalculable surprises.

Needless to say, the answers to the three related questions are complicated. Were there one overwhelmingly obvious message to history, then it would have been identified long ago. In general, it is good advice to be suspicious of interpreters with a single nostrum, such as:

It's all really sex, à la D.H. Lawrence;[4]
or *It's all really class struggle, à la* Marx and Engels;[5]
or *It's all really the March of Freedom, à la* G.W.F. Hegel;
or *It's all really progress towards American-style liberal democracy, à la* Francis Fukuyama;[6]
or *It's all really the universal living will-to-power', à la* Nietzsche;[7]
or *It's all really the contest for survival between individual human genes, à la* Richard Dawkins.[8]

Reductionist dicta, such as these, may seem beguiling. They certainly make for rousing debates, but they are poor history. There are many more things in the cosmos and upon earth ....

At the same time, while the past is marvellously intricate, history is not so utterly tangled that historians (and the many others who study the long term, such as geologists and astronomers) cannot analyse its intricacies. Instead, complex developments over time repay close scrutiny to probe their shape, momentum, and meaning.

The past, viewed in its entirety, constitutes for all humans a vast reservoir of experience and information. After all, in this cosmos of unidirectional temporality, where time runs onwards and not backwards, people cannot learn from the future. Instead, humans learn from the fleeting present and from the encyclopaedic past. That is what makes history so crucial to study and, always, to debate.

The flight from grand narratives

For much of the twentieth century, analysts of Space rather than Time seemed to be seizing the intellectual initiative. Absolute time was 'dead', killed by Einstein's theories of relativity. Time instead was to be related to Space, which thus claimed intellectual centrality. In anthropology, linguistics, and some models of philosophy, structuralism – or spatialization – focused upon examining synchronic networks and signs, in order to discover the inner logic that confers meaning at any given point in time.[9]

Many historians began to share that preoccupation, providing innumerable and invaluable in-depth studies. For example, much of the strength of recent research in social, cultural, and gender history has been in 'synchronic immersion', which entails analysing specific themes (such as meanings, experiences, identities) within specific places in specifically defined short periods. That analytical approach has enjoyed a great buzz of intellectual fashion and excitement.

By contrast, it may be noted that economic history as a field has remained one of the major exceptions to this generalization. Its practitioners do provide close-focus studies but many also continue to engage with the long term.[10] This particular field, however, remains specialized and has never recaptured the surge of excitement and recruitment that it experienced in the 1960s and early 1970s.[11] In Britain, to take one example, that was the period when many separate Economic History departments were established. Today, however, only one of these survives as a stand-alone unit, while the rest have either merged with old-style History departments or federated into Schools of History or Humanities. In many other university systems, too, the subject has been through a similar intellectual trajectory: from popular boom to a much narrower specialization, often wrapped in austere quantification.

Undoubtedly, one major reason for the flight from the very-long-term in so many aspects of academic history is a practical one. As the quantity of research multiplies, so the discipline has been sub-divided into separate specialisms. In Britain alone, there are over 2,000 academic historians. Worldwide, the number must be well over 100,000. Since no one can keep up with the output of all these busy scholars, the professional answer is to specialize, either in a particular period and/or on a particular theme. Furthermore, these subdivisions of academic history are institutionally incorporated into teaching, examining, research, conferences, journals, professional associations, publishing, reviewing and assessment of all kinds at all levels. History students are generally invited to choose among the specialisms of their academic tutors. Scholars talk to others studying similar or closely-related subjects within shared time-frames. And experts generally decline to answer questions outside their own research fortress, replying with the common formula: *It's not my period.*

Rarely are historians invited to debate the possible long-span frameworks of history – whether cyclical, linear, static, revolutionary or multi-stranded. For example, urban historians rarely discuss the very long history of towns. Studies like Lewis Mumford's *The Culture of Cities* (1938) may remain on reading lists as background briefing. *But how many now read Mumford?* Very few, in my experience. His quest to place cities within the socio-economic-cultural context of their times is no longer something that requires special remark, while his schematic contrast between the new, chaotic industrial city with the old, ordered organic settlement now seems far too simplistic. Research has moved on, adding immense depth and breadth – but diminishing length.

Specialization has been, however, only the obvious symptom rather than the deep-rooted cause of the flight from the diachronic. After all, it is notable that big-picture studies have never actually disappeared. For example, environmental history is breaking new ground. Diachronic studies like Neil Robert's *Holocene* (1998) survey humanity's changing relationship with the natural world from 10,000 BCE until today.[12] This is history with a polemical edge, warning that humans ignore at their collective peril the scientists' analysis of the implications of global warming. *But do such global-environment studies appear in the current History curriculum?* Overwhelmingly, no. Such studies, if accessibly written, appeal to educated readers and contribute to public political discourse. But their data and their arguments have commonly been marginalized for teaching purposes, not deliberately but effectively, by the sub-division of the History curriculum into many sectional courses.

One particularly grand but grandly failed attempt at world history also discouraged imitators. This was the cautionary tale of Arnold Toynbee. Between the years 1934 and 1961, he published his massive 12-volume *Study of History*. It was an epic project, chronicling the rise and fall not of ethnic groups or nation-states but of the entire stock of world 'civilizations'. Of these, he identified 21 (later expanded to 31), as well as eight 'abortive' or 'arrested' civilizations, and at least 650 'primitive' societies. Their contrasting fates were depicted as an unending process of continuous challenge, response to challenge, and fresh challenge once more. Soon, however, well-directed criticisms undermined Toynbee's basic classification of civilizations. Equally, his overall interpretation of history as challenge-response-challenge was rejected as banal and unenlightening. His reputation, once sky-high, collapsed. *Who now has read Toynbee? Even in the abridged text?* Only a few historians; and fewer still would now claim him to be a seminal philosopher of history, as once was done.[13]

Above all, however, the flight from Grand Narratives in favour of synchronic immersion was especially hastened by the erosion in the twentieth century of two global saga-histories that were inherited from the nineteenth century. This important intellectual development encouraged fresh in-depth research, bringing valuable new insights. And it simultaneously appeared to free the subject from stereotyped assumptions that had been nullified by the test of actual historical experience.

Of these two meta-narratives, one was a confident belief in linear 'progress', from barbarism to civilization.[14] That vision, which was found extensively but not exclusively in the West, sank in the twentieth century when confronted with the stark evidence of world wars, tyrannies, famines, killer epidemics, ecological degradation, nuclear bombs, and genocides. *Who now believes in universal and unstoppable progress?* Somewhat surprisingly, some people still do – but very far from a majority. Those who are still optimistic tend to invoke technological innovations and the human capacity for adventure. On the other hand, many others instead fear an unstoppable decline, especially with reference to climate change and environmental degradation. And even those scholars, who balance between the extremes of optimism and pessimism, tend to sniff disparagingly when the word 'progress' is mentioned.[15] In academic life, if used at all, it appears in ironic quotation marks. It may survive in some popular mantras, perhaps in relation to new technology – as in: 'you can't stop progress' – but such remarks are readily countered by the obverse: 'things are going (or have already gone) to the dogs'.

Another grand meta-narrative was the Marxist revolutionary sequence of historical stages, each representing a different economic-and-political system. These successive eras were held to be propelled onwards by the class struggle. One stage would be succeeded by a contrasting alternative, generating a historical pathway that would lead 'inevitably' to a new world of egalitarian communism and, ultimately, the 'withering away' of the state. It too was a progress narrative, but one that incorporated conflict. Yet things did not turn out as predicted, and great harm was also done by policies that tried to speed up history to produce the inevitably coming utopia. So, this model too has fallen by history's wayside, disproved by events. *Who now believes in the inevitable triumph of communism?* Only a few determined Marxists, and they do that by redefining past attempts at establishing the workers' utopia as false-communism or 'Stalino-state capitalism'. However, even such a revised version entails a recognition that history's stages follow less straightforwardly and sequentially than the founding fathers Marx and Engels had specified. There are snares and delusions along the way.

So, the conceptual and organizational difficulties of writing a common story for all humanity are only too apparent. There is still great public appetite for narrative histories. Television programmes about the succession of kings and queens, or about the feats of military heroes and political villains, or about the course of major wars, are very popular. Yet such output retains its distance from the world of academic research, not least because, while TV producers like a straightforward narrative line, historians tend to prefer complexities. That makes it hard to bridge the two worlds of media and scholarship. And particularly so today, in the context of the recent marginalization of macro-history within academic history. The coming challenge, then, is to find new and accessible ways of telling a tangled but not impenetrable global tale, which does justice to research detail but still returns to the big picture.

Returning to through-time interpretations

To acknowledge the collapse of the old Grand Narratives is not to blame today's scholars, who contribute magnificently to the richness, depth and professionalism of research knowledge. On the contrary, this is a very exciting time for historians – precisely because so much more is being discovered about so many new or hitherto neglected themes, like (say) gender history and (expanding now) environmental history or animal history. As a result, the aim is not to abandon what is now done well. Nor is the aim simply to announce another Grand Narrative in a take-it-or-leave-it fashion.

Instead, there is a good case for better augmenting and framing these accumulating insights by devising and debating new and better ways of approaching big-picture history. Currently, the timing for this enterprise is especially suitable, given the collapsing state of postmodernist theories. Those ideas, which had some currency in the West in the later 1980s and 1990s, held that time itself was broken or ruptured, so that history within time was disordered and randomized. It was a viewpoint that marginalized the efforts of historians, on the grounds that their interpretations remain no more than fictional.[16] However, the model of ruptured temporality is a fallible one. Things do manifestly happen through time – like sustained speech, in which sounds make sense in sequence – or sustained writing, which is understood by sustained reading, both taking place moment by moment.

Moreover, causes and effects do operate. Space itself is not only located in Time, it is integrally yoked with it. So the anti-philosopher Jacques Derrida's attempt at rejecting temporality as purely 'metaphysical' and substituting *chora* (or ***khōra***) as an atemporal spatiality,[17] remains a curiosity that has not won converts. Indeed, it may be noted that even postmodernist theorists who approve his views, do themselves offer a narrative of sorts. They claim to have identified 'the death of the Enlightenment project'.[18] In that belief, they announce the advent of a new 'postmodernist age'. It is true that these theorists differ notably as to the timing of such a notional transformation.[19] But their analysis of death and rebirth, from an old world-view to a new and better one, is itself a transformation story, based upon a simple binary, which looks to a rejected past to explain/approve cultural progress in the present.

Historians, meanwhile, have overwhelmingly, if not unanimously, rejected the anti-historical thrust of postmodernism.[20] They recognize that all those who study the past do give an imaginative as well as intellectual input into their histories. They are emphatically not, however, writing pure fictions. Nor are they operating in isolation. Historical data and interpretations are debated and refined within and between successive generations. As part of that process, some over-simplified Grand Narratives have been rightly discarded. But it is now time to return to thinking long as well as deep.

In that context, one primary issue to confront is the old question of periodization. That requirement applies not only to the study of history but to many subjects across the humanities and social sciences, which borrow from history. Because the old Grand Narratives collapsed but were not displaced by alternatives, many of the old standard narrative stages of history have survived unchallenged. Thus, the discipline remains divided, both for research and teaching purposes, into broad segments, which sub-divide the long-run into a schematic sequence of chronological periods, each with an outline name. These sub-divisions have a long history and are institutionalized throughout the profession. In other words, the meta-narratives have gone, but the sub-divisions, which they once sustained, are outstaying their welcome.

Often, the established periodization is divided into a set of supposedly discrete historical stages, which act as mental 'default' systems. When questioned about their value, historians usually reply: *We know that these period divisions are purely artificial but they are useful heuristically, for teaching purposes.* However, such unruffled confidence should be questioned. By using outmoded period divisions, historians all too easily end up reifying historical stages about whose 'existence' they are otherwise sceptical, in another part of their minds. And, more importantly still, they and their students avoid thinking about alternatives.

It is true that some new specialist fields have consciously discussed the need to revise traditional periodization. In women's history, for example, there were initial high hopes that there might be a new 'women's history of the world', with a new chronology of change.[21] However, after much research and debate, the familiar and institutionally standardized divisions of 'ancient', 'medieval', and the various permutations of 'modern' have proved hard to budge. Feminist scholars themselves disagree about any alternative schema; and new big-picture accounts of a separate trajectory for women through time have been thin on the ground.

Similarly, some scholars of urban history wrote reflectively about the challenging light that comparative urban development threw upon traditional questions of periodization.[22] But there was very little response from other urban historians. And certainly no new 'urban' stage history has emerged that can be applied globally. The apparent failure of these new approaches suggests that what is wanted is not a new set of rival stages, but instead a different approach.

Common sets of historical stages are usually implicitly accepted rather than freshly justified. Even when there are, from time to time, stinging criticisms, such as Barraclough's 1955 attack upon 'medievalism',[23] the standard periodization remains unchanged – as much through its institutionalized status within the profession for strong intellectual reasons. A standard triad is thus *ancient/medieval/modern*, with the option of *postmodernism* as a contested extra with reference to very recent times.[24] Or, for Marxists, there is an alternative sequence. After many variants were canvassed, Stalin decreed that there were five main stages, each with a distinct form of economic production: *primitive communism (shared labour)/ancient (slave labour)/feudalism (bonded labour)/capitalism (waged labour)/communism (communal labour)*- with the unwelcome (for Marxists) extra option of *post-communism* in the post-1989 era.[25]

Stadial models of this type allow historians to keep chronological control, without anachronistically scrambling events or examples from one period of history with another. Each stage can then gain its own definitional label, hence allowing for straightforward contrasts between different periods and *Zeitgeists*. Furthermore, these segments of history can be fitted implicitly into either linear or cyclical accounts. With such assumptions, one country or world region can then be deemed 'ahead of' or 'behind' another, in terms of the expected stadial sequence – say, from 'barbarism' to 'civilization', or from pre-industrial to industrial, or from predominantly rural to urbanized.

Yet stage theories obscure as much as they illuminate. For a start, such schema make inadequate acknowledgement to any deep historical continuities that may persist over millennia. Instead, stage theories tend to encourage the erroneous idea that everything will change in synchronization, at the end of one stage and the start of the next.

Historical continuity is thus one great fatality within all stage theories, whether of rise or decline. The elements that persist through time have received much less theoretical attention than have theories of either revolution or evolution.[26] Yet without some constants it would be impossible to calibrate the extent of change on some comparative scale. There is, after all, a constant (c) at the heart of Einstein's famous formula $e = mc^2$, so the great guru of relativity theory did not himself eschew all absolutes.[27] In the study of history, historians might be expected to take an interest in the power of continuity, especially as they display great tenacity in holding onto long-standing historical periodizations[28] – but the stadial sub-divisions discourage giving attention to such considerations.

Very long-term incremental changes are also short-changed by the traditional stage divisions. As a result, it often happens that historians proclaim a novel trend in one period, while historians of prior or succeeding periods (or sometimes even both) are discovering the same novel trend in a quite different period. The 'rise of the middle class' was one such omnipresent development whose actual history was obscured rather than illuminated by grand claims for its role.[29] But historians should not be obliged to disaggregate long trends into smaller stages some micro-trends in human history, such as biological evolution, may indeed persist over millennia.

Problematic for all stage theories is the selection of defining criteria to start and end each finite stage. If one factor is highlighted, other important elements – which may persist, or which may change at other times – are ignored or underestimated. Interestingly, that point was noted long ago by Oswald Spengler – a stringent critic of the three-fold division of history into ancient, medieval, and modern. It is too arbitrary for historians to insert into history their own concerns, he insisted, and then to expect those concerns to govern all human development.[30]

Muddled 'modernity' provides one very central example of intellectual confusion. The concept is widely used and as widely diffused.[31] Historians often remark that the term is opaque but then continue to use it. Different experts have detected the 'birth of the modern' at numerous different points between the later twelfth century and the mid-twentieth century: a very prolonged period indeed for birth-pangs. There is also uncertainty as to whether and when 'modernity' has ended, if it has ended. Even the postmodernists, who agree that it has disappeared, disagree as to when its demise occurred – suggesting a range of dates from the 1950s to the 1990s.[32] Within the Anglo-American tradition, there is sometimes incorporated a further sub-division, known as the 'early modern', again with fluid start and end dates. Or for medievalists, there are variant options, with the so-called 'Middle Ages' partitioned into its 'early' and 'high' stages. In practice, therefore, a cheerful eclecticism rules. But the standard default systems continue alongside, inexorably institutionalized within the profession. Little wonder that History's reading public becomes either bemused or frankly sceptical.

Marxism offered the most famous set of historical stages, which were supposed to apply globally. These discrete historical eras came complete with their own in-built economic denominators and an in-built mechanism for change (often left unexplained in other stadial theories), in the form of the class struggle.[33] Convinced believers felt able, on the strength of this historical model, not only to understand the past but also to predict the future. Thus communist leaders, ruling in the name of Marxism, were confident that they held the key to history's grand trajectory. Many were thereby emboldened to impose draconian policies, in order to propel society more rapidly in the direction towards which, they believed, it was 'due' to go. In some cases, townspeople and intellectuals were forced into the countryside in the name of rural simplicity (Mao's China; Pol Pot's Cambodia). Yet, elsewhere country-people were herded into new towns in the name of socialist development (Stalin's Russia; Ceausescu's Romania). Thus, paradoxically, even an agreed historical framework could lead to very different, though equally high-handed, policy applications in practice.

Meanwhile, sincere Marxist researchers faced the same definitional and 'boundary' problems as did all those who accepted stadial models. There was no consensus about the number of stages or the key mechanisms and dates of change. Marxist historians of Britain disagreed about even key developments such as the transition from feudalism to capitalism.[34] Within that latter category, there were further problems. Some economic historians, like Russia's Mikhail Pokrovsky, bravely argued for an early stage of 'commercial capitalism' (international trade) which preceded 'industrial capitalism' (the factory system). Yet such revisionism incurred the wrath of Stalin, for muddying the inexorable march of history. He also rejected an alternative attempt to introduce a separate Asian mode of production (state-directed labour), to apply to China and the East, in lieu of feudalism.

Too many variations would generate too many variant pathways. As a result, stage theories tend to concentrate upon a relatively small number of organizing categories.[35] However, these great eras then seem unconvincing under close scrutiny, with too many internal complexities subsumed into one. Indeed, stage theories raise as many questions as they resolve. What, after all, is their general message? Upon close inspection, they often dwindle into *earlier; later; later still.* Moreover, the common names for the great stages are bald and open to challenge. In practice, a precise meaning has ebbed from the terminology of *ancient/medieval (feudal)/modern (capitalist)*, which now means little more than a historical time-spans *One – Two –Three – (and onwards).* The hollowness of the existing terminology strongly suggests the case for some creativity with 'naming' different eras. The term 'prehistory', in particular, seems particularly bizarre in application to pre-literate human existence, since those origins were absolutely integral to what followed.

No periodization 'summit' could or should resolve these dilemmas. As already noted, while historians currently work within the institutionalized frameworks, more and more individual researchers freely adopt their own timelines and historical frameworks. What can be expected, however, is a more explicit debate about these choices and justifications for the use of terminology. There is scope for more conferences and discussion forums that focus upon diachronic themes to compare and contrast across periods, as well as those that focus upon synchronic immersion within specified periods. What assumptions are being made about trends over time? Is history linear? Or cyclical? Or some combination of the two? Or some other shape entirely? To be sure, such debates need careful thought, to avoid the Scylla of banality and the Charybdis of *Oh, it's all so complex*.

Senior scholars, who sometimes turn to historiography, should be especially encouraged also to reflect upon historical periodization, in the light of a lifetime's research and teaching. That sub-division acknowledges that research neophytes have enough to do without taking on the cosmos as well. But young scholars, when turning a doctoral thesis into a publication, could also analyse how they see their own subject as fitting into a broader picture.

Collectively, too, there may be scope for many more diachronic linkages via collective research projects. Currently, there is in official thinking a modish stress – indeed, a positively dogmatic stress – upon the need for such enterprises to demonstrate interdisciplinarity. That innovation has been signally important in regenerating some subject areas, like biochemistry. But far from all ills are cured by the same medicine. For historians (and for all scholars working on longitudinal subjects, like historical geography), it would make as much or more sense to encourage inter-temporality. That is, there is a need for collective projects to study history 'in the long' as well as history 'in the round'. Conferences and research projects should be encouraged not just to review long spans of consecutive time but also to compare and contrast common themes or trends from disparate and separate periods of time. Such innovations should be the proper medicine for the subject. They constitute a challenge, certainly, but also a needed elixir.

Teaching also needs to be adjusted to provide a seedbed for diachronic debates. Too often, these days, students get a diet of rich synchronic detail but too little overview. They need such framework courses, to complement current 'pick-and-mix' programmes. Again, it should be stressed that overviews must not be taught as dogma, whether nationalist, religious, or ideological. They should provide concepts and themes for debate – not edicts about the inevitable course of history. Students need to encounter such interpretative schema, even if only (or especially if) to disagree. Ideally, indeed, they should have had framework courses at school, with some engaging long-span narratives that will help them to 'locate' the other courses which they study. The long-term has yet to be restored to the syllabus for pre-18s. But some university history departments are now filling the yawning gap with new or refreshed overview courses for first-year students – with positive feedback. There is no prescribed formula, needless to say. Some courses in the newly-named Big-History stretch back to the origins of the cosmos. Others content themselves with human affairs, whether from the primordial eras of pre-literate (misleadingly known as prehistory) or from any later point on the timeline up until today.[36]

Other teaching innovations should also look at different ways of incorporating the diachronic into the syllabus. Courses do not necessarily have to be organized around traditional linear trajectories. Instead, students can be invited to view a subject in synchronic detail alongside an analysis of the same subject's diachronic reputation (including forgetting as well as remembering).[37] Such measures enable students to assess how experiences in one period may either fit into or be revised in the longer-term story. Otherwise, without some explicit study of the different historical frameworks, people fall back on old mythic and belief patterns that subsist as sub-consciously held cultural traditions. In other words, unless they are challenged, the old Grand Narratives – whether cyclical or linear – live on determinedly in ghostly guise.

Three dimensionality

My own view is that the past can be studied with an improved notation, known as three-dimensionality. It does not exclude the macro-changes which are often taken to provide great turning points, as in various stage theories. Yet it does not assume that such revolutionary transformations will happen all the time, or in regular sequence. Also acknowledged in every period are the unduly neglected forces of deep continuity and the slow, incremental processes of micro-change. Alterations and adaptations between these great dimensions form the stuff of history.

Such an approach, first outlined in *Time and the Shape of History*,[38] is post-Progress, post-Marxist, and also post-Braudelian. That is, it accepts the important perception from the eminent French historian Fernand Braudel that historical interpretations must be longitudinal. His model of the diachronic is the most substantial to have been produced in the later twentieth century, restoring and indeed celebrating *la longue durée*. But if differs significantly from Braudel's assumption that history can be divided into three parallel layers, specified as *events (surface)/trends (intermediate)/ and geo-history (foundational).*[39] His model is too schematic in dividing the surface from the depths, and allocating different aspects of history to each separate level. Moreover, he accords to geography a greater continuity than it actually has; and it notably underplays the structural power of events. Neither Braudel in his later works[40] nor his successors in the *Annales* School of French historians actually used his tripartite system.[41]

Having examined the worldwide range of historical interpretations, it became apparent to me that it is more helpful to think in terms of longitudinal *dimensions* that interlock, rather than stratified and near-autonomous layers. One dimension is the power of continuity or persistence. It is found in many guises, not just in the form of geography. Examples can be found in the laws of physics, which do not change from day to day, or the rules of mathematics. They are not strictly time-less; but they are time-invariant. Other forms of persistence can be seen in long-lasting patterns of land use that continue through changing generations. Another example can be seen in the underlying structures of languages, which survive deep-rootedly throughout the many medium-term and short-term adaptations to both written and spoken linguistic forms. In fact, given that continuities seep everywhere, with porous boundaries between continuities and changes of all kinds, framing factors that hold things together in through-time persistence turn out, on closer analysis, to be markedly widespread.

Also recurrent is the power of gradual, incremental change or 'micro-change'. That dimension can be seen, for instance, in the slow pace of biological evolution, when species adapt over long aeons. The gradual transformation of human languages between successive generations gives another case-history, although linguistic mutations are occasionally abrupt, as in moments of language birth and death.

And the third process is the power of short, sharp drastic change, often termed 'revolution', also known as 'macro-change'. The extent of turbulence and discontinuity within history, both global and cosmic, is thus incorporated. An example is the Big Bang that began this universe, some 15 billion years ago. It is true that scientists like Fred Hoyle reject this once-off theory of cosmic origins. Yet, even in his rival model of successive universes, there are still drastic changes when one universe departs and the next arrives.

Putting together the three forces of continuity (persistence), micro-change (momentum) and macro-change (turbulence) makes a three-dimensional web or grid, which frames all history. Each aspect is seamlessly linked into the others, but their mutual relationships keep shifting, sometimes radically, making an interlocking but unruly braid of historical experience.

Continuity gives ballast to the system. It provides the benchmark against which other variations can be assessed. Often underestimated by historians and certainly under-theorized, its importance is very great. In people's personal lives, it can be manifested in the force of habit and repetition. Life in fact would be totally bewildering if everything had to be invented *de novo* from day to day. But instead people rely upon large swathes of existence remaining quietly unchanged – or broadly unchanged – from one moment to the next: like the meaning of words; like the physical environment; like the human genetic inheritance. Continuity, furthermore, tugs at the forces of change, and works to 'domesticate' and assimilate them.

Micro-change, being gradual and incremental, then adds its own gentle dynamism. It prevents the system from clogging. And its long-term trends are slow, subtle, easily absorbed. Some – like biological evolution – take place over millennia, so that living individuals are unaware of the quiet in-built momentum that occurs over the very long term. Micro-changes, which may be plural in any era, are thus characteristically hard to detect and often difficult to 'date', as they spread over long periods of time, from gestation to maturation.

Radical transformation, meanwhile, provides sharp impetus as well as turmoil. It may release some tensions but equally generate new ones, as when a political revolution settles old scores but also initiates new contests. Its force is dramatic, often shocking, always noticeable. Such great upheavals, however, are also imperceptibly assimilated by the forces of micro-change and continuity. Indeed radical discontinuity can then become the basis of a new continuity. Hence, at all times the three dimensions inter-relate, in an ever-changing balance.

None of these three dimensions, it should be emphasized once more, can be allocated rigidly to different features of life, since all three dimensions apply potentially to everything. Accordingly, it is misleading to think *à la Braudel* that geography (for example) must always represent continuity, since the earth has not only experienced major shocks in the past (and likely to face more in the future) but also continually undergoes subtle small modifications such as erosion, continental drift, and so forth (also unlikely to cease). Furthermore, it is equally blinkered to ignore other, non-geographical continuities. For example, human languages, which often adapt slowly, and sometimes change rapidly and surprisingly, also contain persistent features in their basic structures and grammars. Thus, alongside the power of revolution and upheaval, the forces of persistence and micro-change also need systematic evaluation.

Deep persistence, onwards momentum, drastic turbulence: these features frame everything. As a triad, they match the three dimensions of space. While that comprises the seamlessly interlocking triad of latitude, longitude and altitude, so there are simultaneously three longitudinal dimensions of history over time. And these interwoven and ever-varying dimensions can be tested (and debated) and assessed in application to every period or culture around the world.

Coda: past and future

Tracing patterns in the past encourages the hope that they can also be projected forward to help foretell the future. Among the famous prophetic models of history was the Marxist vision of the coming *Kingdom of Freedom.* Out of today's oppression would come tomorrow's liberation. Alas, the perfect society did not arrive on earth, as it was supposed to do. Because so many predictions of the future have failed to come true,[42] there is a rival litany of scepticism. People intone that: 'You can't learn from the past'. History is held to lack all meaning, other than that of chaos and confusion, rather as Macbeth defined life: 'a tale, told by an idiot, full of sound and fury, signifying nothing',[43] a counsel of despair updated in the song lyric by Sting: 'History will teach us nothing'.

Yet, humans routinely act in the assumption that there is and will continue to be a smooth continuity from the past into future. That steadfast (and justified) belief allows people to generate precise plans which anticipate specific events-to-come, as well as to estimate less precise but still calculable estimates of probabilities, with reference to events-likely-to-come. For example, buildings in earthquake zones can be fortified against the probability of future shocks, without knowing exactly when these will happen. Or, future financial risks can be quantified by bankers and hedge-fund experts, as a means of providing secure underpinning for otherwise speculative investments. Of course, in that latter case, the current credit crisis reveals that the formula was applied over-confidently. The unexpected did happen and the calculations proved to be faulty.

Understanding the three-dimensional nature of past and future provides a clear warning to that effect. There are always surprises, whether stemming from the unexpected generated by humans or the unexpected generated within the wider world. These upheavals lead to macro-changes, which constitute macro-turbulence within the system. The extent of radical change is unpredictable, except in the general sense of predicting that there will be some future 'unknown unknowns'.

Set against that, three-dimensionality also teaches that there will be some developing micro-changes, in the form of trends stretching from past to present and into the future. The details are not known with any precision. Yet these are 'known' unknowns. Two (linked) examples from human history in the past three centuries have been the global spread of mass literacy and the process of urbanization, leading to a rising proportion of the world's population living in towns. Understanding such trends, in the animate and inanimate worlds, provides a general framework for future planning. But such long-term trends are particularly hard to stop or to divert, as humans are currently realizing in terms of taking measures to halt the human contribution to climate change.

Throughout all this, three-dimensionality also offers a reminder that continuity will also work to 'domesticate' upheavals, both major and minor. It offers ballast to the system. In positive terms, it is stabilizing, even if to keen advocates of change it can also be seen as inertia. Thus the known 'knowns' of deep continuity will continue to interact in complex ways with the forces of micro- and macro-change. In other words, persistent 'normality' adds an element of 'drag' or resistance into all calculations or estimates of future transformation. Every dimension interacts with and gives feedback to the others.

Returning to the diachronic does *not* seek to halt what historians currently do. It positively seeks to enrich the subject and its public application. The clear need is to view all human history without trapping it into the 'timetable' of just one cultural tradition. To avoid that, historians need to study and debate outside as well as inside the familiar timeframes. And the answers should look not for single universals but for interlocking dimensions, which combine persistence (continuity) with micro-change and macro-change. In that way, humans can improve their greatest mental asset – their capacity to 'think long'.

Notes

1 With thanks to Tony Belton and Gelina Harlaftis for critical readings of the text.

2 An earlier version of this essay is also forthcoming in Italian translation: see Corfield, P.J., 'Tornare di nuovo al grande quadro storico', *Italia Contemporanea*, 250 (2008), pp. 89–102.

3 For introductory guides, see Cable, V., *The Storm: the world economic crisis and what it means* (London, 2009); Turner, G., *The Credit Crunch* (London, 2008); and

Phillips, K., *Bad Money: reckless finance, failed politics, and the global crisis of American capitalism* (New York, 2008).

4 D.H. Lawrence's sense of omnipresent sexual symbolism was famously challenged by Katherine Mansfield: 'And I shall *never* see sex in trees, sex in the running brooks, sex in stones, and sex in everything [as he does]': Meyers, J., *Katherine Mansfield: a biography* (London, 1978), p. 88.

5 Marx, K. and F. Engels, *Manifesto of the Communist Party* (1848), in K. Marx and F. Engels, *Selected Works* (Moscow, 1962), Vol. 1, p. 34: 'The history of all hitherto existing society is the history of class struggles'.

6 See Hegel, G.W.F., *The Philosophy of History*, transl. J. Sibree, ed. C.J. Friedrich (New York, 1956), p. 456: 'For the History of the World is nothing but the development of the Idea of Freedom'; and the Hegel-influenced Fukuyama, F., *The End of History and the Last Man* (New York, 1992).

7 Nietzsche, F., *Beyond Good and Evil* (1886), cited in idem, *The Will to Power*, transl. A.M. Ludovici (Edinburgh, 1909), Vol. 1, p. xi: 'A living thing seeks above all to discharge its strength – life itself is *Will to Power*'.

8 Dawkins is not alone among neo-Darwinists in applying competition to all aspects of human life; but his formulation, much disputed by geneticists, is a particularly clear version of this extrapolation: see Dawkins, R., *The Selfish Gene* (Oxford, 1976), pp. 38–9: 'Genes are competing directly with their alleles [rivals] for survival, since the alleles in their gene pool are alternatives for their slot on the chromosome of future generations … The gene is the basic unit of selfishness'.

9 Structuralism was an approach rather than a school of thought. Its heartland was within linguistics, semiotics, and anthropology; but there were attempts at establishing a structuralist Marxism, structuralist feminism, and structuralist history. See for variant overviews, Sarup, M., *An Introductory Guide to Post-Structuralism and Postmodernism* (London, 1988; 1993); Hawkes, T., *Structuralism and Semiotics* (London, 2003); and Harland, R., *Superstructuralism: the philosophy of structuralism and post-structuralism* (London, 1987).

10 Two ambitions examples include Jones, E.L., *Growth Recurring: economic change in world history* (Oxford, 1988); and Cameron, R.E., *A Concise Economic History of the World: from palaeolithic times to the present* (Oxford, 2003).

11 The general account by Coleman, D.C., *History and the Economic Past: an account of the rise and decline of economic history in Britain* (Oxford, 1987) applies in broad outlines to many other countries too.

12 Roberts, N., *The Holocene: an environmental history* (Oxford, 1998). Others in this genre include Ponting, C., *A Green History of the World* (London, 1991), extended as *World History: a new perspective* (London, 2000).

13 For critiques of Arnold J. Toynbee (1889–1975), see Montagu, M.F.A. (ed.), *Toynbee and History: critical essays and reviews* (Boston, Mass., 1956), plus Gargan, E.T. (ed.), *The Intent of Toynbee's History: a cooperative appraisal* (Chicago, 1961); and Silvestri, P., *Arnold Toynbee e la storia intera: un'importante ipotesi storica che abolisce ogni coordinato spazio-temporale* (Florence, 1991).

14 For such theories, see Bury, J.B., *The Idea of Progress: an inquiry into its origin and growth* (London, 1920); Spadafora, D., *The Idea of Progress in Eighteenth-Century Britain* (New Haven, 1990); and Lasch, C., *The True and Only Heaven: progress and its critics* (New York, 1991).

15 The question *Did science (or medicine) progress in your period?*, if asked at any conference on the history of science or medicine, gets a general response of disbelieving looks, chiding words, and accusations of thoughtless anachronism. It remains, however, a valid question to ask, although without blaming (or lauding) people in the past for differences between their knowledge and that of today.

16 See Drolet, M. (ed.), *The Postmodernism Reader: foundational texts* (London, 2003); and, in application to historical studies, Jenkins, K., *Re-Thinking History* (London, 1991); idem (ed.), *The Postmodern History Reader* (London, 1997); and Munslow, A. (ed.), *The Routledge Companion to Historical Studies* (London, 2000).

17 See Derrida, J., *Khôra* (Paris, 1993), pp. 58, 75–6, 96, for *Khôra* as an immanent, intangible, timeless framing for the cosmos. For commentaries, see too Wood, D., *The Deconstruction of Time* (Evanstown, Ill., 2001), pp. 260–1, 269, 270–3; and Hodge, J., *Derrida on Time* (London, 2007), pp. ix-x, 196–203, 205–6, 213–14.

18 Celebrating the 'death of the Enlightenment Project' forms part of postmodernist thought at its most polemical. Now critics return the compliment by identifying the 'death of postmodernism'. Or, alternatively, postmodernist thought is seen stillborn – 'slipping into the strange history of those futures that did not materialise': see Myerson, G., *Ecology and the End of Postmodernism* (Cambridge, 2001), p. 74.

19 For divergent dates suggested for the advent of postmodernism, see Corfield, P.J., *Time and the Shape of History* (London, 2007), pp. 124–31.

20 One of many rejections, penned by a historian, is Evans, R., *In Defence of History* (London, 1997). See also Gunn, S., *History and Cultural Theory* (Harlow, 2006).

21 See variously Miles, R., *The Women's History of the World* (London, 1988); Smith, B.G. (ed.), *Women's History: a global perspective* (Urbana, Ill., 2004); and, focusing upon cultural imprints rather than a temporal history, French, M., *From Eve to Dawn: a history of women in the world* (New York, 2008).

22 See especially Rozman, G., *Urban Networks in Russia, 1750–1800, and Premodern Periodisation* (Princeton, 1976); and idem, *Urban Networks in Ch'ing China and Tokugawa Japan* (Princeton, 1973).

23 Barraclough, G., '*Medium Aevum*: Some reflections on medieval history and on the term "The Middle Ages"', in his *History in a Changing World* (Oxford, 1955), pp. 54–63. The response from colleagues studying the relevant period of history was very frosty and Barraclough turned his attention to twentieth-century affairs instead.

24 For a critique of the Modernity triad, see Corfield, *Time and Shape of History*, pp. 131–48. See also Rabb, T.K., 'Narrative, periodization and the study of history', *Historically Speaking: Bulletin of the Historical Society [Boston University]* 8 (2007).

25 On the Marxist stages, see Corfield, *Time and Shape of History*, pp. 178–83.

26 The foremost historian theorist of continuity was Fernand Braudel (1902–85), on whom see especially Hexter, J.H., 'Fernand Braudel and the *Monde Braudellien*', in idem, *On Historians: reappraisals of some of the makers of modern history* (Cambridge, 1978), pp. 61–145. See also Burke, P., *The French Historical Revolution: the Annales school, 1929–89* (Cambridge, 1990), pp. 32–53; and Corfield, *Time and Shape of History*, pp. 29–32, 208–10.

27 Einstein's formula incorporates E (energy), M (mass) and C (*celeritas* = Latin for speed, measured as the constant speed of light in a vacuum, at just under 300,000 kilometres per second).

28 The difficulties as well as the challenges of continuity-history are seen in T. Zeldin's *An Intimate History of Humanity* (London, 1994), where human sexuality is confusingly explored without reference to any historical sub-divisions whatsoever.

29 For a critique, see Hexter, J.H., 'The myth of the middle class in Tudor England', *Explorations in Entrepreneurial History* 2 (1950), pp. 128–40; revised in idem, *Reappraisals in History* (London, 1961), pp. 71–116, esp. pp. 112–16.

30 Cited in Corfield, *Time and Shape of History*, p. 184.

31 Ibid., pp. 131–48.

32 See ibid., pp. 127–31; and Corfield, P.J., '*POST-Medievalism/Modernity/Postmodernity?*', forthcoming in *Rethinking History* (2010).

33 Marx and Engels took the motor concept of friction (the dialectic) from Hegel but gave the dialectic a material rather than an ideological basis, to form dialectical materialism: see Marx, K., 'Afterword to Second Edition of *Das Kapital, Vol. 1*' (1873), in Marx and Engels, *Selected Works*, Vol. 1, p. 456: 'The mystification which dialectic suffers in Hegel's hands, by no means prevents him from being the first to present its general form of working in a comprehensive and conscious manner. With him, it is standing on its head. It must be turned right side up again, if you would discover the rational kernel within the mystical shell'.

34 Highly illuminating are the rival views of the Communist Historians Group in the 1940s and early 1950s, as they debated the nature of the English state in the sixteenth century and whether there was or was not a 'bourgeois revolution' in the mid-seventeenth century: see Parker, D. (ed.), *Ideology, Absolutism and the English Revolution: debates of the British Communist Historians* (London, 2008).

35 A review of the most popular numbers for stage theories of history is provided in Corfield, *Time and the Shape of History*, pp. 164–73. See also for Western thought, Butler, C., *Number Symbolism* (London, 1970); and for Far-Eastern traditions, Guénon, R., *The Great Triad*, trans. P. Kingsley (Cambridge, 1991).

36 A compendious example of big history, which starts with the earth before getting to humans, is available in Christian, D., *Maps of Time: an introduction to big history* (Berkeley, 2004), although the unproblematic identification of the industrializing world post-1750 as 'Modernity' is disappointingly conventional for such an unconventional study. For a classic overview of the problems and

challenges of diachronic analysis, see too Barraclough, G., 'Universal history', in H.P.R. Finberg (ed.), *Approaches to History: a symposium* (London, 1962), pp. 83–109; and for other models of the long-term, Zerubavel, E., *Time Maps: collective memory and the social shape of the past* (Chicago, 2003).

37 This technique has been used successfully by myself when teaching a course on early nineteenth-century British history. Students were asked to select (with advice) a suitable topic to be studied in two separate essays, one assessing the subject's synchronic reputation and the other its diachronic reputation (including both the fall as well as rise of fame over time). After some initial trepidation, students warmed to the task and produced particularly original work on the diachronic dimension.

38 For detailed arguments, see Corfield, *Time and the Shape of History*.

39 Summarized in Braudel, F., *On History*, transl. S. Matthews (London, 1980), pp. 27–33, 74–8: from two related essays 'History and the Social Sciences' (1960) and 'History and Sociology' (1958–60).

40 Braudel later propounded an alternative three-layered economic model, with deep infrastructure/ intermediate market economy/ and surface commercial and financial transactions: see Braudel, F., 'Introduction', *Civilisation and Capitalism: fifteenth to eighteenth century – Vol. 1, the structures of everyday life*, transl. M. Kochan, revised S. Reynolds (London, 1981), pp. 23–4.

41 Burke, *French Historical Revolution*, pp. 107, 110–11, notes that, over time, the informal *Annales* 'school' of historians diversified and eventually dissolved.

42 Predictions, forecasts, planning, prophecies, and fortune-telling come in many forms, both sober and fanciful. For very diverse approaches, see Campion, N., *The Golden Age of Astrology: a cultural history of western astrology – the medieval and modern worlds* (London, 2009); Bobrick, B., *The Fated Sky: astrology in history* (New York, 2005); Armytage, W.H.G., *Heavens Below: utopian experiments in England, 1560–1960* (London, 1961); Boesky, A., *Founding Fictions: utopias in early modern England* (Athens, GA., 1996); Claeys, G. (ed.), *Modern British Utopias, 1700–1850* (London, 1997), 8 vols; Rescher, N., *Predicting the Future: an introduction to the theory of forecasting* (Albany, 1998); Strathern, O., *A Brief History of the Future : how visionary thinkers changed the world and tomorrow's trends are 'made' and marketed* (New York, Berkeley, 2007); and Goodman, D., *A History of the Future* (New York, 2009).

43 Shakespeare, W., *Macbeth* (1605/6), Act 5, sc. 5.

Bibliography

Barraclough, G., 'Universal history', in H.P.R. Finberg (ed.), *Approaches to History: a symposium* (London, Routledge, 1962), pp. 83–109.

Braudel, F., 'History and sociology' (1958–60), in F. Braudel, *On History*, transl. S. Matthews, (London, Weidenfeld, 1980), pp. 64–84.

—, 'History and the social sciences: the *longue durée*' (1960), in F. Braudel, *On History*, transl. S. Matthews, (London, Weidenfeld, 1980), pp. 25–54.

Burke, P., *The French Historical Revolution: the* Annales *school, 1929–89* (Cambridge, Polity, 1990).

Bury, J.B., *The Idea of Progress: an inquiry into its origin and growth* (London, Macmillan, 1920).

Cameron, R.E., *A Concise Economic History of the World: from Paleolithic Times to the Present* (Oxford, Oxford University Press, 2003).

Christian, D., *Maps of Time: an introduction to big history* (Berkeley, University of California Press, 2004).

Coleman, D.C., *History and the Economic Past: an account of the rise and decline of economic history in Britain* (Oxford, Clarendon, 1987).

Corfield, P.J., *Time and the Shape of History* (London, Yale University Press, 2007).

—, 'Tornare di nuovo al grande quadro storico', *Italia Contemporanea*, 250 (2008), pp. 89–102.

—, '*POST-Medievalism/Modernity/Postmodernity?*' in *Rethinking History* (2010 forthcoming).

Drolet, M. (ed.), *The Postmodernism Reader: foundational texts* (London, Routledge, 2003).

Evans, R., *In Defence of History* (London, Granta, 1997).

French, M., *From Eve to Dawn: a history of women in the world* (New York, Feminist Press, 2008).

Fukuyama, F., *The End of History and the Last Man* (London, Hamilton, 1992).

Goodman, D., *A History of the Future* (New York, Monacelli, 2009).

Gunn, S., *History and Cultural Theory* (Harlow, Pearson Longman, 2006).

Hegel, G.W.F., *The Philosophy of History*, transl. J. Sibree, ed. C.J. Friedrich (New York, Dover Publications, 1956).

Hexter, J.H., 'Fernand Braudel and the *Monde Braudellien*', in J.H. Hexter, *On Historians: reappraisals of some of the makers of modern history* (Cambridge, MA, Harvard University Press, 1979), pp. 61–145.

Hodge, J., *Derrida on Time* (London, Routledge, 2007).

Jenkins, K., *Re-Thinking History* (London, Routledge, 1991).

Lasch, C., *The True and Only Heaven: progress and its critics* (New York, Norton, 1991).

Marx, K. and Engels, F., *Selected Works*, 2 vols, (Moscow, Foreign Languages Publishing House, 1962).

Miles, R., *The Women's History of the World* (London, Joseph, 1988).

Montagu, M.F.A. (ed.), *Toynbee and History: critical essays and reviews* (Boston, Mass., Porter Sargent, 1956).

Mumford, L., *The Culture of Cities* (London, Secker and Warburg, 1938).

Munslow, A. (ed.), *The Routledge Companion to Historical Studies* (London, Routledge, 2000).

Parker, D. (ed.), *Ideology, Absolutism and the English Revolution: debates of the British Communist Historians* (London, Lawrence and Wishart, 2008).

Ponting, C., *A Green History of the World* (London, Sinclair-Stevenson, 1991), extended as *World History: A New Perspective* (London, Chatto and Windus, 2000).

Rescher, N., *Predicting the Future: an introduction to the theory of forecasting* (Albany, NY, State University of New York Press, 1998).

Roberts, N., *The Holocene: an environmental history* (Oxford, Blackwell, 1998).

Rozman, G., *Urban Networks in Ch'ing China and Tokugawa Japan* (Princeton, Princeton University Press, 1973).

—, *Urban Networks in Russia, 1750–1800, and Premodern Periodisation* (Princeton, Princeton University Press, 1976).

Smith, B.G. (ed.), *Women's History: a global perspective* (Urbana, IL, University of Illinois Press, 2004).

Spadafora, D., *The Idea of Progress in Eighteenth-Century Britain* (New Haven, Yale University Press, 1990).

Toynbee, A.J., *A Study of History*, 12 vols (Oxford, Oxford University Press, 1934–61).

Zeldin, T., *An Intimate History of Humanity* (London, Sinclair-Stevenson, 1994).

Zerubavel, E., *Time Maps: collective memory and the social shape of the past* (Chicago, Chicago University Press, 2003).

2

Changing Ancient Greek History

Robin Osborne

It is never easy to see trends until they have passed, and any account of current trends in any historical field is going to be both subjective and in danger of being less a description than a matter of wishing it were so. However, the nature of ancient history perhaps makes this exercise at least slightly less problematic in this case than in others. For, whereas in other fields of history much endeavour brings to light or to public prominence evidence which has previously languished unexploited, if not unknown, in archives, in the case of ancient history the body of data is relatively small and expands relatively slowly. Of course, fresh historical documents are being discovered all the time – particularly inscriptions – and archaeologists' discoveries make important contributions, as we shall see; but it remains the case that ancient history is changed much more by a changing agenda of questions than by changes in the evidential base.

Looking back at the history being written in the 1960s and 1970s, two things seem to me notable. The first is the continued dominance of political history. This is apparent not just in such exercises as Donald Kagan's re-writing of the history of the Peloponnesian War, or C.D. Hamilton's work on early fourth-century BC Sparta, but in such books as Meiggs' classic *The Athenian Empire* and de Ste Croix's *Origins of the Peloponnesian War.*[1] In both cases it is to a modern reader astonishing, I think, that questions of economics play so small a part. De Ste Croix does have an interest in economics, in as far as he wants to deny that the crucial inflammatory Athenian decree excluding the Megarians from the Athenian agora (market place and civic centre) had anything to do with regulation of trade. But he never thinks it relevant to examine Athenian economic resources or to think how Athenian prosperity might have affected Athenian willingness to enter what was bound to be a long war – this despite one ancient source, Diodorus, hinting very strongly that this was important.[2]

The second notable feature of 1960s and 1970s history is how static everything other than politico-military history is. Sometimes this static view is made explicit and defended. That is the case for one of the most striking of static views, the view of the ancient economy propounded by Moses Finley, in his 1973 book of that title.[3] Here, Finley maintains a fundamental identity to the whole of the ancient world, Roman as well as Greek. At other times, the static view is simply implicit in the general structure of accounts. That is the case for the important Thames and Hudson series on *Aspects of Greek and Roman Life*: *Festivals of the Athenians*, *Charities and Social Aid*, *Law in Classical Athens*, *Craftsmen in Greek and Roman Society*, *the Family in Classical Greece* – all of these become predominantly a matter of an unchanging situation.[4]

These two features have rather different pedigrees. Narrowly political and military narratives ignoring economics or cultural factors stood in a long tradition. This is how ancient history had largely been done in universities, and not only in the English-speaking world, for a century and more. Non-political history, by contrast, was something of a newcomer. The Thames and Hudson series greatly expanded the range of topics on which there were discussions accessible to undergraduates and general readers. Behind it stood both changes in what historians of other periods were studying and, perhaps more importantly, a growing interest by ancient historians in anthropology. This interest had burst upon the scene with Finley's *World of Odysseus*, in the 1950s, and was most straightforwardly manifested in the series of papers by Sally Humphreys, brought together in her *Anthropology and the Greeks*, of 1976.[5]

Behind these two different pedigrees were two common assumptions. The first of these is one implicit in much narrative history but sometimes explicit in social history: the assumption that writing the history of the ancient world should be done in the categories of the actors themselves. Meiggs and de Ste Croix ignored economic factors because Thucydides, their major source, also largely ignored them. Finley makes the absence among the Greeks of a category equivalent to our economics a reason for not applying the categories of modern economics to the ancient world. And his preference for 'orders and status' over 'class', as analytical terms, relates closely to this same preference for using the terms used by the ancients themselves. Citizen, metic (resident foreigner), and slave are the categories employed in Athenian Law; working class, middle class and upper class are not categories for any Athenian author. The 'actor's categories' of the anthropologist are simply assumed to be preferable to forcing upon another society the categories of the observer – a view which confuses the anthropologists' problems of description with the historians' need for analysis.

The second assumption is one for which anthropologists cannot be blamed. This is the assumption shared by both sorts of history that texts can be divided up without anything being lost. What I mean by that is the assumption that ancient texts are treated as simply made up of a series of separate statements, which can be taken one by one and re-deployed to illustrate different aspects of ancient life, without there being any loss. That assumption is most obviously problematic when we consider the texts of the Attic orators, texts of speeches delivered to persuade an Athenian jury to acquit or condemn someone on some particular charge. A good law-court speech constitutes a persuasive argument to which even its most throwaway claims can be seen to contribute. Taking those claims out of the text, without paying attention to what they were there for in the original context, is not only a rash thing to do, it is also to overlook their most valuable contribution to history – as indicators of the assumptions which an audience could be persuaded to hold, rather than facts which an audience already knew. But the problems of using sentences culled from law-court speeches apply to all other literary texts too, if to varying degrees and in varying manners.

I think that there are three major changes that we can observe happening in ancient Greek history over the past 20 years or so – though there remains plenty of ancient Greek history written in the manner I have identified as characteristic of the 1960s and 1970s. The first is a growing awareness that change over time is not just a feature of political and military history but of all history. The second is a willingness to ask of antiquity our questions, not simply to ask again the questions which the ancients themselves asked. And the third is a greater sensitivity to the constructedness of all history.

Let me take and illustrate these in turn, and try to show how, together, they serve not simply to tell us something about the changing priorities of the academy but also something important about the Greek past.

The most obvious example of the introduction of change over time into non-political histories of Greece concerns the history of the Greek countryside. Here, the influence of archaeology has been fundamental. The rise of intensive archaeological survey of the Greek countryside, from the late 1970s on, has revealed that that countryside was not marked by unchanging or slowly changing occupation, but by rapid changes in both settlement and exploitation. Just how surprising this is can be is best brought out by looking back to the Braudelian framework of '*histoire evenementielle*', '*moyen durée*' and '*longue durée*'. The changes to settlement and exploitation in the countryside are precisely the sorts of things that have been expected to occur over the medium term. Archaeology shows that they occur over the short term. Not only that, it has shown that there are very broad general trends to those changes. It is not a matter of more or less random fluctuations of settlement and exploitation, but of heavily patterned developments.

Some of the early work exploiting survey archaeology played down such change – in my *Classical Landscape*, of 1987, change is made a matter for discussion in only one chapter, the chapter on the politics of settlement, but van Andel and Runnels' *Beyond the Acropolis*, of 1987, and Victor Hansen's *The Other Greeks*, of 1994, have rightly insisted that the changing countryside has to be central to all discussions of Greek history, even if some of their particular interpretative claims are open to dispute.[6]

Nonetheless, the introduction of change over time is not simply something historians have had thrust upon them by archaeologists. Most significant of all here, I think, has been the influence of Foucault. It was Foucault who not only generally revealed the possibility that something traditionally not reckoned to have a history – sexuality – had one, but in writing that history he demonstrated generally the possibility, and necessity, of writing history in and of our terms, and specifically turned the essentially static account of Greek homosexuality by Dover into a dynamic story.[7]

But again, the introduction of a sense of changing history has extended to areas hardly influenced by Foucault. Take the history of Greek religion. Greek religion was written about in the 1970s as if there was a narrative of change from prehistory to history (from the second to the first millennium BC), but after that there was an essentially unchanging picture, where practices went on just the same, even if increasing scepticism was expressed by increasingly 'rational' Greeks. The different schools of thought about the origins and meaning of Greek animal sacrifice shared an assumption that Greek animal sacrifice in the Archaic period was essentially the same as Greek animal sacrifice in the Roman period.[8] In the 1990s, however, we began to see works on Greek religion which focus specifically on what changes over time – Robert Garland's *Introducing New Gods* and Robert Parker's *History of Athenian Religion*.[9]

I shall return to the question of the nature of these accounts of change over time, but I need first to explore the second area of change that I have identified: the willingness to ask questions of antiquity which were not antiquity's questions. There have, of course, continued to be plenty of explorations of ancient Greek concepts. We have had monographs on

Hybris and on *Aidos* (shame), for example.[10] It is notable that alongside work on *hybris*, we have also had work on violence, with the debate, largely initiated by Gabriel Herman, about whether or not ancient Athens was a violent society.[11] That is a debate which is related to the debate about the nature of *hybris*, but violence covers much more than *hybris* and covers a range of behaviour which no single Greek term encompasses. Likewise, alongside work on *aidos*, we have had James Davidson's work on 'the consuming passions', a work that achieves its eye-opening effects by bundling together courtesans and fishcakes, that is, bundling together aspects of life which works focusing on particular Greek categories would have kept apart.[12] As this example shows, one major consequence of moving from actors' categories to our categories is that what falls outside actors' categories can be moved to centre stage; most dramatically, this has put women onto an agenda from which their ancient exclusion from politics had removed them.

The prime example of a question that has come to dominate the recent agenda but was not on the ancient agenda is, however, the question we have learned from Foucault's earlier work, the question of power. In some senses, of course, this is a question familiar enough from the beginnings of the writing of Greek history. But only in very restricted senses. Herodotus' concerns with the great and marvellous works of Greeks and Persians, or Thucydides' concerns with telling the story of the greatest of all wars, are not fundamentally concerns to understand the nature of power either in Greek city-states or in the Persian Empire. Herodotus' ethnography is not focused upon the issue of power; Thucydides' analysis of military events, though concerned to explain success and failure, and to explain how things came about, is not focused upon the nature of power, and even his discussion of internal politics, though very concerned with how individuals handle power, takes only a very narrow view of the nature of that power.[13] Nor did twentieth-century ancient historians concern themselves with analysing power structures, except in passing or in as far as that was unavoidable. The reluctance of ancient historians to employ Marxist class analysis can be seen as part of a resistance to analysing the basis of power; Finley's preference for Weberian status over Marxist class is, in part, a preference for description of the social order over analysis of power dynamics.

What was essential for ancient historians to turn their attention to questions of power was their willingness to extend the bounds of history to encompass forms of evidence of which they had traditionally taken little notice – above all works of literature. Only when the full range of ancient Greek cultural production is taken into account does the ancient historian have the material available to observe the play of power in society. Ironically, perhaps, it is only when the ancient historian asks about the nature of power, and in doing so asks a question perhaps impossible to translate into ancient Greek, that the full range of Greek culture becomes grist to the mill, and materials held to have no importance for the writing of history become central in the story. Kurke's 'Traffic of Praise' is a good example.[14] Earlier twentieth-century historians had paid attention to Pindar (only) in as far as he gave possible information about the political regimes of cities other than Athens and Sparta. In the last 20 years, Pindar's odes have come to be seen as central evidence for the way in which individuals, families, and cities staked their claims to power.[15] Similarly, the rising scholarly interest in the Second Sophistic has come from the awareness that the discourse of the Greek writers of the first to the third century AD constitutes a negotiation of power relations with Roman overlords. Fascinatingly here, the work of a literary scholar, Ewen Bowie, written without any knowledge of Foucault's explorations of power and knowledge, and published in the early 1970s, had to wait more than a decade before others realized its central historical importance.[16]

The extension of the bounds of history has indeed led to a blurring of the demarcation lines between historians, literary critics, archaeologists and even, to some extent, ancient philosophers. This is something fundamental to the so-called 'Paris School' – the group of scholars associated with the Centre Louis Gernet, of whom Jean-Pierre Vernant and Pierre Vidal-Naquet were the leading figures in the 1960s and 1970s.[17] In the English-speaking world, however, this blurring of boundaries has been a feature only of the 1980s, the 1990s and the current decade, manifested in the work of such scholars as Jack Winkler, Leslie Kurke, Ian Morris and Richard Neer, in the USA, of Simon Goldhill, Peter Wilson, and me, in the UK[18]. And this blurring of boundaries between literature and history links in with the point I have already made about the insistence on reading texts whole and of looking at them in their full context.

It has not least been because of the interest in power relations and how they are constituted, and the interest in discourse which those questions generate, that ancient Greek history has taken a linguistic turn. The Foucaultian agenda here has joined with an agenda derived from the work of the philosopher J.L. Austin and associated in modern history with Quentin Skinner: the question of what people do with words. We have come to see that the contents of statements made by ancient sources, whether ancient historians or other ancient writers, may be less interesting than (and only to be understood in the context of) what they are doing in making that statement. What they are doing does not necessarily mean what they were intending to do, but rather what a statement like that in that context will have done, whether the author of the statement was conscious of it or not. Indeed, one of the important perceptions has been the way in which certain genres of statement effect a power relationship of which those uttering the statement may be quite unconscious.

This renewed interest in the overall tenor of a text, and in the way in which particular parts of a text affect the tenor of the whole, has served to narrow the gap between studies of history and studies of historiography. This applies not merely to ancient historiography but also to the more recent history of writing Greek history. Since the pioneering work of Richard Jenkyns and, even more importantly, Frank Turner, on the Victorians and Ancient Greece, there has been an explosion of interest in how the Greeks were constructed in the nineteenth century, with Grote and Burckhardt returning to the focus of scholarly attention, and the history of scholarship being rescued from the dry-as-dust pedants who previously had dominated the field.[19] One of the major motivations of such studies has been to understand what doing ancient Greek history achieves, or, more generally, to cite the felicitous formulation used by Simon Goldhill, to discover 'Who needs Greek?'.[20] One beneficial product of this renewed interest in the history of the writing of Greek history has been the beginnings, at least, of a rapprochement between scholars who work on Greek history and those who work on modern history. Even in countries such as Britain and North America, where ancient Greek history is primarily studied in Classics departments rather than History departments, ancient Greek history has moved distinctly closer to the writing of history more generally.

Another benefit of this move has been a distinctly changed understanding of ancient Greek history writing. Nowhere is this more apparent than in our understanding of Herodotus. Twenty years ago, Herodotus was the last archaic Greek and a writer with a ragbag mind, reproduced indiscriminately in the pages of his history. The only alternative to believing him to be naively credulous was Detlev Fehling's notion that he was a deliberate liar.[21] Since the publication of François Hartog's *Le miroir d' Hérodote*, and even more since 1989, the year in which John Gould's brilliant short introduction to Herodotus was published, Herodotus has completely changed.[22] He has become a sophisticated writer deeply embedded in late fifth-century BC intellectual developments, whose history is a carefully constructed exploration not only of relations between Greeks and others, but also of the nature of imperial power.[23] Appreciation of how Herodotus constructs his work as a work of literature and appreciation of his historical endeavour have gone hand in hand here, as understanding of oral history has enabled a much more sensitive discrimination of what it is, and what it is not, reasonable to expect Herodotus to know and do.

The Thucydidean revolution has been only marginally less profound. Whereas earlier twentieth-century scholarship had been inclined to leave Herodotus to the literary critic, Thucydides had been claimed by historians as their own. Loraux's insistence to fellow historians, in the early 1980s, that '*Thucydide n'est pas un collègue*', was a necessary one.[24] But in the 1990s the literary critics answered back, above all through the narratological discussion of his text, whose importance was signalled by Hornblower and then demonstrated by Rood.[25] Against the orthodoxy embodied in Andrewes's comments in the last volume of Gomme's *Historical Commentary on Thucydides*, that Thucydides' history was made up of sections written separately at different times and incompletely edited, Rood and Gribble, above all, have laid down a unitarian challenge by demonstrating the overall coherence of the work.[26] That coherence is important historically, as well as in literary terms, since it shows how we can reasonably ask, and answer, the question of what Thucydides is doing in his text.

In calling this chapter 'Changing Greek History', I wanted to do more than simply signal that different things have been done in Greek history in the past two decades, from what was being done in the previous two. I wanted also to suggest that Greek history has become much more of a story of change than it ever used to be. For, to the narrative of changing political events so long familiar, has been added a sense that values, ideology and outlook were constantly changing, as a result both of internal forces (a more volatile demography than has in the past been assumed) and of external forces (as Greeks as individuals and Greek cities adjusted to changing conditions elsewhere in the Greek and non-Greek Mediterranean). For, the contextual reading of all sorts of texts – the application to texts of the interpretative methods basic to archaeology – has led to a clear perception of those texts as both products of and active agents in the construction of a particular historical moment. In the 1960s and 1970s, to be progressive in Greek history was to aspire to write the anthropology of Greece. In the last two decades, we have, I believe, rediscovered just how vital change is to all aspects of history. In more senses than one, Greek history in the past two decades has become a more dynamic subject.

Notes

1 Kagan, Donald, *The Outbreak of the Peloponnesian War* (Ithaca, 1969); idem, *The Archidamian War* (Ithaca, 1974); idem, *The Peace of Nicias and the Sicilian Expedition* (Ithaca, 1981); Hamilton, Charles D., *Sparta's Bitter Victories. Politics and diplomacy*

in the Corinthian War (Ithaca, 1979); Meiggs, Russell, *The Athenian Empire* (Oxford, 1972); Ste Croix, Geoffrey E.M. de, *The Origins of the Peloponnesian War* (London, 1972).

2 Diodorus 12.40, following the 4th-century BC historian Ephorus (see 12.41.1), has Pericles give as an encouragement to Athenians to go to war, the speech on resources, which Thucydides (2.13) has Pericles give only after the initial Spartan invasion, where it serves to reassure the Athenians that they can survive the war.

3 Finley, Moses I., *The Ancient Economy* (Berkeley, 1973).

4 Parke, Hubert W., *Festivals of the Athenians* (London, 1976); Hands, Anthony R., *Charities and Social Aid* (London, 1968); MacDowell, Douglas M., *The Law in Classical Athens* (London, 1978); Burford, Alison, *Craftsmen in Greek and Roman Society* (London, 1972); Lacey, W. Keith, *The Family in Classical Greece* (London, 1968). To be fair, various of these authors (Hands, MacDowell) make some acknowledgement of change over time.

5 Finley, Moses I., *The World of Odysseus* (London, 1954); Humphreys, Sally C., *Anthropology and the Greeks* (London, 1976).

6 Osborne, Robin G., *Classical Landscape with Figures: the ancient Greek city and its countryside* (London, 1987); Van Andel, Tjeerd and Curtis N. Runnels, *Beyond the Acropolis: a rural Greek past* (Stanford, 1987); Hanson, Victor D., *The Other Greeks. The Family Farm and the Agrarian Roots of Western Civilization* (New York, 1994).

7 Dover, Kenneth J., *Greek Homosexuality* (London, 1978); Foucault, Michel, *The Uses of Pleasure. The History of Sexuality*, vol. 2 (London, 1985); and, on the relationship between the two, Davidson, James, 'Dover, Foucault and Greek homosexuality: penetration and the truth of sex', *Past and Present* 170 (2001), pp. 3–51, reprinted in R. Osborne (ed.), *Studies in Ancient Greek and Roman Society* (Cambridge, 2004), pp. 78–118 and Davidson, James, *The Greeks and Greek Love* (London, 2007).

8 Burkert, Walter, *Homo Necan* (1972, Eng. trans. Berkeley, 1983); idem, *Greek Religion* (1978, Eng. trans. Oxford, 1985); Detienne, Marcel and Jean-Pierre Vernant (eds), *The Cuisine of Sacrifice among the Greeks* (1979, Eng. trans. Chicago, 1989).

9 Garland, Robert, *Introducing New Gods: the politics of Athenian religion* (London, 1992); Parker, Robert C.T., *A History of Athenian Religion* (Oxford, 1996).

10 Fisher, Nicholas R.E., *Hybris: a study of the values of honour and shame in ancient Greece* (Warminster, 1992); Cairns, Douglas, *Aidos. The psychology and ethics of honour and shame in ancient Greek literature* (Oxford, 1993).

11 Herman, Gabriel, 'Tribal and civic codes of behaviour in Lysias 1', *Classical Quarterly* 43 (1993), pp. 406–19; idem, 'How violent was Athenian society?', in R. Osborne and S. Hornblower (eds), *Ritual, Finance, Politics* (Oxford, 1994); and *Morality and Behaviour in Democratic Athens: A Social History* (Cambridge, 2006); note also Van Wees, Hans, 'The mafia of early Greece. Violent exploitation in the seventh and sixth centuries BC', in K. Hopwood (ed.), *Organized Crime in Antiquity* (London, 1999), pp. 1–51.

12 Davidson, James, *Courtesans and Fishcakes. The Consuming Passions in Classical Athens* (London, 1997).

13 See Woodhead, Geoffrey A., *Thucydides on the Nature of Power* (Cambridge, Mass., 1970).

14 Kurke, Leslie, *The Traffic of Praise: Pindar and the poetics of social economy* (Ithaca, 1991).

15 Hornblower, Simon, *Thucydides and Pindar* (Oxford, 2004).

16 Bowie, Ewen, 'The Greeks and their past in the second sophistic', *Past and Present* 46 (1970), pp. 3–41 reprinted in M.I. Finley (ed.), *Studies in Ancient Society* (London, 1974), pp. 166–209; followed by Gleason, Maud, *Making Men. Sophists and self-presentation in ancient Rome* (Princeton, 1995); Swain, Simon, *Hellenism and Empire: language, classicism, and power in the Greek world, AD 50–250* (Oxford, 1996); Whitmarsh, Timothy, *Greek Literature and the Roman Empire: the politics of imitation* (Oxford, 2001); Goldhill, Simon (ed.), *Being Greek under Rome: the Second Sophistic, cultural conflict and the development of the Roman Empire* (Cambridge, 2001).

17 Particularly seminal was Vernant, Jean-Pierre and Pierre Vidal-Naquet, *Mythe et tragédie en Grèce ancienne* (Paris, 1972).

18 Winkler, John J., *The Constraints of Desire. The anthropology of sex and gender in ancient Greece* (London, 1990); Kurke, Leslie, *Coins, Bodies, Games, and Gold: the Politics of Meaning in Archaic Greece* (Princeton, 1999); Morris, Ian M., *Archaeology as Cultural History* (Oxford, 2000); Neer, Richard T., *Style and politics in Athenian vase-painting: the craft of democracy, ca. 530-460 B.C.E.* (Cambridge, 2003); Goldhill, Simon, 'The Great Dionysia and civic ideology', *Journal of Hellenic Studies* 107 (1987), pp. 58–76; Wilson, Peter J., *The Athenian Institution of the Khoregia: the Chorus, the City and the Stage* (Cambridge, (2000).

19 Jenkyns, Richard, *The Victorians and Ancient Greece* (Oxford, 1980); Turner, Frank M., *The Victorian Heritage of Ancient Greece* (Yale, 1981).

20 Goldhill, Simon, *Who Needs Greek?* (Cambridge, 2001).

21 Fehling, Detlev, *Herodotos and his sources: citation, invention and narrative art* (Leeds, 1989).

22 Hartog, François, *Le miroir d'Hérodote* (Paris, 1980); Gould, John, *Herodotos* (London, 1989).

23 Thomas, Rosalind, *Herodotos in Context* (Cambridge, 2000); Munson, Rosario, *Telling Wonders: Ethnographic and Political Discourse in the Work of Herodotus* (Ann Arbor, 2001).

24 Loraux, Nicole, 'Thucydide n'est pas un collègue', *Quaderni di Storia* 12 (1980), pp. 55–81.

25 Hornblower, Simon, 'Narratology and narrative technique in Thucydides', in S. Hornblower (ed.), *Greek Historiography* (Oxford, 1994), pp. 131–66; Rood, Timothy, *Thucydides: narrative and explanation* (Oxford, 1998).

26 Gribble, David, 'Narrator interventions in Thucydides', *Journal of Hellenic Studies* 118 (1998), pp. 41-67.

Bibliography

Bowie, Ewen, 'The Greeks and their past in the second sophistic', *Past and Present* 46 (1970), pp. 3–41 reprinted in M.I. Finley (ed.), *Studies in Ancient Society* (London, Routledge and Kegan Paul, 1974), pp. 166–209.

Burford, Alison, *Craftsmen in Greek and Roman Society* (London, Thames and Hudson, 1972).

Burkert, Walter, *Homo Necan* (1972, Eng. trans. Berkeley, University of California Press, 1983).

—, *Greek Religion* (1978, Eng. trans. Cambridge, MA, Harvard University Press, 1985).

Cairns, Douglas, *Aidos. The psychology and ethics of honour and shame in ancient Greek literature* (Oxford, Oxford University Press, 1993).

Davidson, James, *Courtesans and Fishcakes. The Consuming Passions in Classical Athens* (London, St Martin's Press, 1997).

—, 'Dover, Foucault and Greek homosexuality: penetration and the truth of sex', *Past and Present* 170 (2001), pp. 3–51, reprinted in R. Osborne (ed.), *Studies in Ancient Greek and Roman Society* (Cambridge, Cambridge University Press, 2004), pp. 78–118 and in Davidson, James, *The Greeks and Greek Love* (London, Weidenfeld and Nicolson, 2007).

Detienne, Marcel and Jean-Pierre Vernant (eds), *The Cuisine of Sacrifice among the Greeks* (1979, Eng. trans. Chicago, University of Chicago Press 1989).

Dover, Kenneth J., *Greek Homosexuality* (London, Yale University Press, 1978).

Fehling, Detlev, *Herodotos and his sources: citation, invention and narrative art* (Leeds, Francis Cairns, 1989).

Finley, Moses I., *The World of Odysseus* (London, 1954).

—, *The Ancient Economy* (Berkeley, University of California Press, 1973).

Fisher, Nicholas R.E., *Hybris: a study of the values of honour and shame in ancient Greece* (Warminster, Aris and Phillips, 1992).

Foucault, Michel, *The Uses of Pleasure. The History of Sexuality*, vol. 2 (London, Harvester, 1985).

Garland, Robert, *Introducing New Gods: the politics of Athenian religion* (London, Duckworth, 1992).

Gleason, Maud, *Making Men. Sophists and self-presentation in ancient Rome* (Princeton, Princeton University Press, 1995).

Goldhill, Simon, 'The Great Dionysia and civic ideology', *Journal of Hellenic Studies* 107 (1987), pp. 58–76.

— (ed.), *Being Greek under Rome: the Second Sophistic, cultural conflict and the development of the Roman Empire* (Cambridge, Cambridge University Press, 2001).

—, *Who Needs Greek?* (Cambridge, Cambridge University Press, 2001).

Gould, John, *Herodotos* (London, Weidenfield and Nicolson, 1989).
Gribble, David, 'Narrator interventions in Thucydides', *Journal of Hellenic Studies* 118 (1998), pp. 41–67.
Hamilton, Charles D., *Sparta's Bitter Victories. Politics and diplomacy in the Corinthian War* (Ithaca, Cornell University Press, 1979).
Hands, Anthony R., *Charities and Social Aid* (London, Thames and Hudson, 1968).
Hanson, Victor D., *The Other Greeks. The Family Farm and the Agrarian Roots of Western Civilization* (New York, Free Press, 1994).
Hartog, François, *Le miroir d'Hérodote* (Paris, Gallimard, 1980).
Herman, Gabriel, 'Tribal and civic codes of behaviour in Lysias 1', *Classical Quarterly* 43 (1993), pp. 406–19.
—, 'How violent was Athenian society?', in R. Osborne and S. Hornblower (eds), *Ritual, Finance, Politics* (Oxford, Oxford University Press, 1994).
—, *Morality and Behaviour in Democratic Athens: A Social History* (Cambridge, Cambridge University Press, 2006).
Hornblower, Simon, 'Narratology and narrative technique in Thucydides', in S. Hornblower (ed.), *Greek Historiography* (Oxford, Oxford University Press, 1994), pp. 131–66.
—, *Thucydides and Pindar* (Oxford, Oxford University Press, 2004).
Humphreys, Sally C., *Anthropology and the Greeks* (London, Routledge and Kegan Paul, 1976).
Jenkyns, Richard, *The Victorians and Ancient Greece* (Oxford, Oxford University Press, 1980).
Kagan, Donald, *The Outbreak of the Peloponnesian War* (Ithaca, Cornell University Press, 1969).
—, *The Archidamian War* (Ithaca, 1974).
—, *The Peace of Nicias and the Sicilian Expedition* (Ithaca, Cornell University Press, 1981).
Kurke, Leslie, *The Traffic of Praise: Pindar and the poetics of social economy* (Ithaca, Cornell University Press, 1991).
—, *Coins, Bodies, Games, and Gold: the Politics of Meaning in Archaic Greece* (Princeton, Princeton University Press, 1999).
Lacey, W. Keith, *The Family in Classical Greece* (London, Thames and Hudson, 1968).
Loraux, Nicole, 'Thucydide n'est pas un collègue', *Quaderni di Storia* 12 (1980), pp. 55–81.
MacDowell, Douglas M., *The Law in Classical Athens* (London, Thames and Hudson, 1978).
Meiggs, Russell, *The Athenian Empire* (Oxford, Oxford University Press, 1972).

Morris, Ian M., *Archaeology as Cultural History* (Oxford, Oxford University Press, 2000).

Munson, Rosario, *Telling Wonders: Ethnographic and Political Discourse in the Work of Herodotus* (Ann Arbor, University of Michigan Press, 2001).

Neer, Richard T., *Style and politics in Athenian vase-painting: the craft of democracy, ca. 530–460 BCE* (Cambridge, Cambridge University Press, 2003).

Osborne, Robin G., *Classical Landscape with Figures: the ancient Greek city and its countryside* (London, George Philip, 1987).

Parke, Hubert W., *Festivals of the Athenians* (London, 1976).

Parker, Robert C.T., *A History of Athenian Religion* (Oxford, Oxford University Press, 1996).

Rood, Timothy, *Thucydides: narrative and explanation* (Oxford, Oxford University Press, 1998).

Ste Croix, Geoffrey E.M. de, *The Origins of the Peloponnesian War* (London, 1972).

Swain, Simon, *Hellenism and Empire: language, classicism, and power in the Greek world, AD 50–250* (Oxford, Oxford University Press, 1996).

Thomas, Rosalind, *Herodotos in Context* (Cambridge, Cambridge University Press, 2000).

Turner, Frank M., *The Victorian Heritage of Ancient Greece* (New Haven, Yale University Press, 1981).

Van Andel, Tjeerd and Curtis N. Runnels, *Beyond the Acropolis: a rural Greek past* (Stanford, Stanford University Press, 1987).

Van Wees, Hans, 'The mafia of early Greece. Violent exploitation in the seventh and sixth centuries BC', in K. Hopwood (ed.), *Organized Crime in Antiquity* (London, Duckworth, 1999), pp. 1–51.

Vernant, Jean-Pierre and Pierre Vidal-Naquet, *Mythe et tragédie en Grèce ancienne* (Paris, F. Maspero, 1972).

Whitmarsh, Timothy, *Greek Literature and the Roman Empire: the politics of imitation* (Oxford, Oxford University Press, 2001).

Wilson, Peter J., *The Athenian Institution of* the Khoregia: the *Chorus, the City and the Stage* (Cambridge, Cambridge University Press, 2000).

Winkler, John J., *The Constraints of Desire. The anthropology of sex and gender in ancient Greece* (London, 1990).

Woodhead, A. Geoffrey, *Thucydides on the Nature of Power* (Cambridge, MA, Harvard University Press, 1970).

3

New Perspectives in Greek Archaeology in the Last Twenty Years

John Bintliff

It is a great honour to have been invited to join this gathering of international scholars, who are celebrating the twentieth anniversary of the Ionian University History Department by presenting some of the key developments in History and Archaeology over this last generation of research.

My brief was to focus on what has been happening in the archaeology of Greece. Naturally, my choice of notable developments will be a personal one, but I believe that the new research I will summarize includes some of the most striking new discoveries, new methods and new ways of interpretation. I shall also be covering – very generally with the space available – all the periods of Greek prehistory and history, as indeed this is perhaps *the* most significant innovation in Greek Archaeology over the last 20 years – the extension of mainstream archaeological research across the whole time-range of human presence in Greece, from the Palaeolithic hunters through to the Greek and Roman civilizations, and on into Byzantine, Crusader, Ottoman and even Early Modern times.

The Palaeolithic and Mesolithic hunter-gatherers in Greece

Two excellent conferences have summarized a new wave of Greek and foreign-school research on the Palaeolithic and Mesolithic of Greece – convened by Bailey[1] and by Galanidou and Perlès,[2] respectively. Central to current research projects is the remarkable example set by the final publication of the Anglo-Greek Epirus project, which ran from the early 1960s to the 1990s and was brought together in a fine two-volume synthesis edited by Geoff Bailey in 1997.[3] Bailey skilfully exposes the changing adaptation of hunting peoples, and the animals they hunted, to the difficult and dynamic climate and landscape of the rugged northwest Greek mainland during the last Ice Age and the beginning of our current interglacial era, preferring a Darwinian and an ecological perspective to fashionable post-modern approaches. His justification for such a biological approach is presented in a final conclusion, which has an impressive philosophical argument.

The first farmers – the Greek Neolithic Age

For me, the greatest impact in this long – 4,000-year – period, when settled mixed farming established itself everywhere in Greece, has come from the monograph by Catherine Perlès.[4] The special focus here is on the more than 1,000-year-long early period, and the remarkable evidence from Thessaly, where hundreds of long-lived tell-villages sit packed densely together in the fertile plains (on average just 1–2 kilometres apart) (Figure 3.1). Perlès convincingly argues that in this region an unparalleled society developed and persisted over an immense time-span. Artistically creative, peaceful and highly social, small-scale and manageable, it was kept this way by regular fissioning of the villages if they grew too large.

Europe's first civilization – the Minoan palace states of Bronze Age Crete

The last generation has seen the discovery or reinterpretation of several new minor palatial or town centres on the island of Crete. But more significant for me has been a radical critique of existing models of how the Minoan palaces functioned, their relations with each other, and the socio-political organization which revolved around these elaborate urban centres. A key part in this 'rethinking' of the Minoan civilization has been played by Jan Driessen, Colin MacDonald and Ilsa Schoep.[5] It is well-argued that each palace has its own historical path, that the larger centres competed against each other, even at times suppressing their rivals, and, most controversial, that only in their final phases were the palaces the residences of a royal dynasty, before which they were political and ritual theatres in which competing regional elite families residing *around* the palaces shared or alternated in power. Whereas in the later use of the 'palaces' access was restricted and the general public displaced by a dominant elite, for much of their life – and this now extends at Malia, if not elsewhere, back into the mature Early Bronze Age – the ceremonial rituals in the Central and West Courts may have performed district integration roles.

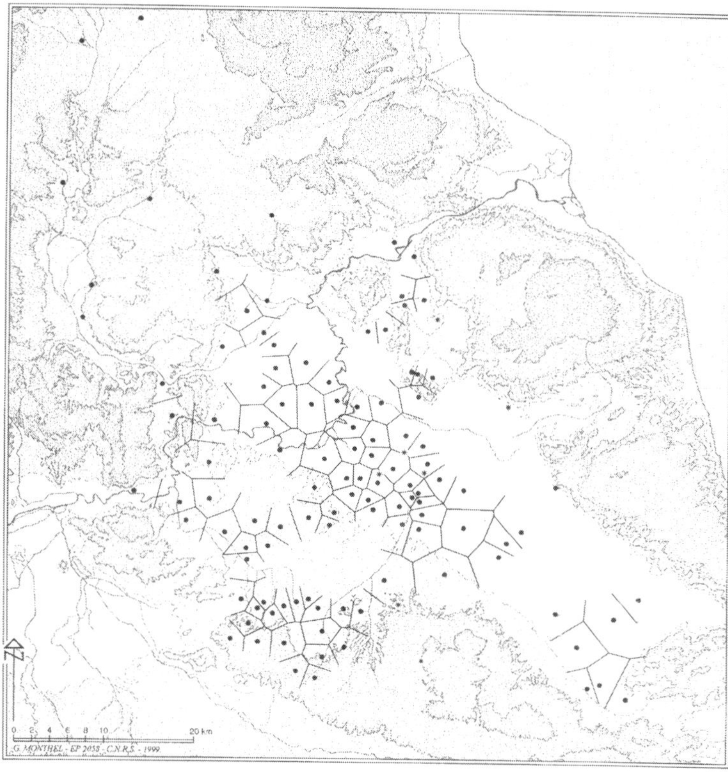

Figure 3.1: Early Neolithic tell-villages packed densely in the Thessalian fertile plains (Perlès 2001)

The Mycenaean civilization of the Bronze Age mainland

The most interesting development here has been intensive research into the origins of the Mycenaean states, focusing both on their background in preceding Middle Helladic societies and the earliest stages of the emergence of civilization, at the beginning of the Late Bronze Age. Restudy of the first elite burials at key sites involves anthropological work on the dynastic groups, with DNA now being applied to test for kinship relations within elite cemeteries and between the elites of different centres.[6] The symbolism of emerging power has been traced in the elaboration, over time, of forms of prestigious dress and personal equipment, creating new 'identities' of class division as the state arises out of local chiefdom societies.[7] The number and location of elite burial monuments has been used to trace the crystallization of larger territorial states out of numerous smaller chiefdoms and village-level societies.[8] Re-examination of the Pylos palace excavations has suggested that the earliest palace may have resembled a Minoan court-centred complex, only being replaced by a typical megaron-centred Mycenaean mainland design in a second phase, perhaps coinciding with the expansion of the Pylian State into the neighbouring region of eastern Messenia.[9] A generalized 'rethinking' of the scale and the geographical scope of Mycenaean palaces and states has been carried out, with a fruitful debate between those who still consider there to have been a series of palatial powers with comparable-sized kingdoms and a general control over surplus production, others who minimize the impact of palaces on their regional populations, and others, perhaps the majority, adopting an intermediate position.[10]

Dark Age Greece

Just over a generation ago, the collapse of Bronze Age civilization was seen as followed by some 500 years of a 'year-zero' society of low population and primitive culture, after which came such a rapid cultural recovery, in Late Geometric times, that it was dubbed the 'eighth-century renaissance'. Anthony Snodgrass's chart of burial numbers (1977, 1987) seemed to confirm the population stagnation and dramatic takeoff.[11] However, two key discoveries have changed this picture forever. The first occurred in 1980 but its impact has been growing ever since – the chieftain's house and elite burial at Lefkandi on Euboea,[12] proving, to most people's surprise, that even at the supposed lowest point of the Dark Age, around 1000 BC, society was probably focused on local chieftains and their retinues rather than being dispersed and egalitarian.[13] This was reinforced by a second key discovery – this an intellectual one – when Ian Morris demonstrated, to most people's satisfaction, that the low numbers of buried people over the Dark Age was due to the exclusion of half the population – the lower class or '*kakoi*', from formal burial.[14] This underlined the powerful control of the chiefly elite or '*basileis*' and their armed followers over a peasant majority throughout the period, encouraging us to consider that the Homeric legends were sung in these great houses to associate the Dark Age power structure with that of the Bronze Age. The implications of these discoveries have now been intelligently discussed in an authoritative review of the period by Oliver Dickinson.[15]

The Classical Greek Age

Although traditional concerns such as the interpretation of fine art and architecture continue to form the bulk of Classical Greek archaeology publications, increasingly rich results are being obtained by applying mainstream archaeological approaches to everyday life. The potential of anthropological and analytical approaches to ordinary material culture can be judged by the finest recent book on everyday life in Classical Greece, that of Cahill on the city of Olynthus.[16] Even more remarkable is the fact that our best large-scale sample of ancient Greek houses and their contents comes from the joint American-Greek excavations here in the 1920s and 1930s, but such was the quality of the work, that Cahill has reanalysed and reinterpreted the finds to produce new and exciting insights into patterns of household behaviour, gender spaces in the home, variable wealth levels and economic specialization across the city as a whole. Even richer information has been obtained from recent high-quality urban excavations, even though the areas excavated are, of course, far smaller.[17] Parallel work on the social meaning of space in domestic buildings is advancing rapidly and providing concrete evidence for issues often left unclear from textual sources.[18]

In the Classical Greek countryside, intensive field-by-field surface survey has also revealed a degree of settlement and land use often unparalleled in any later period, as well as fine detail of farm plans and the function and social status of rural settlements. The richest information was revealed in the outstanding monograph by Hans Lohmann on his survey in the Athenian *demos* of Atene.[19]

More obviously spectacular, not least for the public, has been a series of excavations in Macedonia, at urban sites such as Pella and Dion, of royal palaces at Aigai-Vergina and Pella, and, of course, in the dynastic tombs of the ruling elite at Vergina, including the claimed tomb monument of Philip II.[20] The high level of art, architecture and urban planning, and its much earlier beginnings than previously thought, challenge the old perception, fed by ancient Athenian propaganda, that Macedonia was a backward region till the later fourth century BC. The stupendous rich gifts in the dynastic tombs, and the unprecedented and vast scale of the royal palace complexes, give powerful evidence of the early development of a symbolic art and architecture of absolute power, which can now be seen to form the roots of Hellenistic monarchical prestige display, as well as of the new plans of residences of wealthy people throughout the Hellenistic world.[21]

Roman Greece

Long neglected, except for its fine sculpture and public architecture, research into Greece under Roman rule has blossomed dramatically in the last 20 years. The most abundant new information has been gained through the revolutionary spread of intensive surface survey, and nothing demonstrates the power of combining regional survey with historical texts than Sue Alcock's classic study of '*Graecia Capta*', where we gained for the first time a closer understanding of how the Roman impact transformed Greece, for the good, but equally to its detriment.[22] Moreover it has become clear that some regions benefitted, others lost out drastically, whilst there was a total contrast between life in Greece in early Roman times and in late Roman Imperial times.

Since the surveys reviewed by Alcock, a new level of much greater detail has become available for reconstructing changing life in town and country, through the application of a higher level of resolution in surface survey data. Let me illustrate this through a small area of countryside belonging to the Graeco-Roman city of Thespiai, in Boeotia.[23] South of the city, some 18 rural settlements were identified, for each of which we collected sufficient detail to reconstruct what we can call 'the biography' of each farmstead or villa. Take the site called LSE1, for example: Classical Greek pottery is everywhere, showing a large estate centre (Figure 3.2); in Early Roman times (Figure 3.3, left) characteristic pottery is mostly confined to a dense but small western focus – the farm shrank to a small establishment; then, in Late Roman times (Figure 3.3, right) very rare and dispersed pottery finds indicate the abandonment of the site as a residence, whilst the location became a temporary field shed or place for dumping manure.

If we put all the site biographies together, we can compose the biography of the whole landscape, and this is how it looks: an unsurpassed population level for Classical Greek times, with rural farms and villages surrounding a giant, 100-hectare city. In final Hellenistic and Early Roman times a catastrophic decline of population and land use: the city loses 60 per cent of its size and rural sites shrink or disappear. In Middle Roman times a slight recovery of rural sites is marked by a new landscape of villas and villages, and this expands much further by Late Roman times, although the city never recovers its size. We see in this sequence the collapse of a large city with a considerable population of independent peasants, into a small city from where most peasants commute to work on villa estates, which though large have, arguably, a very small resident population.

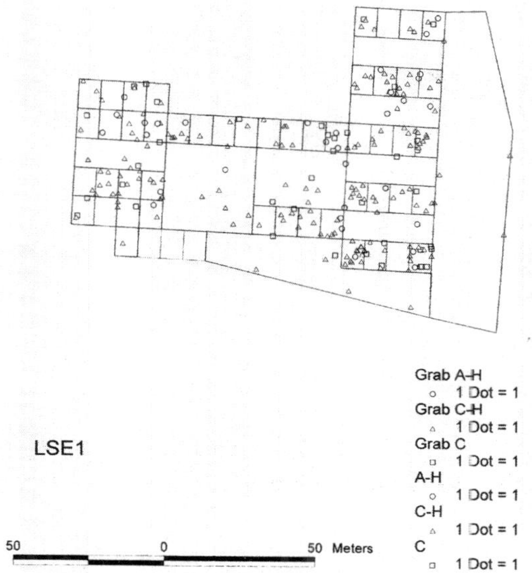

Figure 3.2: Distribution of Classical Greek ceramics at site LSE1 in the countryside of the Greco-Roman city of Thespiae

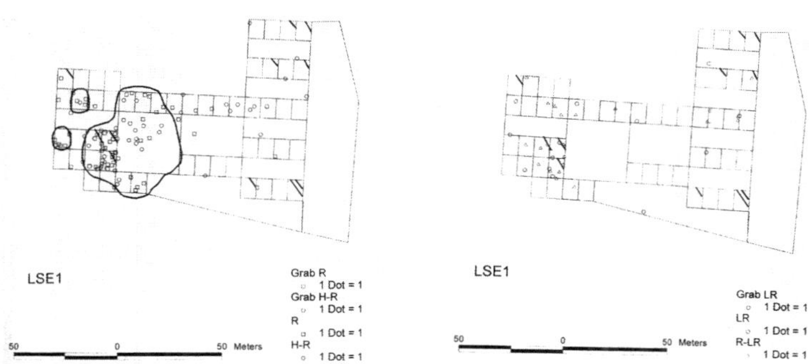

Figure 3.3: Distribution of Roman ceramics at site LSE1 in the Early Roman (left) and Late Roman times (right), showing the shrinking and finally the abandonment of the site as a residence

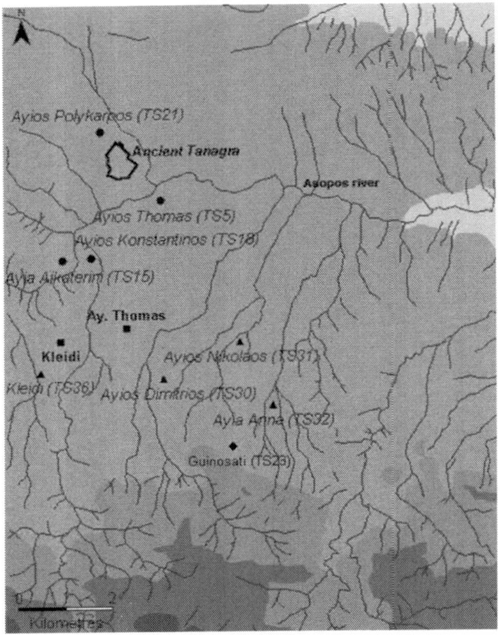

Figure 3.4: Deserted medieval villages studied close to ancient Tanagra and marked with survey TS numbers

Byzantine and Crusader Greece

It is not unfair to say, and indeed Timothy Gregory has written (in the *Oxford Dictionary of Byzantium*), that the archaeology of Byzantine Greece has barely been born. What he means by this is that almost all research until the 1980s was focused on the rich monuments – churches and icons – with rare attention to everyday life and material culture. Once again I would like to highlight the major contribution that has been made in the last 20 years through surface survey, in bringing us close to the Byzantine man in the street, or rather man and woman in the village! Take the case of the deserted rural village of Agios Thomas, close to ancient Tanagra and in a way its replacement, where we shall look at the research of Athanasios Vionis (Figure 3.4: deserted Medieval villages studied marked with survey TS numbers).[24] The abandoned Byzantine village forms a large sherd scatter north of the standing eleventh-century church, which was later converted into a Crusader tower dominating the village. The study grid placed over

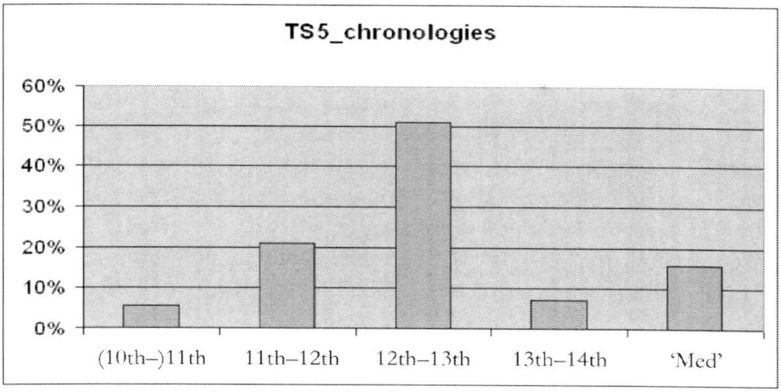

Figure 3.5: Dated ceramics from the Byzantine village of Agios Thomas (TS5) illustrate the life-cycle of the village

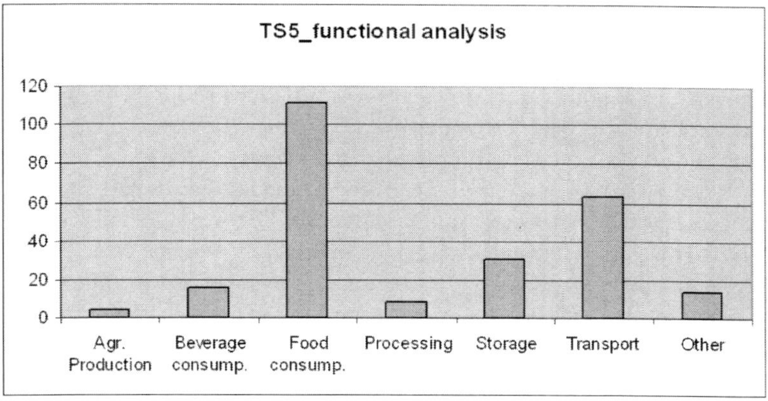

Figure 3.6: Functional analysis of ceramics collected from the Byzantine village of Agios Thomas (TS5)

its surface yielded a rich harvest in diagnostic pieces of ceramics, allowing Vionis to demonstrate that the settlement was founded with the church in the late tenth or the eleventh century (Figure 3.5), grew to its maximum in late Middle Byzantine times and the early Crusader period (when it was apportioned to a Frankish estate-holder residing at the site), and, like most others of its type, was abandoned in the fourteenth century as a result of the Black Death and endemic warfare. Vionis, however, goes beyond settlement history to use the ceramics to investigate everyday life (Figure 3.6): the village, though small, had access to imported pottery and invested heavily in social dining – tableware comprises the largest category of broken pots.

Venetian and Ottoman era Greece

Perhaps the fastest-moving new field of Greek Archaeology is a sub-discipline that does not formally exist for Greece: Post-Medieval Archaeology. The most exciting results are now emerging through combining very detailed research in historical archives with regional surface survey and standing building recording.[25] The records kept by the Venetian Empire for Crete and, for a brief period, also for the Peloponnese, offer data on population, economy, and uniquely for landholding.[26] In the Ionian University History Department Professor Tsougarakis is a leading scholar in this field of Byzantine and Venetian archival research, participating in exactly such a collaboration with survey archaeologists in Crete. The Pylos Project in Messenia has also been combining Venetian and Ottoman archives in its regional surface survey of the Post-Medieval countryside.

Equally exciting research has emerged in the last generation from the swift emergence of an Ottoman archaeology for Greece.[27] No one has done more to bring to our consciousness the built heritage of the 500 years of Ottoman rule in Greece than Machiel Kiel, equally expert in the reading of Ottoman imperial archives,[28] so it is fitting to introduce his work by mentioning perhaps his most important contribution, a joint book with a Greek colleague on the Ottoman monuments, extant and ruined, and archives for the island of Lesbos, rich in scholarship and finely illustrated.[29]

Let me show how specialists such as Kiel are contributing also to the new landscape history of Greece, being produced by regional intensive surface survey, by linking his archival research to study on the ground of villages listed in the tax defters (registers) from the fifteenth to the eighteenth century.[30] In the next figure we see the villages of Boeotia in the first surviving tax record, showing large Greek refuge villages (in black) from the population collapse we referred to above, in the fourteenth century, but surrounded by a sea of newly-arrived Albanian colonists in small clan-hamlets (in white) (Figure 3.7). One hundred years of the *Pax Ottomanica*, and both Greek and Albanian settlements have multiplied and grown in size (Figure 3.8). Another one hundred years, and the local effects of the decline of the empire, immortalized in a much-cited article by Inalcik are apparent – abandonment and shrinkage of settlements everywhere (Figure 3.9).[31] And this is how we can follow the big picture at the individual settlement level: the village of Panagia, one of the large Greek survivor communities in the foothills of Mount Helikon, begins – as our grid-based ceramic survey of its surface makes clear – as a small community at the foot of a Crusader feudal tower. During the early Ottoman era, it swells to maximum size (Figure 3.10), its population estimated on archaeological data at more than 1,000 people neatly matched by its taxable inhabitants in the defters The wealthy villagers founded two monasteries and one dozen watermills, and we have found the religious foundations and six of the sixteenth-century mills. The seventeenth-century decline hits Panagia especially hard – its population drops by two-thirds, and the free community is broken up into 13 tied estates or çifliks. The location is soon abandoned.

The traditional houses of Greece

There has been a strong tradition of Folklore Studies in Greece, and many excellent books have appeared on public and private architecture. We single out especially the many volumes on Greek domestic architecture, organized by region, published by the Melissa Printing House.[32] However, a growing interest by architectural historians and archaeologists in traditional houses, which are disappearing rapidly, is now leading to the regional cataloguing of the surviving examples.[33] Nonetheless, as archaeologists, what we have needed is a detailed study combining excavated houses from as early as Byzantine and Frankish times, houses described or portrayed by historical writers and painters, and the surviving domestic buildings of pre-modern date. Ideally it would also treat the house as a social rather than a merely typological environment. We now have this pioneering work, in the excellent monograph by Eleftherios Sigalos.[34] Particularly noteworthy is the evidence for the predominance of the longhouse in southern mainland Greece, in both country and town. This common home for the family and its livestock is well-represented not only in surviving examples, but also at archaeological sites, as we discovered on the acropolis of the ancient city of Tanagra, where a ruined hamlet of four longhouses was discovered in a single row, associated with a localized concentration of seventeenth- and early eighteenth-century ceramics.

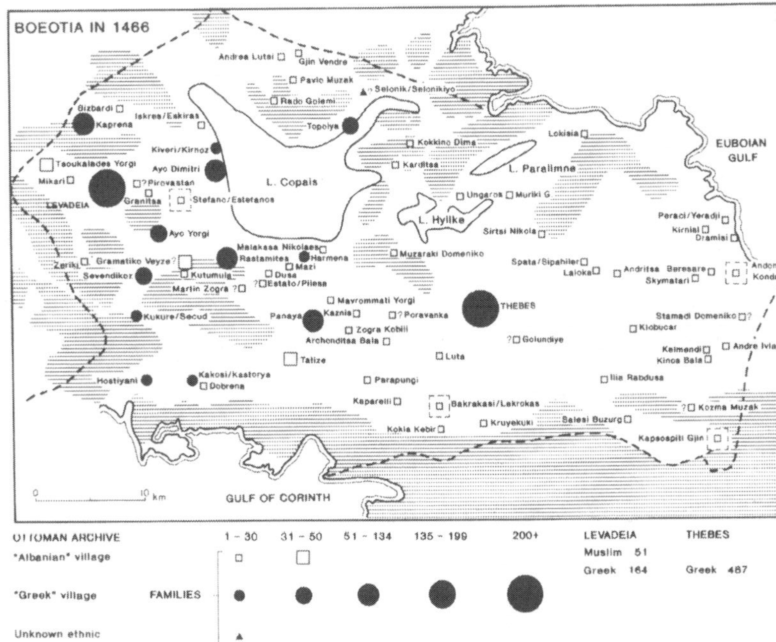

Figure 3.7: Villages of Boeotia in the first survived Ottoman tax record of 1466 (large Greek refuge villages in black and newly-established Albanian villages in white)

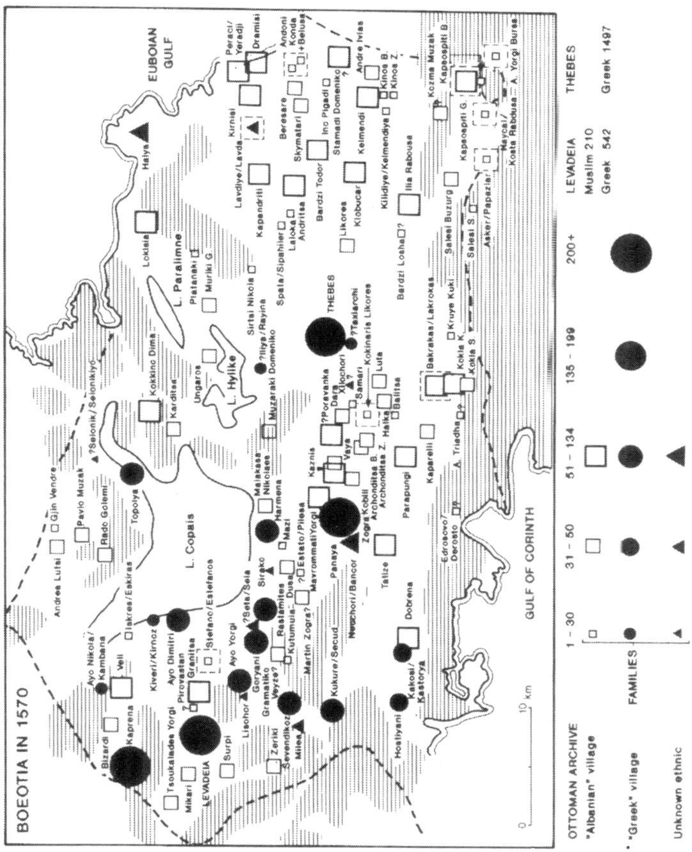

Figure 3.8: Villages of Boecotia in the tax record of 1570

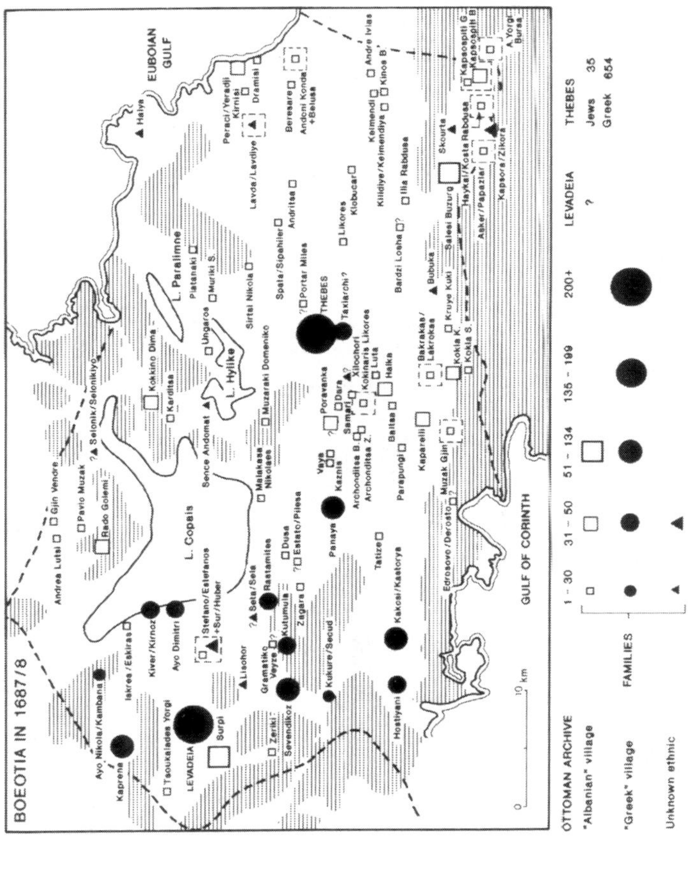

Figure 3.9: Villages of Boeotia in the tax record of 1687/8

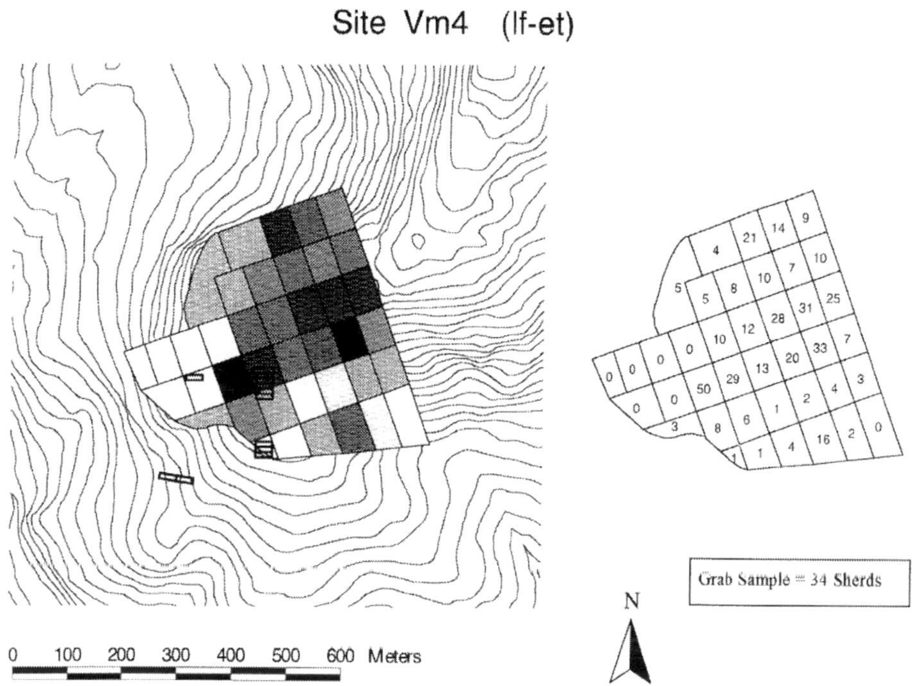

Figure 3.10: Distribution of Early Ottoman ceramics at the village of Panagia (site VM4) in the foothills of Mount Helicon

The historiography of Greek history and archaeology

Finally, the last 20 years have seen a rich harvest of self-reflection into the social and political factors which have influenced the study of the Greek past. Critical studies of European travellers, for example, have clarified the ways in which their perceptions of early Modern Greece and its past were coloured by imperialist and Orientalist prejudices. One of the best of this genre is the thoughtful analysis of British travellers by our host Professor Tsougarakis's wife, Mrs Angelomatis-Tsougarakis.[35] The influence of factors such as Greek nationalism and politics on the history of Greek archaeology has likewise been explored by scholars such as Michaelis Fotiadis,[36] and Yannis Hamilakis. A striking if chilling example comes from the article by Hamilakis and Yalouri, where political prisoners on the island of Makronisos, in the 1940s and 1950s, were re-educated from their allegiance to Communism by being compelled to construct model Parthenons, so as to realign themselves with European democratic history.[37] Ian Morris has also thoughtfully explored the burden placed on Greek studies by the role thrust on it by Western Europeans since the eighteenth century, as the paradigm of the origins of European civilization (1994, 2004).[38]

Notes

1 Bailey, G.N., E. Adam, et al. (eds), *The Palaeolithic Archaeology of Greece and Adjacent Areas*, British School at Athens Studies 3 (London, 1999).

2 Galanidou, N. and C. Perlès (eds), *The Greek Mesolithic. Problems and Perspectives*, British School at Athens Studies 10 (London, 2003).

3 Bailey, G. N. (ed.), *Klithi: Palaeolithic Settlement and Quaternary Landscapes in Northwest Greece* (Cambridge, 1997), vols 1–2.

4 Perlès, C., *The Early Neolithic in Greece* (Cambridge, 2001).

5 Driessen, J., I. Schoep, et al. (eds), *Monuments of Minos. Rethinking the Minoan Palaces* (Liège, 2002); Schoep, I., 'Architecture and power: the origins of Minoan "palatial architecture"', in J. Bretschneider, J. Driessen and K. van Lerberghe, *Power and Architecture. Monumental Public Architecture in the Bronze Age Near East and Aegean* (Leuven, 2007), pp. 213–36.

6 Brown, T.A., et al., 'DNA analysis of bones from Grave Circle B at Mycenae', *Annual of the British School at Athens* 95 (2000), pp. 115–19; Voutsaki, S., 'Age and gender in the southern Greek mainland, 2000–1500 BC', *Ethnogr.-Archaeol.Z.* 45 (2004), pp. 339–63.

7 Kilian-Dirlmeier, I., 'Beobachtungen zu den Schachtgräbern von Mykenai und zu den Schmuckbeigaben Mykenischer Männergräber', *Jahrbuch Des Römisch-Germanischen Zentralmuseums (JRGZM)* 33 (1986), pp. 159–98.

8 Voutsaki, S., 'Mortuary evidence, symbolic meanings and social change: a comparison between Messenia and the Argolid in the Mycenaean period', in

K. Branigan, *Cemetery and Society in the Aegean Bronze Age* (Sheffield, Sheffield Academic Press, 1998), pp. 41–58.

9 Nelson, M.C., 'Pylos, block masonry and monumental architecture in the Late Bronze Age Peloponnese', in Bretschneider, Driessen and van Lerberghe, *Power and Architecture*, pp. 143–59.

10 Galaty, M.L. and W.A. Parkinson (eds), *Rethinking Mycenaean Palaces II* (Los Angeles, Cotsen Institute of Archaeology, University of California, 2007).

11 Snodgrass, A., *Archaeology and the Rise of the Greek State* (Cambridge, 1977); Snodgrass, A., *An Archaeology of Greece* (Stanford, 1987).

12 Popham, M., E. Touloupa, et al., 'The hero of Lefkandi', *Antiquity* 56 (1982), pp. 169–74.

13 Morris, I., *Archaeology as Cultural History* (Oxford, 1999).

14 Morris, I., *Burial and Ancient Society. The Rise of the Greek City-State* (Cambridge, 1987).

15 Dickinson, O.T.P.K., *The Aegean from Bronze Age to Iron Age* (London, 2006).

16 Cahill, N., *Household and City Organisation at Olynthus* (New Haven and London, 2002).

17 Ault, B.A., *The Excavations at Ancient Halieis 2: The House. The Organisation and Use of Domestic Space* (Bloomington, 2005).

18 Ault, B.A. and L.C. Nevett (eds), *Ancient Greek Houses and Households* (Philadelphia, University of Pennsylvania Press, 2005); Westgate, R.C., 'Space and decoration in Hellenistic houses', *Annual of the British School at Athens* 95 (2000), pp. 391–426; Westgate, R.C., 'House and society in Classical and Hellenistic Crete', *American Journal of Archaeology* 111 (2007), pp. 423–57.

19 Lohmann, H., *Atene. Forschungen zu Siedlungs- und Wirtschaftsstruktur des klassischen Attika* (Köln, 1993).

20 Andronikos, M., *Vergina. The Royal Tombs* (Athens, 1989). (Greek edition 1984).

21 Etienne, R., C. Müller, et al., *Archéologie Historique de la Grèce Antique* (Paris, 2000).

22 Alcock, S.E., *Graecia Capta. The Landscapes of Roman Greece* (Cambridge, 1993).

23 Bintliff, J. and P. Howard, 'Studying needles in haystacks - Surface survey and the rural landscape of Central Greece in Roman times', *Pharos. Journal of the Netherlands Institute in Athens* 7 (1999), pp. 51–91; Bintliff, J.L., P. Howard, et al. (eds), *Testing the hinterland: The work of the Boeotia Survey (1989–1991) in the southern approaches to the city of Thespiai* (Cambridge, 2007).

24 Bintliff, J.L., E. Farinetti, et al., 'The Tanagra project: investigations at an ancient city and its countryside (2000–2002)', *Bulletin de Correspondence Hellènique* 2004–5 (2008), pp. 541–606.

25 Davies, S. and J.L. Davis (eds), *Between Venice and Istanbul. Colonial Landscapes in Early Modern Greece*, Hesperia Supplement 40 (Athens, 2007).

26 Cf. for the northeast Peloponnese, Dokos, K. and G. Panagopoulos, *To Venetiko Ktimatologio tis Vostitsas* (Athens, 1993).

27 Bintliff, J.L., 'Considerations for Creating an Ottoman Archaeology in Greece', in Davies and Davies, *Between Venice and Istanbul*, pp. 222–36.

28 Cf. Kiel, M., 'The rise and decline of Turkish Boeotia, 15th–19th century', in J.L. Bintliff, *Recent Developments in the History and Archaeology of Central Greece* (Oxford, 1997), pp. 315–58.
29 Karidis, D.N. and M. Kiel, *Mytilinis Astigraphia kai Lesvou Chorographia* (Athens, 2002).
30 Bintliff, J.L., 'The Two Transitions: Current Research on the Origins of the Traditional Village in Central Greece', in J.L. Bintliff and H. Hamerow, *Europe Between Late Antiquity and the Middle Ages. Recent Archaeological and Historical Research in Western and Southern Europe* (Oxford, 1995), pp. 111–30.
31 Inalcik, H., 'The Ottoman decline and its effect upon the Reaya', in H. Birnbaum and S. Vryonis, *Aspects of the Balkans, Continuity and Change* (The Hague, 1972), pp. 338–54.
32 *Elliniki Paradosiaki Architektoniki* (Athens, 1984 et seq.), 8 vols.
33 Kizis, G., *Pilioreitiki Oikodomia* (Athens, 1994); Cooper, F., *Houses of the Morea: Vernacular Architecture of the Northwest Peloponnesos (1205–1955)* (Athens, 2002); Bintliff, J.L., B. Slapsak, et al., 'The Leiden-Ljubljana Ancient Cities of Boeotia Project. Summer 2007–Spring 2008', *Pharos. Journal of the Netherlands Institute in Athens* 15 (2009 (2007)), pp. 18–42.
34 Sigalos, E., *Housing in Medieval and Post-Medieval Greece* (Oxford, 2004).
35 Angelomatis-Tsougarakis, H., *The Eve of the Greek Revival* (London, 1990).
36 Fotiadis, M., 'Modernity and the past-still-present: Politics of time in the birth of regional archaeological projects in Greece', *American Journal of Archaeology* 99 (1995), pp. 59–78; idem, 'Imagining Macedonia in prehistory, ca. 1900–1930', *Journal of Mediterranean Archaeology* 14/2 (2001), pp. 115–35.
37 Hamilakis, Y. and E. Yalouri, 'Antiquities as symbolic capital in modern Greek society', *Antiquity* 70 (1996), pp. 117–29.
38 Morris, I., 'Archaeologies of Greece', in I. Morris, *Classical Greece: ancient histories and modern archaeologies* (Cambridge, 1994), pp. 8–47; idem, 'Classical Archaeology', in J.L. Bintliff, *The Blackwell Companion to Archaeology* (Oxford, 2004), pp. 253–71.

Bibliography

Alcock, S.E., *Graecia Capta. The Landscapes of Roman Greece* (Cambridge, Cambridge University Press, 1993).

Andronikos, M., *Vergina. The Royal Tombs* (Athens, Ekdotike Athenon, 1989). (Greek edition 1984).

Angelomatis-Tsougarakis, H., *The Eve of the Greek Revival* (London, Routledge, 1990).

Ault, B.A., *The Excavations at Ancient Halieis 2: The House. The Organisation and Use of Domestic Space* (Bloomington, In., Indiana University Press, 2005).

— and L.C. Nevett (eds), *Ancient Greek Houses and Households* (Philadelphia, University of Pennsylvania Press, 2005).

Bailey, G.N. (ed.), *Klithi: Palaeolithic Settlement and Quaternary Landscapes in Northwest Greece*, Vols 1–2 (Cambridge, McDonald Institute for Archaeological Research, 1997).

—, E. Adam, et al. (eds), *The Palaeolithic Archaeology of Greece and Adjacent Areas*, British School at Athens Studies 3 (London, The British School at Athens, 1999).

Bintliff, J.L., 'The Two Transitions: Current Research on the Origins of the Traditional Village in Central Greece', in J.L. Bintliff and H. Hamerow, *Europe Between Late Antiquity and the Middle Ages. Recent Archaeological and Historical Research in Western and Southern Europe* (Oxford, Tempus Reparatum. BAR International Series 617, 1995), pp. 111–30.

—, 'Considerations for Creating an Ottoman Archaeology in Greece' in S. Davies and J.L. Davis, *Between Venice and Istanbul: Colonial Landscapes in Early Modern Greece* (Athens, The American School of Classical Studies at Athens. Hesperia Supplement 40, 2007), pp. 222–36.

—, E. Farinetti, et al., 'The Tanagra project: investigations at an ancient city and its countryside (2000–2002)', *Bulletin de Correspondence Hellènique* 2004–5 (2008), pp. 541–606.

— and P. Howard, 'Studying needles in haystacks - Surface survey and the rural landscape of Central Greece in Roman times', *Pharos. Journal of the Netherlands Institute in Athens* 7 (1999), pp. 51–91.

—, P. Howard, et al. (eds), *Testing the hinterland: The work of the Boeotia Survey (1989–1991) in the southern approaches to the city of Thespiai* (Cambridge, MacDonald Institute Monographs, University of Cambridge, 2007).

Bintliff, J.L., B. Slapsak, et al., 'The Leiden-Ljubljana Ancient Cities of Boeotia Project. Summer 2007–Spring 2008', *Pharos. Journal of the Netherlands Institute in Athens* 15 (2009 (2007)), pp. 18–42.

Brown, T. A. et al., 'DNA analysis of bones from Grave Circle B at Mycenae', *Annual of the British School at Athens* 95 (2000), pp. 115–19.

Cahill, N., *Household and City Organization at Olynthus* (New Haven and London, Yale University Press, 2002).

Cooper, F., *Houses of the Morea: Vernacular Architecture of the Northwest Peloponnesos (1205–1955)* (Athens, Melissa Publishing House, 2002).

Davies, S. and J.L. Davis (eds), *Between Venice and Istanbul. Colonial Landscapes in Early Modern Greece*, Hesperia Supplement 40 (Athens, American School of Classical Studies, 2007).

Dickinson, O.T.P.K., *The Aegean from Bronze Age to Iron Age* (London, Routledge, 2006).

Dokos, K. and G. Panagopoulos, *To Venetiko Ktimatologio tis Vostitsas* (Athens, Morphotiko Institouto Agrotikis Trapezas, 1993).

Driessen, J., I. Schoep, et al. (eds), *Monuments of Minos. Rethinking the Minoan Palaces* (Liège, Université de Liège, 2002).

Elliniki Paradosiaki Architektoniki (Athens, Melissa Publishing House, 1984 et seq.), (8 vols).

Etienne, R., C. Müller, et al., *Archéologie Historique de la Grèce Antique* (Paris, Ellipses, 2000).

Fotiadis, M., 'Modernity and the past-still-present: Politics of time in the birth of regional archaeological projects in Greece', *American Journal of Archaeology* 99 (1995), pp. 59–78.

—, 'Imagining Macedonia in prehistory, *ca.* 1900–1930', *Journal of Mediterranean Archaeology* 14(2) (2001), pp. 115–35.

Galanidou, N. and C. Perlès (eds), *The Greek Mesolithic. Problems and Perspectives.* British School at Athens Studies 10 (London, The British School at Athens, 2003).

Galaty, M.L. and W.A. Parkinson (eds), *Rethinking Mycenaean Palaces II* (Los Angeles, Cotsen Institute of Archaeology, University of California, 2007).

Hamilakis, Y. and E. Yalouri, 'Antiquities as symbolic capital in modern Greek society', *Antiquity* 70 (1996), pp. 117–29.

Inalcik, H., 'The Ottoman decline and its effect upon the Reaya', in H. Birnbaum and S. Vryonis, *Aspects of the Balkans, Continuity and Change* (The Hague, Mouton, 1972), pp. 338–54.

Karidis, D.N. and M. Kiel, *Mytilinis Astigraphia ke Lesvou Chorographia* (Athens, Olkos, 2002).

Kiel, M., 'The rise and decline of Turkish Boeotia, 15th–19th century', in J.L. Bintliff, *Recent Developments in the History and Archaeology of Central Greece* (Oxford, Tempus Reparatum, 1997), pp. 315–58.

Kilian-Dirlmeier, I., 'Beobachtungen zu den Schachtgräbern von Mykenai und zu den Schmuckbeigaben Mykenischer Männergraeber', *Jahrbuch Des Römisch-Germanischen Zentralmuseums* 33 (1986), pp. 159–98.

Kizis, G., *Pilioreitiki Oikodomia* (Athens, Politistiko Technologiko Idryma ETBA, 1994).

Lohmann, H., *Atene. Forschungen zu Siedlungs- und Wirtschaftsstruktur des klassischen Attika* (Köln, Böhlau Verlag, 1993).

Morris, I., *Burial and Ancient Society. The Rise of the Greek City-State* (Cambridge, Cambridge University Press, 1987).

—, 'Archaeologies of Greece', in I. Morris, *Classical Greece: ancient histories and modern archaeologies* (Cambridge, Cambridge University Press, 1994), pp. 8–47.

—, *Archaeology as Cultural History* (Oxford, Blackwell, 1999).

—, I., 'Classical Archaeology', in J.L. Bintliff, *The Blackwell Companion to Archaeology* (Oxford, Blackwell, 2004), pp. 253–71.

Nelson, M.C., 'Pylos, block masonry and monumental architecture in the Late Bronze Age Peloponnese', in J. Bretschneider, J. Driessen and K. van Lerberghe, *Power and Architecture* (Leuven, Peeters Press, 2007), pp. 143–59.

Perlès, C., *The Early Neolithic in Greece* (Cambridge, CUP, 2001).

Popham, M., E. Touloupa, et al., 'The hero of Lefkandi', *Antiquity* 56 (1982), pp. 169–74.

Schoep, I., 'Architecture and power: the origins of Minoan "palatial architecture"', in J. Bretschneider, J. Driessen and K. van Lerberghe, *Power and Architecture* (Leuven, Peeters Press, 2007), pp. 213–36.

Sigalos, E., *Housing in Medieval and Post-Medieval Greece* (Oxford, British Archaeological Reports, 2004).

Snodgrass, A., *Archaeology and the Rise of the Greek State* (Cambridge, Cambridge University Press, 1977).

—, *An Archaeology of Greece* (Stanford, Stanford University Press, 1987).

Voutsaki, S., 'Mortuary evidence, symbolic meanings and social change: a comparison between Messenia and the Argolid in the Mycenaean period', in K. Branigan, *Cemetery and Society in the Aegean Bronze Age* (Sheffield, Sheffield Academic Press, 1998), pp. 41–58.

—, 'Age and gender in the southern Greek mainland, 2000–1500 BC', *Ethnogr.-Archaeol.Z.* 45 (2004), pp. 339–63.

Westgate, R.C., 'Space and decoration in Hellenistic houses', *Annual of the British School at Athens* 95 (2000), pp. 391–426.

—, 'House and society in Classical and Hellenistic Crete', *American Journal of Archaeology* 111 (2007), pp. 423–57.

4

Twenty Years of Medieval History in France: A Preliminary Assessment

Anita Guerreau-Jalabert

It is not possible in a few pages to make a comprehensive survey of the developments in medieval historiography over the last 20 years. Instead, with more modest aims, I intend to focus my attention on France. This is still somewhat ambitious, and I cannot hope to produce more than a brief sketch that will inevitably overlook certain complex subtleties.

Nevertheless, I believe that my comments about French medieval historiography will be relevant to other countries. My analysis of the situation in France, although perhaps not applicable to the precise content of the subject in each country, which is influenced by different intellectual and research traditions, will relate more widely to the position that universities, politics and public debate give to medieval history.[1] It is clear that these factors, which almost all European countries share and which are constantly changing, have more influence on historiography than we care to acknowledge. It is, therefore, necessary to compare the importance of the medieval period with that of other periods, and to consider how the academic status of other history-based social sciences has developed and changed. Above all, I want to look at the way society scrutinizes our relationship with the past and history; and at how this might effect research and the politics surrounding cultural heritage.[2]

Research areas

If there is one thing that all scholars readily agree on, it is decline. Decline has plunged economic history into, for want of a better term, semi-oblivion. This fate is shared by medieval, ancient, modern (that is, before the nineteenth century) and perhaps even contemporary history. Medieval scholarship in France developed largely thanks to the historian Marc Bloch and the journal *Annales – Economies, Sociétés, Civilisations.* Until the 1970s, numerous books and theses had been written about this period. Now, unfortunately, it has little more than a residual influence and fails to arouse the slightest interest among the next generation of academics. At that time, archaeologists were making their own contributions to medieval history, from different but consistent and imaginative angles. The study of habitat, a topic that had emerged earlier, when medieval archaeology was just beginning to take hold, is an example of this, as are the recent and impressive innovations in archaeological techniques. The latter have revolutionized our knowledge of land, soil properties and methods of crop growth, production and consumption. However, for reasons I shall analyse later, archaeology's real finds have only received limited response. They have hardly been incorporated into the body of medieval knowledge or been used to question and scrutinize existing ideas about the material foundations of medieval society. This failure means that we have now almost abandoned the study of 'social groups', such as merchants, peasants, city-workers and even those on the fringes of society, so central to social history. Nonetheless, we do continue to research the clergy and the aristocracy. However, the focus has changed even here. This can be explained by the development of certain trends over the last 20 years:

1 Firstly, our focus has been influenced by the emergence of 'political' history. This no longer refers to war and dynasty, but is rather the history of power, institutions and social norms.
2 Secondly, there is little real interest in Church history. That which exists focuses more on analysing ecclesiastic discourse (sermons, theology and icons) than on its social and economic dominance. The extensive archives devoted to the Church's history, which would facilitate such research, and are indeed essential for medieval historians (since the power of the Church was not, after all, simply symbolic), receive little attention.
3 Finally, there has been a growing tendency towards cultural history, or the history of representation, (replaced in the 1980s by a 'history of mentalities'). This reason is closely related to the two previous points, since it is the cultural products of those with secular or religious power which remain more easily available to the historian.

Unfortunately, it is not possible here to carry out a more detailed inquiry into the different directions of research undertaken by medieval historians over the last two decades. However, the basic surveys carried out by the *Bibliographie* of the *Société des médiévistes de l'enseignement supérieur public*, available online dating from 1989, confirm the trends I have just identified.[3] Further confirmation of this can be found in a collective volume comparing the findings of French and German medieval historians.[4] We have hardly any reason, therefore, to question why it is important for medievalists to study dominant social groups: the historical evidence and documentation we have about them stretches impressively far back. They played an essential role in society, even if as a group they were small in number. Nevertheless, even when research does reaffirm the historical nature of cultural phenomenon, it fails, for the most part, to acknowledge its relationship to social constructions. Without a social perspective of history, we are led to analyse systems of representation for their own sake. This stops us from fully understanding their wider implications and meaning – which is what, after all, constitutes the principal interest for historians rather than 'specialists' of literature, art or law. More generally, I would argue that this narrowing of focus also maintains and reinforces restrictive and shortsighted perspectives that preclude the possibility of a global approach. Worse still, such an approach is vehemently condemned by many as both practically unrealistic and intellectually unfounded. This serves to overlook any sense that the remaining traces we have of the Middle Ages are the products of one society; indeed, even the very idea of society, as a structured organization, is dismissed. There are, however, certain methodological tools available to re-address this situation.

Some possible methodological tools: quantitative methods: measurements and statistics

'Quantitative' or 'serial' methods were abandoned at the same time as the study of economic and social history. This is, in part, because the way in which these methods were employed was particularly weak. However, instead of trying to rectify this situation, we have preferred to give up. The indifference, or rather defiance, expressed against accepting any form of measurement as evidence, is a serious methodological failing. It has led to an inability to discriminate. The same importance and, therefore, meaning, is given to all phenomena, whether they played a large or small part in medieval society. Abandoning quantitative methods of research is all the more worrying as it prevents us from benefiting from the digital era – one of the key technological developments, not to say revolutions, of the last 15 years. Developments in digital technology and the Internet have provided historians with extremely precise tools of assessment, as well as vast quantities of all kinds of documents, such as texts, images and archaeological data, in conditions which we could hardly have imagined in the early the 1980s. Yet, because of their sheer quantity, these data cannot be read and treated in the same way as physical archival material. Instead, they demand that we rethink and recreate elements of the *instrumentarium* used by medievalist historians. We need to create the right software for such sources. However, before doing so, we must consider what purpose measurement and statistics serve in history. In opposition to the prevailing argument, which suggests that 'quantitative' history is only relevant for certain sources and subjects, namely inflation and demography, I would suggest that all social phenomena can be quantified (whether this refers to frequency, order, size or distance) and that their measurement is intrinsic to their very meaning. Imposing a formula in this way furnishes us with an excellent means of organizing certain topics. It allows us to apply the same means of measurement to different subjects, so that we can draw effective comparisons. This approach is particularly well suited to medieval works. Thanks to the work of a new generation of academics, its benefits are already apparent in the study of images (or rather 'art'), which bodes well for its more obvious application to textual sources.[5] This also demonstrates how using statistical measurements, applicable to all sorts of data, can help create a more global approach towards medieval society, providing a common methodology for research, which the traditional practices of history and its related academic disciplines have actually somewhat segregated. It is also necessary to adapt undergraduate and graduate teaching to this approach.

It would be apt here to make a comparison with historical anthropology, as this is another discipline whose method and approach have developed in France over the last two or three decades.

'Historical anthropology'

Despite their lack of interest in 'micro-history' and the 'linguistic turn', following developments in the 'history of mentalities', French historians have helped to establish historical anthropology. Historians of the Medieval and Ancient Greek[6] periods played a significant role in promoting this movement, at the time when anthropology was at its height in France. One of the founding principles, initially proposed by Jacques le Goff, was based on the idea that pre-capitalist Western societies were strongly linked to those studied by anthropologists, and that their particular methods of analysis would prove useful for historians of the medieval period.[7] This was an extremely interesting hypothesis, which we have every reason to follow, even if it was and continues to be met with stubborn resistance. As is also the case for 'quantitative' methods, putting it into practice has never been a priority. This might explain, if not justify, such ongoing reluctance. There are very few French medieval historians who are willing to adapt to the demands of a discipline that is complicated and so different from their own; nor is there any teaching in place to encourage this from students. Too many of the projects which lay claim to bridging this gap are only very superficially anthropological. We have, thus, hardly benefitted from the potential methodological value of this interdisciplinary approach. Its absence is obvious. For example, historians have undertaken little research into kinship, an anthropological subject *par excellence*; and that which has been done is of rather poor quality. In contrast, historical anthropology (which subdivides into religious, educational, legal and political anthropology) has been central in exploring new topics – such as the body, sexuality and women – or in reviving areas of interest, such as politics, power, ritual, justice, mores and representations. The latter are all, as I have suggested, quintessentially anthropological. These are all fruitful and thought-provoking subjects, and yet none of them has given rise to any real development in methodology. I will highlight two reasons for this failure:

4 We have not sufficiently questioned the traditional frameworks that historians use. Doing so would have improved our ability to criticize or, at least, to evaluate more exactly, and in context, the scope and use of some of the ideas and approaches used by anthropology. To take an obvious example, it is not simply because it was an anthropologist, Georges Balandier, who created the idea of political anthropology in France that this is valid, or at least not entirely. Instead, it is almost universally accepted that the undeniable ethnocentricity governing a large part of anthropology should legitimize the use of incongruous anachronism, usually reserved for historians, with respect to economy, politics and religion. This is proof, if we still need it, that intellectual practice does little good in its own right. It must always be subjected to consistent and systematic criticism.

5 In an apparent paradox, this appreciation of anthropology has not led us to rethink the necessity of approaching social phenomenon more globally, although this is still one its principal aims. For scholars of the medieval period, the division of research into categories and sub-categories is widespread and manifest; too often, subjects are studied for themselves, without considering the influence of structures, social and

> other organizational systems. Medieval historians have not adopted the most basic component of this structural approach, which is probably the most valuable aspect of French anthropology – namely, the central role of social relationships in explaining and categorizing human behaviour.

The fact that the works of Maurice Godelier, Claude Levi-Strauss and Jack Goody have had so little influence on medieval research, however often these authors might be cited, highlights this lack of dialogue and interchange. And yet, Godelier is without doubt the foremost proponent of the theoretical foundations necessary for analysing society, and more specifically pre-capitalist societies.[8] Furthermore, we are frequently all too happy to apply indiscriminately and unquestioningly the results of an anthropological study to medieval material. In so doing, historical anthropology has only been used for anecdotal and unconvincing evidence. This serves to undermine utterly the very methods it hopes to promote. I should also point out that anthropologists themselves have made little effort to engage in a real dialogue with historians.[9]

Over the last 20 years, medieval historians have developed interest in new subjects or have often returned, with different perspectives and methods, to topics that were looked at years earlier. Yet, this comes at the cost of looking at different areas of research. Indeed, the choice of subjects themselves suggests that historians were following trends rather than conducting more independent inquiries. The results of such research are still important, but we should question the conviction that medieval societies must remain opaque. This conviction probably stems from 'anthropological decentralization' (inspired by the 'otherness' of these societies), and a way of thinking constructed and shaped as much by theory and methodology as by the very subject of medieval history.

I am aware of the dangers in making these comments: criticism is often considered inconvenient or, worse, as motivated by personal tensions. This is evidently not the case. It seems, however, that all medieval historians have a more or less confused sense of their period as difficult. This is apparent in a veiled but pointed comment in a text by Georges Duby from 1990–1991.[10] It is important to remember that, at this time, Georges Duby, along with Jacques le Goff, was one of the best known French historians of the medieval period, holding one of the most prestigious academic posts as a professor at the *Collège de France* and member of the *Académie française*. In several densely argued pages, he paints a very negative portrait of academic institutions and their current situation. He highlights the decline in paradigms, which had so dominated the previous period. Even so, he envisages the beginnings of a new era for the discipline, based on three principal axes; a return to scholarship, abandoning the positivist approach adopted by certain texts, and using archaeological finds to further our knowledge. These were excellent aims, even if now we have to adapt them to the digital age. Unfortunately, it must be said that 15 years later, the improvements suggested by Georges Duby have not been taken up. This is most likely for organizational and institutional reasons, which, due to recent developments, have become more pressing. I will refer briefly to these now, to draw this chapter to an end.

A critical look at institutions

Analysing causes of a crisis does not entail casting blame on any particular establishment or group; but rather requires us to understand how an *ensemble* of social, political, institutional and ideological structures can produce these effects. I will now consider three elements.

The organization of universities creates distinct separation between different disciplines, as we have seen already regarding anthropology. Yet, it is also true that historians, for the most part, work exclusively on texts and have little, if any, linguistic training; they do not have the intellectual tools necessary to understand, and even less resolve, what semantics might reveal. As Georges Duby demonstrated in the extract quoted earlier, archaeology is a case in point. Medieval archaeology, which developed as late as the 1960s in different Western European countries, has produced findings which serve to question what economic and social history can establish through working solely with textual data. However, the approach adopted by institutions, such as the inflexible segregation of different fields in teaching and research, subject-specific journals and common strategies for protecting the autonomy of each 'separate' discipline, has been instrumental in creating collective prejudices and division.

A comparison can be made here with visual and architectural disciplines. The majority of art historians have shown, and indeed continue to show, significant hostility towards the research conducted since the 1980s by 'mere' historians, who are interested in the historical value and meaning of art objects, instead of their aesthetic properties. Similarly, since the 1970s there seems to be a decline in dialogue between historians and specialists of 'literary' texts written in the vernacular, which make up a large portion of medieval works.[11] The way institutions are organized and our adherence to an anachronistic distinction between literature, art and law, come together to maintain such staunch division.

The pressure to study contemporary history

There has been a disproportionate rise in the number of university students studying twentieth-century history, particularly the period since 1930. This situation has inevitably led to questions about the necessity of the standard general education offered in France, which requires all students and trainee teachers to learn about four major periods: ancient history, medieval history, modern history (before 1789) and contemporary history (after 1789). Although this could be described as somewhat nationalist and Eurocentric, it did maintain an important balance; now, however, the ancient periods, including medieval history, have to fight for their survival. The day when we abandon entirely any principle of general education in teacher-training courses and exams, leading to significantly fewer jobs and posing great difficulty for research, looms threateningly on the horizon. Indeed, this is already beginning to happen. Since 2008, the basic training of primary- and secondary-school teachers has been subject to review in France. A similar situation has already emerged in Germany, albeit in a different institutional framework. This is somewhat unexpected in a country where the study of medieval history was as certain as in France, if not more so. (It is important to remember the influence of German academics on early medieval scholarship, in the late nineteenth century.) It has also clearly begun to occur in Italy.

However, this focus on the contemporary, (and here 'contemporary' is particularly narrow since it does not even include the nineteenth century), is not only gathering strength in universities, it is also being adopted in conservation and archive services. All their efforts are devoted to recent documents, under the pretext that they have wider appeal and are more highly sought after. Not only can this argument easily be refuted (this apparent demand largely comes from media and political pressure, rather than from anything inherent) but it has even been completely contradicted by a survey in 2001, conducted by a specialized institute and the newspaper *Le Monde*. According to this survey, the Middle Ages come second to the period of the Second World War among French specializations. However, if archives and library services are no longer much concerned with documents from the medieval period, it is also because the overall situation for such services is not good. This is a result of choices made by political 'decision-makers'.

Political and social decisions

These choices are governed by financial and ideological concerns. In this respect, the crisis is ubiquitous. It affects universities and research organizations, as well as libraries and archives. It demonstrates a particular lack of long-term political vision and stems from never-ending short-term financial motivations. As soon as we can only digest what immediately 'relates' to us (a criterion that is used to define from on high what society needs), we are no longer interested in social sciences – they are seen as potentially threatening to the *status quo*. Instead, we prefer more bite-size knowledge. History, therefore, shares its fate with a number of social sciences. It struggles for the same reasons, such as, for example, the consistent pressure from different governments to get rid of the *Département des Sciences de l'homme et de la société du Centre national de la recherche scientifique* in France. On this point too, the situation in our neighbouring European countries is no more encouraging.

The all-encompassing question that needs to be acknowledged and analysed by social sciences relates to the way our society's relationship to the past has changed, and how this development has affected different fields of historical research. This is a vast question, which cannot be tackled here and to which François Hartog has made the most significant contribution.[12] Let me just highlight the fact that, with the political misappropriation of references to history came also the replacement of history with memory. The ever-growing invasion of public space by a discourse of remembrance and a demand for ceremonies, maintained by various groups and carried out by political leaders, can be seen as more worrying from a lay point of view than for conservation services or even historians. One could argue that this phenomenon, which has appeared in different forms in various European countries over the last two decades, is even validated by the EU, thanks to its legislation regarding 'remembrance laws' – for which France, apparently, provided the inspiration.[13]

Some concluding thoughts

The situation facing medieval scholarship in France consists of paradoxes, ambiguity and ambivalence. The contributions of Marc Bloch and the *Annales* journal have left it with a very strong heritage, which is certainly less fractious than it could have been. However, such harmony is not wholly positive; debate is essential for any academic discipline. Unlike its German counterpart, the situation for the university in France has remained more or less untouched: but how long will this last? The last few decades have witnessed an important revival of medieval topics and themes, but this proliferation of areas, which borders on disintegration, is not necessarily a good sign.

Although it has been considered inconvenient to state this explicitly, French medieval historians are aware of the gradual disappearance of the principles that have formed the basis of this discipline since the 1950s and 1960s, leaving it in a difficult position. To combat this, they have considered it necessary to rethink these foundations, focusing particularly on the 'digital revolution' (mainly in terms of communication and availability of information), which has transformed our access to, and relationship with, sources. This feeling was strong enough to lead the *Société des médiévistes de l'enseignement supérieur* to entitle its 2007 conference, 'The Position of a Medieval Historian in the 21st Century'.[14] Such effort must be praised, even if it reveals a deep insecurity. However, we must also acknowledge that such essential ambitions have not yet, at least, been achieved.

Translated from French by Helena Taylor

Notes

1 For a more detailed discussion of this, see Oexle, Jean-Claude and Otto Gerhard (eds), *Les tendances actuelles de l'histoire du Moyen Âge en France et en Allemagne. Actes des colloques de Sèvres (1997) et Göttingen (1998)* (Paris, 2002). This study brings together the work of French and German historians, comparing both their choice of subject matter and methodological approach. Despite some differences, which proved to be somewhat minor, they share a number of concerns and questions. This 654-page volume proves how useful it is to make such a detailed assessment of the research undertaken by medieval historians from these two countries over the last 30 years.

2 For a more thorough introduction to these questions, see Guerreau, Alain, *L'avenir d'un passé incertain. Quelle histoire du Moyen Âge au XXIe siècle?* (Paris, 2001); and Morsel, Joseph, avec Christine Ducourtieux, *L'Histoire (du Moyen Âge) est un sport de combat. Réflexions sur les finalités de l'Histoire du Moyen Âge destinées à une société dans laquelle même les étudiants en Histoire s'interrogent* (Paris, 2007), available online at: http://lamop.univ-paris1.fr/W3/JosephMorsel/Sportdecombat.pdf.

3 The *Société des médiévistes de l'enseignement supérieur public* brings together all the medieval specialists who consider themselves as historians, that is, who train future history professors and teachers. Since 1989, the research conducted by its members is available online at http://sid.ish-lyon.cnrs.fr/shmesp/index.php. It is also available in Balard, Michel (ed.), *L'histoire médiévale en France. Bilan et perspectives* (Paris, 1991). This is a 567-page description of research areas and publications of members of the *Société*, compiled to commemorate its twentieth birthday.

4 Schmitt, Oexle, *Les tendances actuelles*.

5 For a further assessment of the current state of research in France, see, in terms of text, Bertrand, Paul, Marjorie Burghart, et alii, 'L'historien médiéviste et la pratique des textes: le enjeux du tournant numérique', in *Être historien du*

Moyen Âge au XXIe siècle. XXXVIIIe Congrès de la SHMESP (Paris, 2008), pp. 273–301, and of image; Baschet, Jérôme, Dominique Rigaux, 'Le médiéviste et les images à l'ère de l'écran global', ibid., pp. 259–72. Both of these provide useful bibliographical information. There are also two recent and forthcoming theses which address this issue: Lepape, Séverine, *Représenter la parenté du Christ et de la Vierge: l'iconographie de l'Arbre de Jessé en France du Nord et en Angleterre, du XIIIe au XVIe siècle*; Guerreau, Isabelle, *L'auto-représentation du clergé saxon au Moyen-Age d'après les sceaux*. For the relevant statistics see Guerreau, Alain, *Statistiques pour historiens*, http://elec.enc.sorbonne.fr/statistiques/stat2004.pdf, available on the website of the l'École nationale des chartes. We should note also that the journal, *Histoire et mesure*, was established by the Centre National de la Recherche Scientifique in 1986, by a group of historians from all periods, concerned with developing the possibilities of using measurement and statistics in history.

6 I am thinking particularly of the numerous works of Jean-Pierre Vernant, Pierre Vidal-Naquet and Marcel Detienne.

7 Jacques le Goff first expressed this idea in 1964, in *La civilisation de l'Occident médiéval* (Paris, pp. 17–19). *L'histoire médiévale en France. Bilan et perspectives* (Berlioz, Jacques, Jacques Le Goff, avec Anita Guerreau-Jalabert, 'Anthropologie et histoire', pp. 269–304) provides a summary of his arguments.

8 He did so most notably in *Un domaine contesté: l'anthropologie économique* (Paris, 1974) and *L'idéel et le matériel. Pensée, économies, sociétés* (Paris, 1984).

9 The difficulties, if not impossibilities, of a such a 'dialogue' (this terminology is misleading since 'dialogue' suggests that they have a common reference system) are clear from Magnani, Eliana (ed.), *Don et sciences sociales. Théories et pratiques croisées* (Dijon, 2007).

10 Duby, Georges, 'Préface', in L'*histoire médiévale en France*, pp. 7–9.

11 In France, professional organizations are modelled on the academic disciplines defined by universities. This is not the case, for example, in Germany, where the *Mediävistenverband* brings together all scholars of the Middle Ages, regardless of their field of research.

12 Hartog, François, *Régimes d'historicité: présentisme et expérience du temps* (Paris, 2003). Research on this theme began to emerge in France in the mid-1990s, and has since gathered strength. An emotional approach to the past, evident from the importance placed on memory and the 'reign of the witness', is directly related to the media's demands on our emotions and, more widely, to questioning the rational bases for academic research; it effects fields other than just human and social sciences.

13 This legislation has provoked a strong reaction from historians in France since 2005; see, for example, Nora, Pierre-Françoise Chandernagor, *Liberté pour l'histoire* (Paris, 2008).

14 See *Être historien du Moyen Âge au XXIe siècle*. It is interesting to note that prior to this the *Mediävistenverband* chose a similar theme for its annual meeting: Goetz, Hans-Werner, Jörg Jarnut (eds), *Mediävistik im 21. Jahrhundert. Stand und Perspektiven der internationalen und interdisziplinären Mittelalter Fosrschung* (München, 2003).

Bibliography

Baschet, Jérôme, Dominique Rigaux, 'Le médiéviste et les images à l'ère de l'écran global', in *Être historien du Moyen Âge au XXIe siècle. XXXVIIIe Congrès de la SHMESP* (Paris, 2008), pp. 259–72.

Balard, Michel (ed.), *L'histoire médiévale en France. Bilan et perspectives* (Paris, 1991).

Bertrand, Paul, Marjorie Burghart, et al., 'L'historien médiéviste et la pratique des textes: le enjeux du tournant numérique', in *Être historien du Moyen Âge au XXIe siècle. XXXVIIIe Congrès de la SHMESP* (Paris, 2008), pp. 273–301.

Duby, Georges, 'Préface', in *L'histoire médiévale en France. Bilan et perspectives* (Paris, 1991), pp. 7–9.

Godelier, Maurice, *Un domaine contesté: l'anthropologie économique* (Paris, 1974).

—, *L'idéel et le matériel. Pensée, économies, sociétés* (Paris, 1984).

Goetz, Hans-Werner, Jörg Jarnut (eds), *Mediävistik im 21. Jahrhundert. Stand und Perspektiven der internationalen und interdisziplinären Mittelalter Fosrschung* (München, 2003).

Guerreau, Alain, *L'avenir d'un passé incertain. Quelle histoire du Moyen Âge au XXIe siècle?* (Paris, 2001).

—, *Statistiques pour historiens*, http://elec.enc.sorbonne.fr/statistiques/stat2004.pdf, available on the website of the l'École Nationale des Chartes.

Hartog, François, *Régimes d'historicité: présentisme et expérience du temps* (Paris, 2003).

Le Goff, Jacques, *La civilisation de l'Occident médiéval* (Paris, 1964).

Magnani, Eliana (ed.), *Don et sciences sociales. Théories et pratiques croisées* (Dijon, 2007).

Morsel, Joseph, avec Christine Ducourtieux, *L'Histoire (du Moyen Âge) est un sport de combat. Réflexions sur les finalités de l'Histoire du Moyen Âge destinées à une société dans laquelle même les étudiants en Histoire s'interrogent* (Paris, 2007), available online at: http://lamop.univ-paris1.fr/W3/JosephMorsel/Sportdecombat.pdf.

Nora, Pierre-Françoise Chandernagor, *Liberté pour l'histoire* (Paris, 2008).

Oexle, Jean-Claude and Otto Gerhard (eds), *Les tendances actuelles de l'histoire du Moyen Âge en France et en Allemagne. Actes des colloques de Sèvres (1997) et Göttingen (1998)* (Paris, 2002). http://sid.ish-lyon.cnrs.fr/shmesp/index.php.

5

New Wine in New Bottles: Byzantine Studies Come of Age (c. 1981–c. 2007)

Cecile Morrisson

Εἰς μνήμην Ἀγγελικῆς, μὲ φιλία

Surveying the development of Byzantine studies over the last quarter of the century is no easy task and this will unavoidably be a personal picture, not a comprehensive review.[1] It is a challenge to have a look in retrospect at research trends in one's discipline and to attempt to outline them for a broader audience of historians, beyond the usual internalized genre of reports to specialized congresses. However, the time is ripe for such a self-examination: the last two decades of the twentieth century and the first decade of the twenty-first may be considered as particularly innovative years for Byzantinists, who emerged from a 'classical' environment to take part, sometimes as pioneers, in the general transformation of Medieval studies.

'Byzantinists' have not, in spite of these changes, renounced being called and calling themselves by this title. It is a convenient shorthand label for an ambivalent identity, which allows them to present themselves also as Classicists, Orientalists or Medievalists, according to which audience they are addressing or their personal background. Even if Byzantium still evokes, occasionally, 'the triumph of barbarism and religion', despised by Gibbon and Voltaire, or at least 'useless complexity', rather than the 'glory' displayed in recent spectacular exhibits,[2] it has, hopefully, and thanks also to recent books aimed at the general cultivated public,[3] overcome long-standing prejudice. 'Byzantium' has long been the object of a variety of definitions. They all centred, of course, on the 'Empire of New Rome', and the world around it, down to the Fall of Constantinople in 1453 and the capitulation of the last Byzantine outposts a few decades later, but differed widely about its starting date (the consecration of its capital, Constantinople, in 330, the division of the Empire at the death of Theodosius I, in 396, the seventh-century crisis, etc.). Although I have argued elsewhere for the earliest date,[4] I shall consider here studies dealing with the period starting in the seventh century, when Byzantium lost most of its Late Antique Roman features and became a specific medieval entity and civilization.[5] Late Antiquity, in which the Eastern component is no small part, would have required a chapter on its own, but its abundant historiography has been treated in several surveys to which the reader may turn.[6]

In 1976, in the concluding session of the 15th International Congress of Byzantine Studies, in Athens, Paul Lemerle emphasized that Byzantine Studies were half a century behind their Classical and Western Medieval counterparts in their methodology and tools, a sharp but unfortunately well-founded statement. In 1981, the organizers of the next Congress, in Vienna, commissioned reports to reflect on the requirements for future development in the perspective of the new millennium. In 1982, Giles Constable and Alexander Kazhdan brilliantly outlined the state of Byzantine historiography, from its origins in the seventeenth century, and advocated its modernization, promoting a shift from the hitherto dominant political and diplomatic history to one concerned with the individual, the *Homo byzantinus* and his world.[7] In the following 25 years or so, the discipline took up the challenge, making dramatic progress and innovations regarding tools and sources on the one hand, methods and approaches on the other. These twain sides have sometimes been opposed; in fact they are the two sides of the same coin.

Tools and sources: the instruments of Byzantine studies

In the 1960s and 1970s, many Byzantine historical texts were still only available in the nineteenth-century edition of the Bonn Corpus, while the Teubner series included only a score of titles, and the Byzantine series of the Collection des Universités de France (the so-called 'Guillaume Budé') even fewer – but systematically accompanied by a French translation. The religious and hagiographical literature was read either in the outdated *Patrologia Graeca* or in the *Acta Sanctorum* and often in scattered obscure publications. Archive documents were partially accessible in Austrian or Russian publications of the early twentieth century, though the selection of documents from Mount Athos by Dölger,[8] and the French publication of the *Actes de Lavra* (vol. 1, 1970) and of a few other monasteries were opening immense avenues for research.

The 1980s were a turning point: the number of critical editions of the primary sources grew rapidly thereafter. Far superior in their standards to the nineteenth-century editions, most of them were now accompanied by notes and a translation into a modern language. Besides the continuing series of the Corpus Christianorum (Leuven), the Bollandists and Teubner, the Association Internationale des Études Byzantines began to oversee the *Corpus Fontium Historiae Byzantinae*, responsible to date for some fifty titles since the first in 1967. The archive documents were now systematically and critically edited: in Athens the dossier of Patmos,[9] in Paris the numerous archives of Mount Athos,[10] and in Rome several South Italian archives.[11] Neglected documents, such as collections of letters and, above all, saints' Lives, also attracted due attention and publication. The Dumbarton Oaks Hagiography Database now facilitates searching into the sources of the eighth to the tenth century, and the Institute for Byzantine Research in Athens will soon launch another database for hagiographical sources from 1204 to 1453. Moreover, as the knowledge of classical languages steadily recedes, the amount of translated texts has proportionally increased, including even the 200 or so Byzantine monastic foundation documents assembled in Dumbarton Oaks and available online as well as in print (2000).[12]

Medieval Greek language, for which in the early 1960s researchers had only Du Cange's *Glossarium … infimae Graecitatis* (1688) and Sophocles' insufficient *Greek Lexicon of the Roman and Byzantine Periods (from BC 146 to AD 1100)* (1870), has been lemmatized anew in E. Trapp's *Lexikon zur byzantinischen Gräzität* (1994–2007). It has also been included progressively in the monumental digital resource set up at the University of California, Irvine: the *Thesaurus Linguae Graecae* now allows a full on-line search of the complete corpus of Byzantine Greek authors and has recently begun to integrate the corpus of documentary sources, so rich in rare vernacular or technical words unknown in the other genres.

At the same time, coins and seals, hitherto neglected primary sources, were systematically published or classified, notably in the two major enterprises of Dumbarton Oaks, by Grierson, Hendy, Oikonomides and Nesbitt,[13] supplemented by those of the Austrian Academy of Sciences (Hahn's *Moneta Imperii Byzantini*, Seibt's catalogue of seals in Austrian collections), by the unfinished project of V. Laurent's Corpus and by the private initiative of G. Zacos.[14] Over the last 20 years, J.-Cl. Cheynet has been putting this widely dispersed new material to use for the history of Byzantine society.[15] The record of epigraphy, so plentiful in Late Antiquity, is much less so in our period but is by no means negligible. Unfortunately, the corpus of dated inscriptions from Constantinople and its region, assembled by I. Sevcenko and C. Mango, is still unpublished, and the Epigraphy section in the *BZ* was discontinued a few years ago. But the annual *Chroniques* by D. Feissel, in the *Revue des Études grecques*, cover all material from Late Antiquity through the Byzantine period.[16] This complete array of sources provided material for several, sometimes competing, prosopographical publications covering the whole Byzantine period from the fourth to the fifteenth century.[17] Concurrently, the interest of the 1970s in 'historical geography' materialized in the Austrian series of the *Tabula Imperii Byzantini*, both a dictionary and an atlas, registering textual and archaeological evidence for each region (1976–2008, 11 volumes so far), which has led to important synthetic works by J. Koder and colleagues.[18]

Byzantine archaeology has ceased to be a '*parent pauvre*' of classical archaeology, which so often had scraped off and suppressed Post-Roman remains and layers, without even keeping a record of what was considered an inglorious decadent period. It took part in the general development of medieval archaeology, with its new scientific tools, including the extraordinary advances of ceramology, planned excavations of urban sites – Pergamon, Amorion, Sagalassos, Corinth, Thebes, Butrint, Byllis, etc. – or of modest villages – Panakton (Boeotia), Brucato (Sicily), Scribla, Squillace (Calabria), Dehes (Syria), etc. – together with extensive surveys in Boeotia, the Peloponnese, Bithynia …, so enormously increasing the evidentiary base. All the more, since archaeologists are engaged now in permanent dialogue and collaboration with historians, and are considered as historians in their own right.[19]

With these resources at hand, there has been no shortage of encyclopaedias, dictionaries and handbooks of all kind and sizes. The first and best of the former is again a Dumbarton Oaks project, the *Oxford Dictionary of Byzantium* (1991) (*ODB*), directed by A. Kazhdan and A.-M. Talbot, with its 5,000 entries.[20] For the latter, the exclusive dominance of G. Ostrogorsky, *Geschichte des byzantinischen Staates* (Munich, 1940), with its numerous French, English, Greek and Serbian translations, gave way to a flourish of various syntheses, from the controversial narrative of W. Treadgold (1997)[21] to the recent multi-authored *Cambridge History of the Byzantine Empire* (2008) and the shorter collective 'Nouvelle Clio' history of *Le monde byzantin*.[22] Byzantine *instrumenta studiorum* now stand comparison with the Western Medieval ones, while the new or better-published sources have made available a mine of direct or indirect information to submit to new approaches.

New approaches and their results

It was not this accumulation of better edited and more varied sources that changed so much our perception of Byzantium, but rather the questions that were asked and the ways that were used to provide answers. In the wake of Western Medievalists, Byzantinists, concurring with Kazhdan's and Constable's lines of thought, changed, as we will see below, the focus of their attention to subjects of greater concern at the time: gender, daily life of *Homo byzantinus*, law and order, rebellion, poverty, state and the economy, art and text, their interaction and their reception, etc. A new cultural history of Byzantium emerged in this quarter of a century. The positivist approach, so well exemplified in the founding studies of Paul Lemerle with their critical analyses of sources,[23] was not abandoned, especially in France, and empiricists remained the great majority. However, research evolved in the direction of greater 'contextualization', embedded in the theoretical and conceptual lines of thought of the twentieth century, such as materialism, structuralism or post-structuralism,[24] and, above all, it resorted increasingly to interdisciplinary practice.

Contextual investigation was applied first and foremost to the study of historical works and literature in a wider acception. Historical sources ceased to be sheer repositories of data to explore for 'facts' and were researched for their ideology, the conditions of their production and their readership.[25] A few exemplary studies can be adduced to this point: Averil Cameron's *Procopius and the Sixth Century* (Berkeley, 1985), Beaucamp et al., on the *Chronicon paschale* (1979)[26] and *Recherches sur la chronique de Jean Malalas* (2004), the parallel works on the *Patria* of Constantinople by Dagron, and Cameron and Herrin,[27] Mullett on Theophylact of Ochrid,[28] work in progress on Anna Comnena,[29] or the 'iconoclastic' reading of the *Life of St Stephen the Younger* by M.-F. Auzépy.[30] The last work is typical of a rare application of modern critical theory to the corpus of Byzantine literature; 'literature' being now intended in the widest possible acception, beyond the former straightjacket of classification between '*Hochsprachliche*' and '*Trivialliteratur*', between learned and vernacular literature.[31] In *After Antiquity: Greek Language, Myth, and Metaphor* (Ithaca and London, 2002), Margaret Alexiou studies the main images regarding life that flow through Greek literature from Antiquity to the twentieth century, whether proverbs, satires, ritual or highbrow texts, to demonstrate 'the flexibility and coherence of Greek metaphors' and the constant 'heterogeneity' of the Greek language. The earlier contempt, which even the greatest Byzantinists of former generations would express for Byzantine texts as a poor and contrived imitation (*mimesis*) of the Ancients or a stupid monk's fabric of chronicles, has turned into a more empathic understanding of the authors and their work. Even if a 'new literary history' of Byzantine literature is still only in preparation,[32] the classical *Handbücher* of Beck and Hunger are now supplemented by Kazhdan's two-volume *History of the Byzantine Literature* (with collaborators),[33] and Jan-Olof Rosenqvist's *Byzantinische Literatur* (Berlin-New York, 2007). Text specialists and historians have developed since the 1970s an acute interest in literacy – probably higher in Byzantium than in most other countries of the time[34] – and the subject is still much alive, as a round table in the Paris 2001 Congress demonstrates.[35]

Literature reception, levels of language, networks and milieux of *literati* relate to social history, a field opened in 1977 by É. Patlagean's structuralist approach to economic and social poverty in Early Byzantium.[36] Like literature, it still awaits a synthetic and comparative study, which remains a desideratum. The recent collection assembled by J. Haldon offers some issues and tracks to follow in that direction.[37] To date, there has been a proliferation of empirical studies on social-historical topics, offering the desired material for a 'framing' synthesis. With the end of the Cold War, the harsh and obfuscating debate about Byzantine 'feudalism' between Western historians and their Soviet Marxist colleagues, which had stirred so much passion and misunderstanding in the 1970s, has receded into near oblivion. It has given way to themes better attuned to the preoccupations of society in the 1980s and essentially to gender studies, first promoted by a new generation of scholars, primarily female but not necessarily feminist. The interest in *Homo byzantinus*, advocated by Kazhdan, was now refined by a gender-nuanced approach.[38] An increasing number of women, whether empresses, saints, nuns, whores or anonymous wives or farmers, were brought into the historical picture.[39] Their role and status in society was analysed: the pioneering studies by Beaucamp[40] and Laiou[41] were followed by many essays on sexual practices or the role of women in power and in religious life.[42] The detailed and now contextualized picture[43] of women in Byzantium emphasized the severe restrictions put on their 'public' and even 'private' life. However, women did possess important personal, economic and property rights, guaranteed by law. Women's studies soon lent themselves to theorizing in the perspective of gender, exploring visual evidence, language, social situations and the nexus of power, to research the structure of the Byzantine world. They also led, not unsurprisingly, to a burgeoning of studies about eunuchs, a Byzantine specificity taken for granted in previous historiography, now examined in its own right and full socio-historical developments.[44] Inevitably, 'masculinity' has emerged as a promising field for dissertations.

Family and kinship relationships appear as one of the most fruitful tracks explored in this context. On their 'public' side they impinge on political history, as Cheynet's exemplary analysis of power conflicts in the tenth to the twelfth century illustrates.[45] On the 'private' side, the family structure, strengthened in Byzantium as in the early Medieval West by the combined action of Church and State, with its nuclear rather than patriarchal nature, was undoubtedly a key element in the eighth-century revival and in the peasant household, the cornerstone of rural exploitation. Patterns of inheritance, so important – or at least better apprehended by our sources – for aristocratic marriage strategies, but well known for rural families through late archival documents, have been analysed thoroughly, e.g. in the Paris colloquium on the transmission of property.[46] It is clear that the Byzantine family, like the Western family from 1000 onward, was a monogamous nuclear one in which property was transmitted through bilateral inheritance, which the law distributed equally between its members, male or female, in the framework of many tenets of Roman law.

In fact, many historical themes such as this one, but also other social problems, such as law and order, heresy and exclusion,[47] were approached using legal sources. But it needs true 'legal historians', such as Dieter Simon and the late Marie Theres Fögen, lawyers and classicists who are also historians, to help 'decode' the complex Byzantine tradition, in which, surprisingly to our modern minds, the new law does not take precedence over the old, and to prevent us from taking legal texts systematically at face value. The second difficulty lies in the paucity of sources from which to assess the law's effectiveness in social practice.[48] The 'social history of Byzantine law', desired by Kazhdan, is a tremendous task that awaits an audacious author, but the essays in the 1992 Dumbarton Oaks symposium opened tracks in this direction.[49]

From the 1990s onward, a better understanding and use of the whole range of legal sources, regarding norms as practice, permeated the study of the Byzantine economy, notably of its immaterial structures and framework. Indirectly – or directly in several chapters regarding property as well as banking and trade – legislation features prominently in the milestone three-volume *Economic History of Byzantium* (*EHB*), edited by Angeliki Laiou (1992). This was the first attempt at a synthesis in the field since Michael Hendy's *Studies in the Byzantine Monetary Economy c. 400–c. 1500* (Cambridge, 1985) and the two Paris seminars (1985–86) on *Hommes et richesses*.[50] It provides a paradigm of the increasing multidisciplinarity so characteristic of the last quarter-century, which is not specific to Byzantine studies, but obtains in scientific research in general. Collaboration between disciplines (archaeology, geography, numismatics, economics, climatology), the application of the fast-developing new scientific methods (nuclear activation or other metallographic and petrographic analyses, DNA and biomolecular archaeology, magnetic prospection, ^{14}C dating, dendrochronology, paleobotany, archaeozoology, and so forth) have led to a deepening, indeed to a dramatic rethinking, of our view of the Byzantine world. The results from these 'new directions' for the early Middle Ages have been summed up conveniently in a recent Harvard conference.[51] A comprehensive larger assessment would require more space than is available in the present volume. However, a few points can be highlighted briefly.

The fundamental shift of archaeology from the study of monuments and art objects to an all-inclusive approach to material remains of daily life, production, relations to the surrounding territory, the development of extensive archaeology (see 'Greek archaeology' in this volume), has opened many avenues. The study of settlement patterns has reversed the previous schemes: it is now clear that, after the dramatic decline in the aftermath of the sixth-century plague, recovery began in the mid-eighth century. Palynological and ^{14}C studies show the expansion of culture into previously wooded areas. For the tenth through to the early thirteenth century, surveys concur with the now abundant archival documents to map, for example, the accelerated growth of population and land exploitation in Macedonia or South Italy, before it reached Malthusian limits in the three decades preceding the Great Plague of 1342.[52] The real 'great leap forward' of ceramology, with the discovery of African Red Slip and other fine wares, the identification of sites of production and distribution of transport amphorae,[53] and the ongoing study of regional coarse wares, provide markers for commercial exchanges.[54] The evolution of long-distance trade can now be plotted and quantified, at least relatively, in a more accurate way. McCormick (2001) summoned a vast corpus of travellers and their journeys, of mentions in sources, of coin finds, shipwrecks, etc., to analyse the persisting Mediterranean exchanges, along new routes and networks developed in the eighth and ninth centuries.[55] The equally monumental book by Chris Wickham integrates the new data from archaeology into both a detailed analysis and a comprehensive synthesis of the economic and social history of the early Middle Ages, which includes Byzantium, in a wide frame stretching from the whole Mediterranean to the northern seas, and compares specific regional developments.[56]

Regional commercial networks[57] around productive rather than 'parasitic' cities, and surplus production of marketable staples, are data that have transformed the previous schematic image of the Byzantine economy as a tributary state and 'monopolies'-dominated economy with a few luxury products, resident immobile traders and self-sufficient peasantry. Differing from most previous studies, Angeliki Laiou thought that the concepts of modern economics, notably development economics, had a high explanatory value for many areas of the Byzantine economy. She recognized, however, the regulatory role of the state, and that of redistributive and 'non-economic' factors, whose importance declined after the eleventh century.[58] Her balanced and innovative views are synthesized in her last *opus*, *The Byzantine Economy* (2007), which insists on the broad chronological parallelism of Byzantine economic development with that of the West, until the thirteenth century, and its 'exemplarity' as a dynamic and flexible economy before its ultimate failure for political reasons.[59]

A combination of economics and physics proved instrumental in interpreting the secular evolution of the Byzantine coinage: the earliest phases of the debasement in the 'long eleventh century' are now understood in the context of the increased monetization entailed by economic expansion, which prevented it from having a negative impact on prices.[60] Activation analyses of major and trace elements in the gold coinage enabled J.-N. Barrandon and his collaborators to deduce the achievements of Roman and Byzantine technology in the manipulations of the alloy, whether in its extreme purification or in complex alterations. In a few cases they could trace the input of metal from new sources.[61] However, the history of Byzantine mines and metal availability in Byzantium still awaits more research.

Other 'revolutionary' advances in the natural sciences are beginning to bring other discoveries: data from Greenland or other glaciers enable us to study the climatic variations or events,[62] isotopic ratios in human bones can reveal medieval diets, pathologies and mortality.[63] Soon, ancient DNA will illuminate migrations as well as the spread of pandemics or infections, such as plague or malaria.[64]

Finally, art history followed a path more or less parallel to that of history except that publication of monuments, its primary source, have remained limited to scattered monographs. To date, the corpus initiated in 1982 includes only the volume by Chatzidakis and Bitha on Kythera,[65] and a little book by E. Piltz on two Swedish churches in Byzantine style. Like text historians, art historians resorted to new approaches, of which Hans Belting, *Bild und Kult: eine Geschichte des Bildes vor dem Zeitalter der Kunst*, (Munich, 1990, Fr. trsl., Paris, 1998, 2007) is a remarkable illustration. The need for an inquiry into art's social function and anthropological processes, advocated in 1993 by J.-M. Spieser,[66] was developed by him and A. Cutler in *Byzance Médiévale (700–1204)* (Paris, 1996). The previous dominance of 'style' has given way to a study of the significance, use, function and production of monuments, images and any art object, as well as their reception from Byzantine times to our day.[67] Post-modern interpretations are characteristic of British or American scholars, such as R. Cormack and his school,[68] while H. Maguire has shown in several studies[69] the pertinence of this new approach combined with textual references and stylistic analysis. Style appears now, beyond its chronological or regional frame, to carry a larger significance. Art history at its best now interacts fully with the other branches of Byzantine studies.

Conclusion

Byzantine studies have thus done their best, over the three past decades, to reinsert Byzantium into general history, firstly by making its sources and trends available to the readers unfamiliar with Greek and oriental languages; secondly by taking part in the mainstream progress in historical studies, their methods and the 'paradigm shift' of the period. They have struggled and continue to struggle with the handicap stemming from the relative paucity of their sources and lack of quantitative data compared to the abundance of Western documents. The difficult task I found in writing this essay, which I 'inherited' from Angeliki Laiou after her untimely death,[70] would be rewarded if it would stimulate non-Byzantinists and particularly Western medievalists to take the developments I have outlined into full account and realize that the theatre of European history did not stop at the borders of the Carolingian Empire and its marches, nor at the outposts of the Latin Orient.[71]

Notes

1 See the few general reports published before or after the millennium: McCormick, M., 'Byzantium and Modern Medieval Studies', in Van Engen, J. (ed.), *The Past and Future of Medieval Studies* (Notre Dame, IN, 1994), pp. 58–72; Haldon, J., 'Byzantium after 2000. Post-millenial but not post-modern?', in C. Sode, S. Takács (eds), *Novum Millennium. Studies on Byzantine history and culture dedicated to Paul Speck* (Aldershot, 2001), pp. 1–11; Talbot, A.-M., 'Byzantine Studies at the Beginning of the Twenty-first Century', *Journal of English and Germanic Philology* (Jan. 2006), pp. 26–43. My thanks to them as well as to Margaret Mullett and to J.-M. Spieser for help with documentation and orientation. The gaps and biases in what follows are mine.

2 The pioneering *Byzance. L'art byzantin dans les collections françaises* (Louvre RMN, 1991, J. Durand ed.) was followed by a flourish of events on the same theme. The largest were the two exhibits in the Metropolitan Museum, Evans, H. and

W. Wixom (eds), *The Glory of Byzantium* (1997) and eadem, *Faith and Power* (2004) and now the all inclusive Cormack, R. and M. Vassilaki (eds), *Byzantium 330–1453* (London 2008).

3 Mango, C., *Byzantium: The Empire of New Rome* (London, 1980), Haldon, J., *Byzantium: A History* (Stroud, 2000), Cameron, A., *The Byzantines* (Oxford, 2006), Herrin, J., *Byzantium. The Surprising Life of a Medieval Empire* (Princeton, 2008).

4 As adopted for the handbook *Le monde byzantin* vol. I. *L'empire romain d'Orient (330–641)* (Paris, 2003). See pp. v–VII.

5 Haldon, J., *Byzantium in the Seventh Century. The Transformation of a Culture* (Cambridge, 1990); Whittow, M., *The Making of Orthodox Byzantium. 600–1025* (London, 1996); Laiou, A.E., *Economic History of Byzantium* (hereafter *EHB*) (Washington, DC, 2002), pp. 8–14. É. Patlagean's title *Un Moyen Âge grec (IXe-XIVe siècle)* (Paris, 2007) is somewhat misleading since it obscures the non-Greek components of the Middle Byzantine Empire.

6 Straw, C., R. Lim and G. Bowersock, *The Past Before Us. The challenge of historiographies of Late Antiquity* (Bibl. AnTard 6) (Turnhout, 2005), Averil Cameron, two stimulating books, *The Later Roman Empire AD 284–430* (London, 1993) and *The Mediterranean World in Late Antiquity (AD 395–600)* (London, 1993; 'SO Debate: The world of Late Antiquity Revisited', *Symbolae Osloenses* 72 (1C07), pp. 5–90 (about Peter Brown and his influence) and for a wider perspective: Cameron, A., 'Ideologies and Agendas in Late Antique Studies', in L. Lavan and W. Bowden (eds), *Theory and Practice in Late Antique Archaeology*, Late Antique Archaeology 1 (Leiden, Boston, 2003), pp. 3–21.

7 Kazhdan, A. and G. Constable, *People and Power in Byzantium. An Introduction to Modern Byzantine Studies* (Washington DC, 1982).

8 Dölger F., *Aus den Schatzkammern des Heiliges Berges* (Munich, 1948).

9 *Vyzantina engrapha tes Mones Patmou*, Vranouse, E.L. and M.G. Nyztazopoulou-Pelekidou (eds), (Athens, 1980), 2 vols.

10 In the series 'Archives de l'Athos' (Lethielleux), founded by G. Millet and P. Lemerle, now edited by J. Lefort. Twenty-five volumes have appeared so far and 10 remain to be published.

11 See the reports on 'Instrumenta Studiorum' (in particular W. Hörandner) in *XXe congrès international des Études byzantines (Paris, 2001) Pré-Actes* I, pp. 319–428.

12 Thomas, J. and A. Constantinides Hero (eds), *Byzantine Monastic Foundation Documents: A Complete Translation of the Surviving Founders' Typika and Testaments* (Washington DC, 2001).

13 Bellinger, A.R., P. Grierson and M.F. Hendy, *Catalogue of the Byzantine Coins in the Dumbarton Oaks Collection and in the Whittemore Collection* (Washington DC, 1966–1999), 5 vols; Oikonomides, N. and J. Nesbitt, *Catalogue of Byzantine Seals at Dumbarton Oaks and in the Fogg Museum of Art* (Washington DC, 1991–), 6 vols to date.

14 Zacos, G. and A. Veglery, *Byzantine Lead Seals* (Basle, 1972–1984), 2 vols.

15 Cheynet, J.-Cl., *La société byzantine. L'apport des sceaux* (Paris, 2008), (coll. studies), 2 vols.

16 Feissel, D., *Chroniques d'épigraphie byzantine (1987–2004)* (Paris, 2006).

17 Jones, A.H.M., J.R. Martindale, et al., *The Prosopography of the Later Roman Empire* (Cambridge-London, 1971–92); Lilie, R.J., C. Ludwig and Th. Pratsch (eds), *Prosopographie der mittelbyzantinischen Zeit* I. *(641–867). Prolegomena et I-VI* (Berlin 1998–2002); Martindale, J.R., *The Prosopography of the Byzantine Empire I (641–877)* (Aldershot, 2001) (CD-Rom); Trapp, E., *Prosopographisches Lexikon der Palaiologenzeit* (Vienna, 1976–96) also in a CD-Rom Version (Vienna 2001). An *Encyclopaedic Prosopographical Lexicon of Byzantine History and Civilization* (A. Savvides et al. eds.) is in progress (2 vols to date, Turnhout, 2008).

18 J. Koder's stimulating book on *Der Lebensraum der Byzantiner, Historisch-geographischer Abriß ihres mittelalterlichen Staates im östlichen Mittelmeerraum* (Vienna, 1984, repr. w. update 2001, and new Greek version, 2005); Belke, K., et al. (eds), *Byzanz als Raum* (Vienna, 2000).

19 See e.g. the thematic annual series *Late Antique Archaeology* (L. Lavan, et al. eds) (Leiden, 2003–2008), 5 vols so far; Lefort, J., C. Morrisson and J.-P. Sodini (eds), *Les villages dans l'empire byzantin (V^e^–XVe siècle)* (Paris, 2006) among an ever increasing number of collective works and meetings.

20 There are now on the market encyclopaedic works with longer essays, updating and covering issues which the *ODB* did not consider: Jeffreys, E., et al. (eds), *The Oxford Handbook of Byzantine Studies* (Oxford, 2008). There are also larger and smaller essay collections, covering new approaches to both new and older themes in Byzantine studies, for example Stephenson, P. (ed.), *The Byzantine World* (Routledge, 2010); Harris, J. (ed.), *Palgrave advances in Byzantine History* (Basingstoke, 2005).

21 Reviewed by W. Brandes, *Byzantinische Zeitschrift* 95/2 (2002), pp. 716–25.

22 2 vols published: I. *330–641* (Paris, 2003; w. Greek, Italian and Polish trsl.), II. *641–1204* (2006). III. *1204–1453* ed. by A. Laiou (in preparation).

23 Lemerle, P., *Les plus anciens miracles de saint Démétrius et la pénétration des Slaves dans les Balkans* (Paris, 1981); idem, *Cinq Études sur le XIe siècle byzantin* (Paris, 1977).

24 Haldon, J.F., '"Jargon" vs. "the Facts"? Byzantine History-Writing and Contemporary Debates', *Byzantine and Modern Greek Studies* 9 (1984–1985), pp. 95–132.

25 Ljubarskij, J., 'New Trends in the Study of Byzantine Historiography', *Dumbarton Oaks Papers* 47 (1993), pp. 131–8.

26 Beaucamp, J., R. Bondoux, J. Lefort, M.-Fr. Rouan and I. Sorlin, 'Temps et Histoire I: le Prologue de la Chronique pascale', *Travaux et Mémoires* 7 (1979), pp. 223–301.

27 Dagron, G., *Constantinople imaginaire* (Paris, 1984), Cameron, A. and J. Herrin (eds), *Constantinople in the Early Eighth Century: The Parastaseis syntomoi chronikai: introduction, translation and commentary* (Leiden 1984).

28 Mullett, M., *Theophylact of Ochrid: reading the letters of a Byzantine archbishop* (Aldershot, 1997).

29 Reinsch, D., *Alexias, übersetzt, eingeleitet und mit Anmerkungen versehen* (Cologne, 1996; 2nd edn 2001); Gouma-Peterson, T. (ed.), *Anna Komnena and Her Time* (New York-London, 2000).

30 Auzépy, M.-F., 'Une lecture "iconoclaste" de la *Vie d'Étienne le Jeune*', *Travaux et Mémoires* 8 (1981), pp. 415–36 (repr. in eadem, *L'histoire des iconoclastes* (Paris, 2007), pp. 119–44); eadem, *La Vie d'Étienne le Jeune par Étienne le Diacre* and *L'hagiographie et l'iconoclasme byzantin. Le cas de la Vie d'Étienne le Jeune* (Aldershot, 1997–1999).

31 See Trapp, E., 'Learned and Vernacular Literature in Byzantium: Dichotomy or Symbiosis?', *Dumbarton Oaks Papers* 47 (1993), pp. 115–29.

32 Mullett, M., 'New literary History and the History of Byzantine Literature', in Odorico, P. and P. Agapitos (eds), *Pour une nouvelle histoire de la littérature byzantine* (Paris, 2003), pp. 37–60 (repr. in eadem, *Letters, Literature and Literacy in Byzantium* (Aldershot, 2007, art. XVII)) with other examples and references to her earlier works, and a stimulating reflection on recent developments.

33 Kazhdan, A., with L.F. Sherry and C. Angelidi, *A History of Byzantine Literature*, I. *650–850*, II. *850–1204* (Athens: EIE/KBE, 1999–2006) is rather a collection of essays on paradigmatic authors.

34 For orientation and references, see Mullett, M., 'Writing in early medieval Byzantium', (1990) repr. in eadem *'Letters'* (art. VI) with update p. 4.

35 Mondrain, B. (ed.), *Lire et écrire à Byzance* (Paris, 2006).

36 Patlagean, É., *Pauvreté économique et pauvreté sociale à Byzance, 4e-7e siècles* (Paris-The Hague, 1977), which is analysed together with her ground-breaking Variorum collection, *Structure sociale, famille, chrétienté à Byzance* (London, 1981) by J. Haldon, *Byzantinoslavica* 42 (1981), pp. 203–11.

37 Haldon, J. (ed.), *A Social History of Byzantium* (Chichester, 2009) and especially his epistemological reflection: 'Towards a Social History of Byzantium', pp. 1–30.

38 Author herself of two important studies (*Desire and denial in Byzantium* (London, 1999); *Empresses and Power in Early Byzantium* (London, 2001)), Liz James offers the most recent and authoritative update on 'Men, Women, Eunuchs: Gender, Sex and Power', in Haldon, *Social History*, pp. 31–50.

39 For a complete online bibliography on *Women in Byzantium* (A.-M. Talbot ed.) see http://www.doaks.org/research/byzantine/women_in_byzantium.html.

40 Beaucamp, J., 'La situation juridique de la femme à Byzance', *Cahiers de civilisation médiévale* 20 (1977), pp. 145–76; eadem, *Le statut de la femme à Byzance (4e-7e siècle)* (Paris, 1990–1992), 2 vols.

41 Laiou, A.E., 'The Role of Women in Byzantine Society,' *XVI. Internationaler Byzantinistenkongress (Wien, 1981) Akten I/1 = Jahrbuch der Österreichischer Byzantinistik* 31/1 (1981), pp. 233–60 (repr. in *Gender*, art. I); eadem, *Gender, Society and Economic Life in Byzantium* (Aldershot, 1992)

42 Talbot, A.M., *Women and Religious Life in Byzantium* (Aldershot, 2004); Herrin, J., *Women in Purple* (London, 2001).

43 See the recent exhibition catalogue and its persuasive essays on *Women in Byzantium* (Cambridge, Mass., 2003), I. Kalavrezou (ed.).

44 Tougher, S. (ed.), *Eunuchs in Antiquity and Beyond* (London, 2002); Ringrose, K., *The Perfect Servant* (Chicago, 2003); Tougher, S., *The Eunuch in Byzantine History and Society* (London, 2008); Sidéris, G., 'Approches sur l'historiographie du genre à Byzance', *Genre et Histoire* 3 (2008) (http://www.genrehistoire.fr/document.php?id=358); idem., *Les anges du Palais, eunuques, sexes et pouvoir à Byzance (IVe-VIIe siècle)* (Turnhout, 2009).

45 Cheynet, J.-Cl., *Pouvoir et contestations à Byzance (963–1210)* (Paris, 1990).

46 Beaucamp, J. and G. Dagron (eds), *La transmission du patrimoine: Byzance et l'aire méditerranéenne* (Paris, 1998).

47 Fögen, M.Th. (ed.), *Ordnung und Aufruhr im Mittelalter: historische und juristische Studien zur Rebellion* (Frankfurt a. M. 1995); eadem (ed.), *Fremde der Gesellschaft: historische und sozialwissenschaftliche Untersuchungen zur Differenzierung von Normalität und Fremdheit* (Frankfurt a. M., 1991).

48 For a review of Byzantine legal historiography in our period, see Stolten B., 'Balancing Byzantine Law', *Fontes Minores* XI (2005), pp. 57–75 and his assessment on 'The Social Function of the Law', in Haldon (ed.), *Social History*.

49 Laiou, A. and D. Simon (eds), *Law and Society in Byzantium Ninth-Twelfth Centuries* (Washington DC, 1994).

50 *Hommes et richesses dans l'Empire byzantin* I. *IVe-VIIe siècle*, II. *VIIe–XVe siècle* (Paris, 1989, 1991).

51 Davies, J.R. and M. McCormick (eds), *The Long Morning of Medieval Europe. New Directions in Early Medieval Europe* (Aldershot, 2008).

52 Geyer, B., 'Physical Factors in the Evolution of the Landscape and Land Use', *EHB*, pp. 31–45; Dunn, A., 'The Exploitation and Control of Woodland and Scrubland in the Byzantine World', *Byzantine and Modern Greek Studies (BMGS)* 16 (1992), pp. 235–98; *Villages* (above n. 18); the collected studies of Lefort, J., *Société rurale et histoire du paysage à Byzance* (Paris, 2006); Harvey, A., *Economic expansion in the Byzantine empire 900–1200* (Cambridge, 1989).

53 For the Middle Byzantine period, the Ganos type linked with wine production on the coast of the Sea of Marmara merits special mention: Günsenin, N., 'Medieval Trade in the Sea of Marmara ; the evidence of shipwrecks', in R. Macrides (ed.), *Travel in the Byzantine World* (Aldershot, 2002), pp. 125–35.

54 Vroom, J., *After Antiquity: ceramics and society in the Aegean from the 7th to the 20th century A.C.* (Leiden, 2003); François, V., 'Réalités des échanges en Méditerranée orientale du XIIe au XVIIIe siècle: l'apport de la céramique', *Dumbarton Oaks Papers* 58 (2004), pp. 241–9. In spite of frequently expressed *caveats*, it seemed that the Middle Byzantine trade still relied mostly on ceramic containers.

55 McCormick, M., *Origins of the European Economy. Communications and Commerce AD 300–900* (Cambridge, 2001). See J.-M. Carrié, in *Annales. Histoire, Sciences Sociales* 58/6 (2003), pp. 1369–72, D. Griffiths, http://www.eh.net/bookreviews/library/0511.shtml.

56 Wickham, C., *Framing the Early Middle Ages: Europe and the Mediterranean, 400–800* (Oxford, 2005). See Whittow, M., *Journal of Roman Archaeology* 20 (2007), pp. 697–704.

57 Mango, M.M. (ed.), *Byzantine Trade, 4th-12th Centuries. The Archaeology of Local, Regional and International Exchange* (Oxford, 2009); Morrisson, C. (ed.), *Trade and Markets in the Byzantine World. Dumbarton Oaks Spring symposium 2008* (in preparation).

58 Laiou, A.E., *EHB*, ch. 35, pp. 681–96.

59 Laiou, A.E., C. Morrisson, *The Byzantine economy* (Cambridge, 2007).

60 Morrisson, C., *Monnaies et finances dans l'empire byzantin. Analyses, techniques* (Aldershot, 1994), art. IX (1976); eadem, 'La monnaie source de l'histoire de Byzance', *Praktika tes Akademias Athenon* (2008), pp. 211–23 (assessment of the discipline's results).

61 Morrisson, C., C. Brenot, J.-P. Callu, J.-N Barrandon, J. Poirier and R. Halleux, *L'or monnayé* I. *Purification et altérations de Rome à Byzance* (Cahiers Ernest-Babelon 2), (Paris, 1985).

62 McCormick, M., et al., 'Volcanoes and the Climate Forcing of Carolingian Europe', *Speculum* 82 (2007), pp. 865–95, which, despite its title, includes Byzantium.

63 Bourbou, C., 'On the Bioarchaeology of Birth and Death: Aspects of Childhood and Subadult Mortality Patterns during the Early and Middle Byzantine Periods in Greece', in Papaconstantinou, A. and A.-M. Talbot (eds), *Growing Byzantine: Children and Childhood in Byzantium* (Washington, DC, 2009). See also Bourbou, C. and M.P. Richards, 'The Middle Byzantine menu: Palaeodietary information from isotopic analysis of humans and fauna from Kastella, Crete', *International Journal of Osteoarchaeology* 17 (2007), pp. 63–72.

64 McCormick, M., 'Molecular Middle Ages: Early Medieval Economic History in the Twenty-First Century', in Davies, J.R., *New Directions* (above n. 50), pp. 83–104.

65 Chatzidakis, M. and I. Bitha, *Corpus of the Byzantine Wall- Paintings of Greece. The Island of Kythera* (Athens, 1997, Greek edn, 2003, Engl. edn).

66 Spieser, J.-M., 'Histoire de l'Art et Archéologie de Byzance : de la vie des formes à leur fonction sociale et à leur fonctionnement anthropologique', in Hamesse, J. (ed.), *Bilans et perspectives des Études médiévales en Europe, Actes du 1er Congrès européen de la FIDEM (Spoleto, 27–29 mai 1993)* (Louvain-la-Neuve, 1995), pp. 81–106.

67 Nelson, R., *Later Byzantine Painting: Art, Agency, and Appreciation* (Aldershot, 2007).

68 Cormack, R., *Painting the Soul: Icons, Death Masks, and Shrouds* (London, 1997); Barber, Ch., *Figure and Likeness: on the Limits of Representation in Byzantine Iconoclasm* (Princeton, 2002).

69 Maguire, H., *The Icons of their Bodies: saints and their images in Byzantium* (Princeton, 1996).

70 See Morrisson, C. and A.-M. Talbot, 'Angeliki Laiou (1941–2008)', *Dumbarton Oaks Papers* 63 (2010), forthcoming.

71 Auzépy, M.-F. (ed.), *Byzance en Europe* (Saint-Denis, 2003); Spieser, J.-M. (ed.), *Présence de Byzance* (En Crausaz, Suisse, 2007); Cameron, A., 'Byzantium between East and West', in Spieser (ed.) as above; eadem, 'The Absence of Byzantium',

Nea Hestia 82/i, (January 2008), pp. 4–59; Dagron, G., 'Oublier Byzance, Éclipses et retours de Byzance dans la conscience', *Praktika tes Akademias Athenon* 82/2 (2007), pp. 141–58.

Bibliography

Auzépy, M.-F., *La Vie d'Étienne le Jeune par Étienne le Diacre* and *L'hagiographie et l'iconoclasme byzantin. Le cas de la Vie d'Étienne le Jeune* (Aldershot, Variorum, 1997–1999).

— (ed.), *Byzance en Europe* (Saint-Denis, Presses universitaires de Vincennes 2003).

—, 'Une lecture "iconoclaste" de la *Vie d'Étienne le Jeune*', *Travaux et Mémoires* 8 (1981), pp. 415–36 (repr. in eadem, *L'histoire des iconoclastes* (Paris, Association des Amis du Centre d'Histoire et Civilization de Byzance, 2007), pp. 119–44.

Barber, Ch., *Figure and Likeness: on the Limits of Representation in Byzantine Iconoclasm* (Princeton, Princeton University Press, 2002).

Beaucamp, J., 'La situation juridique de la femme à Byzance', *Cahiers de civilisation médiévale* 20 (1977), pp. 145–76.

—, R. Bondoux, J. Lefort, M.-Fr. Rouan and I. Sorlin, 'Temps et Histoire I: le Prologue de la Chronique pascale', *Travaux et Mémoires* 7 (1979), pp. 223–301.

—, *Le statut de la femme à Byzance (4e-7e siècle)* (Paris, De Boccard, 1990–1992), 2 vols.

— and G. Dagron (eds), *La transmission du patrimoine: Byzance et l'aire méditerranéenne* (Paris, Monographies de Travaux et Mémoires 11, 1998).

Belke, K., et al. (eds), *Byzanz als Raum* (Vienna, Verlag der Österreichischen Akademie der Wissenschaften, 2000).

Bellinger, A.R., P. Grierson and M.F. Hendy, *Catalogue of the Byzantine Coins in the Dumbarton Oaks Collection and in the Whittemore Collection* (Washington DC, Dumbarton Oaks Research Library and Collection, 1966–1999), 5 vols.

Bourbou, C. and M.P. Richards, 'The Middle Byzantine menu: Palaeodietary information from isotopic analysis of humans and fauna from Kastella, Crete', *International Journal of Osteoarchaeology* 17 (2007), pp. 63–72.

—, 'On the Bioarchaeology of Birth and Death: Aspects of Childhood and Subadult Mortality Patterns during the Early and Middle Byzantine Periods in Greece', in A. Papaconstantinou and A.-M. Talbot (eds), *Becoming Byzantine: Children and Childhood in Byzantium* (Washington, DC, Dumbarton Oaks Research Library and Collection, 2009).

Cameron, A., 'Byzantium between East and West', in J.-M. Spieser (ed.), *Présence de Byzance* (En Crausaz, Suisse, 2007).

—, *The Later Roman Empire AD 284–430* (London, Routledge, 1993).

—, *The Mediterranean World in Late Antiquity (AD 395–600)* (London, Routledge, 1993).

—, 'Ideologies and Agendas in Late Antique Studies', in L. Lavan and W. Bowden (eds), *Theory and Practice in Late Antique Archaeology* (Late Antique Archaeology 1) (Leiden, Brill, 2003), pp. 3–21.

—, *The Byzantines* (Oxford, Oxford University Press, 2006).

—, 'So Debate: The world of Late Antiquity Revisited', *Symbolae Osloenses* 72 (2007), pp. 5–90.

—, 'The Absence of Byzantium', *Nea Hestia* 82/i (January 2008), pp. 4–59.

— and J. Herrin (eds), *Constantinople in the Early Eighth Century: The Parastaseis syntomoi chronikai: introduction, translation and commentary* (Leiden, Brill, 1984).

Chatzidakis, M. and I. Bitha, *Corpus of the Byzantine Wall-Paintings of Greece. The Island of Kythera* (Athens 1997, Greek edn, 2003, Engl. edn).

Cheynet, J.-Cl., *Pouvoir et contestations à Byzance (963–1210)* (Paris, 1990).

—, *La société byzantine. L'apport des sceaux* (coll. studies), 2 vols (Paris, 2008).

Cormack, R., *Painting the Soul: Icons, Death Masks, and Shrouds* (London, Reaktion Books, 1997).

— and M. Vassilaki (eds), *Byzantium 330–1453* (London, Royal Academy, 2008).

Dagron, G., *Constantinople imaginaire* (Paris, PUF, 1984).

—, 'Oublier Byzance, Eclipses et retours de Byzance dans la conscience européenne', *Praktika tes Akademias Athenon*, 82/2 (2007), pp. 141–58.

Davies, J.R. and M. McCormick (eds), *The Long Morning of Medieval Europe. New Directions in Early Medieval Europe* (Aldershot, Ashgate, 2008).

Dölger, F., *Aus den Schatzkammern des Heiliges Berges* (Munich, 1948).

Dunn, A., 'The Exploitation and Control of Woodland and Scrubland in the Byzantine World', *Byzantine and Modern Greek Studies* 16 (1992), pp. 235–98.

Durand, J. (ed.), *Byzance. L'art byzantin dans les collections françaises* (Louvre RMN, 1991).

Evans H., *Faith and Power* (New York, Metropolitan Museum of Art, 2004).

Evans, H. and W. Wixom (eds), *The Glory of Byzantium* (New York, Metropolitan Museum of Art New York, 1997).

Feissel, D., *Chroniques d'épigraphie byzantine (1987–2004)* (Paris, 2006).

Fögen, M.Th. (ed.), *Fremde der Gesellschaft: historische und sozialwissenschaftliche Untersuchungen zur Differenzierung von Normalität und Fremdheit* (Frankfurt a. M., 1991).

— (ed.), *Ordnung und Aufruhr im Mittelalter: historische und juristische Studien zur Rebellion* (Frankfurt a. M., 1995).

François, V., 'Réalités des échanges en Méditerranée orientale du XIIe au XVIIIe siècle: l'apport de la céramique', *Dumbarton Oaks Papers* 58 (2004), pp. 241–9.

Geyer, B., 'Physical Factors in the Evolution of the Landscape and Land Use', in A.E. Laiou, *Economic History of Byzantium* (Washington, DC, Dumbarton Oaks Research Library and Collection, 2002), pp. 31–45.

Gouma-Peterson, T. (ed.), *Anna Komnena and Her Time* (New York and London, Garland, 2000).

Griffiths, D., http://www.eh.net/bookreviews/library/0511.shtml.

Günsenin, N., 'Medieval Trade in the Sea of Marmara; the evidence of shipwrecks', in R. Macrides (ed.), *Travel in the Byzantine World* (Aldershot, Ashgate Variorum, 2002), pp. 125–35.

—, '"Jargon" vs. "the Facts"? Byzantine History-Writing and Contemporary Debates', *Byzantine and Modern Greek Studies* 9 (1984–1985), pp. 95–132.

—, *Byzantium in the Seventh Century. The Transformation of a Culture* (Cambridge, Cambridge University Press, 1990).

—, *Byzantium: A History* (Stroud, Tempus, 2000).

—, 'Byzantium after 2000. Post-millenial but not post-modern?', in C. Sode and S. Takács (eds), *Novum Millennium. Studies on Byzantine history and culture dedicated to Paul Speck* (Aldershot, Ashgate, 2001), pp. 1–11.

— (ed.), *A Social History of Byzantium* (Chichester, Wiley-Blackwell, 2009).

Harris, J. (ed.), *Palgrave Advances in Byzantine History* (Basingstoke, Palgrave Macmillan, 2005).

Harvey, A., *Economic expansion in the Byzantine empire 900–1200* (Cambridge, Cambridge University Press, 1989).

Hendy, Michael, *Studies in the Byzantine Monetary Economy c. 400–c. 1500* (Cambridge, Cambridge University Press, 1985).

—, *Hommes et richesses dans l'Empire byzantin* I *IVe-VIIe siècle, II VIIe–XVe siècle* (Paris, Editions P. Lethielleux, 1989, 1991).

Herrin, J., *Women in Purple* (London, Weidenfeld and Nicolson, 2001).

—, *Byzantium. The Surprising Life of a Medieval Empire* (Princeton, Princeton University Press, 2008).

James, Liz, *Desire and Denial in Byzantium* (Aldershot, Ashgate Variorum, 1999).

—, *Empresses and Power in Early Byzantium* (London, Leicester University Press, 2001).

—, 'Men, Women, Eunuchs: Gender, Sex and Power', in J. Haldon (ed.), *A Social History of Byzantium* (Chichester, Wiley-Blackwell, 2009), pp. 31–50.

Jeffreys, E., et al. (eds), *The Oxford Handbook of Byzantine Studies* (Oxford, Oxford University Press, 2008).

Jones, A.H.M., J.R. Martindale, et al., *The Prosopography of the Later Roman Empire* (Cambridge and London, Cambridge University Press, 1971–92).

Kalavrezou, I. (ed.), *Women in Byzantium* (Cambridge, MA, Harvard University Press, 2003).

Kazhdan, A., G. Constable, *People and Power in Byzantium. An Introduction to Modern Byzantine Studies* (Washington, DC, Dumbarton Oaks Research Library and Collection, 1982).

—, with L.F. Sherry and C. Angelidi, *A History of Byzantine Literature,* I. *650–850*, II, *850–1204* (Athens, EIE/KBE, 1999–2006).

Koder, J., *Der Lebensraum der Byzantiner, Historisch-geographischer Abriß ihres mittelalterlichen Staates im östlichen Mittelmeerraum* (Vienna, 1984, repr. w. update 2001, and new Greek version, 2005).

Laiou, A.E., 'The Role of Women in Byzantine Society', *XVI. Internationaler Byzantinistenkongress (Wien, 1981) Akten I/1 = Jahrbuch der Österreichischer Byzantinistik* 31/1 (1981), pp. 233–60 (repr. in *Gender*, art. I).

—, *Gender, Society and Economic Life in Byzantium* (Aldershot, Ashgate, 1992).

—, *Economic History of Byzantium* (Washington, DC, Dumbarton Oaks Research Library and Collection, 2002).

— (ed.), *Le monde byzantin*, 3 vols, I. *330–641* (C. Morrisson (ed.), Paris, 2003), II *641–1204* (J.-C. Cheynet (ed.), Paris, 2006), III. *1204–1453* (A. Laiou and C. Morrisson (eds), in preparation).

— and C. Morrisson, *The Byzantine economy* (Cambridge, 2007), 2 vols published: I. *330–641* (Paris, 2003; w. Greek, Italian and Polish trsl.), II. *641–1204* (2006).

— and D. Simon (eds), *Law and Society in Byzantium Ninth-Twelfth Centuries* (Washington DC, Dumbarton Oaks Research Library and Collection, 1994).

Lefort, J., *Société rurale et histoire du paysage à Byzance* (Paris, 2006).

—, C. Morrisson and J.-P. Sodini (eds), *Les villages dans l'empire byzantin (V^e-XVe siècle)* (Paris, 2006).

Lavan, L. et al. (eds), *Late Antique Archaeology* (Leiden, Brill, 2003–2008), 5 vols so far.

Lemerle, P., *Cinq Études sur le XIe siècle byzantin* (Paris, 1977).

—, *Les plus anciens miracles de saint Démétrius et la pénétration des Slaves dans les Balkans* (Paris, 1981).

Lilie, R.J., C. Ludwig and Th. Pratsch (eds), *Prosopographie der mittelbyzantinischen Zeit* I *(641–867). Prolegomena et I–VI* (Berlin, 1998–2002).

Ljubarskij, J., 'New Trends in the Study of Byzantine Historiography', *Dumbarton Oaks Papers* 47 (1993), pp. 131–8.

Maguire, H., *The Icons of their Bodies: saints and their images in Byzantium* (Princeton, Princeton University Press, 1996).

Mango, C., *Byzantium: The Empire of New Rome* (London, Hackett, 1980).

Mango, M. Mundell (ed.), *Byzantine Trade, 4th–12th Centuries. The Archaeology of Local, Regional and International Exchange* (Farnham, Ashgate, 2009) (not available at the time of writing).

Martindale, J.R., *The Prosopography of the Byzantine Empire I (641–877)* (Aldershot, Ashgate, 2001) (CD-Rom).

McCormick, M., 'Byzantium and Modern Medieval Studies', in J. Van Engen (ed.), *The Past and Future of Medieval Studies* (Notre Dame, University of Indiana Press, 1994), pp. 58–72.

—, *Origins of the European Economy. Communications and Commerce A.D. 300–900* (Cambridge, Cambridge University Press, 2001).

—, 'Molecular Middle Ages: Early Medieval Economic History in the Twenty-First Century', in J.R. Davies, M. McCormick (eds), *The Long Morning of Medieval Europe. New Directions in Early Medieval Europe* (Aldershot, Ashgate, 2008), pp. 83–104.

—, et al., 'Volcanoes and the Climate Forcing of Carolingian Europe', *Speculum* 82 (2007), pp. 865–95.

Mondrain, B. (ed.), *Lire et écrire à Byzance* (Paris, CNRS, 2006).

Morrisson, C., *Monnaies et finances dans l'empire byzantin. Analyses, techniques* (Aldershot, 1994), art. IX (1976).

—, 'La monnaie source de l'histoire de Byzance', *Praktika tes Akademias Athenon* (2008), pp. 211–23 (assessment of the discipline's results).

— (ed.), *Trade and Markets in the Byzantine World. Dumbarton Oaks Spring symposium 2008* (in preparation).

— and A.-M. Talbot, 'Angeliki Laiou (1941–2008)', *Dumbarton Oaks Papers* 63 (2009), forthcoming.

—, C. Brenot, J.-P. Callu, J.-N Barrandon, J. Poirier and R. Halleux, *L'or monnayé* I. *Purification et altérations de Rome à Byzance* (Cahiers Ernest-Babelon 2) (Paris, 1985).

Mullett, M., *Theophylact of Ochrid: reading the letters of a Byzantine archbishop* (Aldershot, Birmingham Byzantine and Ottoman Monographs, 2, 1997).

—, 'New Literary History and the History of Byzantine Literature', in P. Odorico, P. Agapitos (eds), *Pour une nouvelle histoire de la littérature byzantine*

(Paris, 2003), pp. 37–60 (repr. in eadem, *Letters, Literature and Literacy in Byzantium* (Aldershot, Ashgate, 2007, art. XVII))
—, 'Writing in early medieval Byzantium', (1990) repr. in *Letters, Literacy and Literature in Byzantium* (Aldershot, Ashgate, 2007) (art. VI).
Nelson, R., *Later Byzantine Painting: Art, Agency, and Appreciation* (Aldershot, Ashgate Variorum, 2007).
Oikonomides, N. and J. Nesbitt, *Catalogue of Byzantine Seals at Dumbarton Oaks and in the Fogg Museum of Art* (Washington, DC, Dumbarton Oaks Research Library and Collection, 1991–), 6 vols to date.
Patlagean, É., *Pauvreté économique et pauvreté sociale à Byzance, 4e-7e siècles* (Paris-The Hague, 1977).
—, *Structure sociale, famille, chrétienté à Byzance* (London, Variorum Reprints 1981).
—, *Un Moyen Âge grec (IXe–XIVe siècle)* (Paris, 2007).
Reinsch, D., *Alexias, übersetzt, eingeleitet und mit Anmerkungen versehen* (Cologne, 1996, 2nd edn 2001).
Ringrose, K., *The Perfect Servant* (Chicago, University of Chicago Press, 2003).
Savvides, A., et al. (eds), *An Encyclopaedic Prosopographical Lexicon of Byzantine History and Civilization*, in progress (2 vols to date, Brepols, Turnhout, 2008).
Sidéris, G., 'Approches sur l'historiographie du genre à Byzance', *Genre et Histoire* 3 (2008), (http://www.genrehistoire.fr/document. php?id=358).
—, *Les anges du Palais, eunuques, sexes et pouvoir à Byzance (IVe-VIIe siècle)* (Turnhout, Brepols, 2009).
Spieser, J.-M., 'Histoire de l'Art et Archéologie de Byzance : de la vie des formes à leur fonction sociale et à leur fonctionnement anthropologique', in J. Hamesse (ed.), *Bilans et perspectives des Études médiévales en Europe, Actes du1er Congrès européen de la FIDEM (Spoleto, 27–29 mai 1993)* (Louvain-la-Neuve, 1995), pp. 81–106.
— (ed.), *Présence de Byzance* (En Crausaz, Suisse, 2007)
Stephenson, P. (ed.), *The Byzantine World* (London, Routledge, 2010).
Stolten B., 'Balancing Byzantine Law', *Fontes Minores* XI (2005), pp. 57–75.
—, 'The Social Function of the Law', in J. Haldon (ed.), *A Social History of Byzantium* (Chichester, Wiley-Blackwell, 2009).
Straw, C., R. Lim and G. Bowersock, *The Past Before Us. The challenge of historiographies of Late Antiquity* (Bibl. AnTard 6) (Turnhout, Brepols, 2005).
Talbot, A.M., *Women and Religious Life in Byzantium* (Aldershot, Ashgate, 2004).

—, 'Byzantine Studies at the Beginning of the Twenty-first Century', *Journal of English and Germanic Philology* (Jan. 2006), pp. 26–43.

— (ed.), *Women in Byzantium* in http://www.doaks.org/research/byzantine/women_in_byzantium.html.

Thomas, J. and A. Constantinides Hero (eds), *Byzantine Monastic Foundation Documents: A Complete Translation of the Surviving Founders' Typika and Testaments* (Washington, DC, Dumbarton Oaks Research Library and Collection, 2001).

Tougher, S. (ed.), *Eunuchs in Antiquity and Beyond* (London, Duckworth, 2002).

—, *The Eunuch in Byzantine History and Society* (London, Routledge, 2008).

Trapp, E., 'Learned and Vernacular Literature in Byzantium: Dichotomy or Symbiosis?', *Dumbarton Oaks Papers* 47 (1993), pp. 115–29.

—, *Prosopographisches Lexikon der Palaiologenzeit* (Vienna, 1976–96) also in a CD-Rom Version (Vienna 2001).

Vranouse, E.L. and M.G. Nyztazopoulou-Pelekidou (eds), *Vyzantina engrapha tes Mones Patmou* (Athens, 1980), 2 vols.

Vroom, J., *After Antiquity: ceramics and society in the Aegean from the 7th to the 20th century AC* (Leiden, Brill, 2003).

VV.AA., 'Instrumenta Studiorum' (in particular W. Hörandner) in *XXe congrès international des Études byzantines (Paris, 2001) Pré-Actes* I, pp. 319–428.

Whittow, M., *The Making of Orthodox Byzantium. 600–1025* (London, Palgrave Macmillan, 1996).

—, 'Beyond the cultural turn: economic history revived?', *Journal of Roman Archaeology* 20 (2007), pp. 697–704.

Wickham, C., *Framing the Early Middle Ages: Europe and the Mediterranean, 400–800* (Oxford, Oxford University Press, 2005).

Zacos, G. and A. Veglery, *Byzantine Lead Seals* (Basle, 1972–1984), 2 vols.

6

The 'Absence of Byzantium' or the Absence of History in General?[1]

Nikos Karapidakis

In her contemplative article entitled[2] 'Absence of Byzantium', Averil Cameron poses a pivotal question that preoccupies her as a specialist in Byzantine history, namely, the place of Byzantium in contemporary public discourse. In that article, she is interested less in Byzantine Studies *per se* and more, if not exclusively, in what we call 'public history' or, as we would have said earlier, in the perception and the use of 'Byzantium' by a certain public discourse. For her, however (p. 7), this is the 'somewhat eccentric to bring in Byzantium in British, American or European public discourse outside Greece and the other countries which trace a direct historical link with Byzantine history and culture'. Thus, she introduces three different concepts into the discussion. The concept of the specialist Byzantinist (and therefore of scientific history), who knows his subject scientifically (this she considers rather as given and, unfortunately, does not explain what exactly she means); the public discourse on Byzantium in Britain, North America (we presume that this is what she means by writing America) and Europe (here she means Europe excepting Britain); and the countries that have a direct historical relationship with Byzantium (we have good grounds for assuming that various Slav countries are implied (but which ones?) and first and foremost Russia). That is, we are dealing, in a way, with many 'Byzantiums', which are defined by the academic history and the cultural history of each one of the aforesaid zones.[3]

The first example Cameron gives comes from the lecture delivered by Pope Benedict XVI at the University of Regensburg in September 2006. An excellent example, which widens the public discourse from the British,

American and European domain, referred to above, into the religious domain, since the pope departs from these almost national categories and represents a quasi-ecumenical entity. In this lecture, His Holiness quoted an excerpt from an essay by Manuel II Palaiologos (1391–1425) against Islam. The pope used Palaiologos to support his argument that Christianity, in contrast to Islam, is based on the Word (*Logos*). In so doing, he also opened a window for dialogue with the Eastern Orthodox Church and a new cycle in their pre-eternal discussion. On another occasion, if we are not mistaken, the pope asked forgiveness for the change of target of the Fourth Crusade, thus reminding us that he is the continuer of the same history (essentially of the same narrative scheme), but is also sufficiently generous (and so, always the regulator) to seek exoneration. Cameron analyses perspicaciously the issue of the pope's use of the passage from Palaiologos. We have here a characteristic 'use' of a historical text detached from its historical (that is its actual) context, in order to support a particular point of view. So 'successful' a use that it led the opposite side, that is, the Muslims, to protest with alacrity to the pope, so showing that they too use history in a similar way. It would be worth investigating how the Orthodox sides perceived the use of the passage, but this is not our brief here. Nonetheless, the use of history, essentially its abuse, in such a way enjoys exceptional success, since it churns up the same deep-bedded sediments in men's mind. Their ideology and the image they form, on the basis of their ideology, of the other and, primarily, of their rival or potential rival. Cameron implies, quite rightly, that no historian can take seriously this kind of unhistorical uses of historical examples. However, we would disagree with her statement (p. 18) that: 'The whole episode of the lecture and its reception is a vivid example of the absence of understanding of Byzantium'. We would say, on the contrary, that the whole episode is a striking example of the uses and the abuses that history in general suffers, so as to serve, in public discourse of this kind, the intentions of its agent. Intentions that are mainly ideological and hegemonic. This is the usual danger of history in public discourse. Indeed, it is curious that although Cameron criticizes so pointedly the pope's use of an excerpt from Manuel II Palaiologos, she is not particularly surprised by the fact that the seminar at which she was invited to present her paper on the 'absence of Byzantium', was preceded by a lecture by the British conservative politician (the label 'conservative' is hers) B. Johnson, entitled 'The Dawn of Rome: a comparison of the Roman Empire with the European Union'. Johnson has published a book entitled *The Dream of Rome*, in which he argues that 'The Roman empire could offer lessons for building a better European Union'. His Holiness is concerned with the superiority of his Church in the Word, and this is what he promotes; the honourable gentleman is concerned with stabilizing the power of the European Union. The pope uses, to this end, a passage from a scholarly Byzantine emperor; the politician uses ancient Rome, symbol of all powers and all empires, at least in Western thought. There would have been very little difference if the latter had used Byzantium to help in the stabilization of European power. In this case too he would have resorted to using a mirror. In both cases, 'history' is a tool, a rhetorical metaphor and a reflection of the ideology of its user, but in no case does the user need scientific understanding of the object about which he speaks. The rhetorical use of the object is enough; the exemplum and the interpretations that the orator reserves for it.

Cameron writes (p. 18), somewhat contradictorily in our opinion, that 'Byzantium is generally absent from the current public discourse of western Eurpean countries'. And we say contradictorily because she adds, immediately after, that 'Of course it is possible to cite exceptions, for instance the appeal of certain themes in French and Italian drama and opera, and the attraction of the sixth-century Empress Theodora to novelists. In nineteenth-century England, Byzantine architecture, with its gold mosaic and its polychromy, made some impact and was debated''. We would add the numerous novels in English on Byzantine subjects – the traveller still comes across them in the bookcases of tourist inns in Scotland – or the historiographical syntheses, such as those by John Julius Norwich, which succour to the public's appetite for blood and intrigue, and also the allure of Byzantine art, even today, for the Anglo-Saxon public (and not only), judging by recent major exhibitions on Byzantium in New York and in London. Only that this attraction of the public – and not only the Anglo-Saxon – towards the artworks and the 'mysteries' of Byzantium, is not due particularly to the history of Byzantium or of the Middle Ages in general, but to a conception of history associated with the ideology of the organizers of each exhibition – which ideology is sometimes abandoned, fortunately, for the sake of history – and the ideology of the spectators as agents of culture. Culture, which, addressed to their spirituality, makes them stand out culturally (that is, also socially). And since Byzantine art is linked with Christianity, a certain public is identified with the spirituality and the mysticism of Byzantium, and therefore other uses that public history reserves for Byzantium. In which case, we would prefer to say that Byzantium is not exactly absent from the public discourse, but that it undergoes each time the transformations with which the public discourse recognizes it. And this does not apply only to Byzantium but to other periods of history too, and in our view, of British, of American or of European history. We would add of Islam, of China and of Japan. A brief visit to the fortunes of the concept Middle Ages or to the fortunes of the concept Europe would be sufficient to convince of the truth of this view.

At this point things become somewhat confused, since the public discourse on history is frequently constructed by the historians themselves. Cameron writes (p. 18): 'English-speaking scholarship has for example historically identified with the classical tradition and inherited a Gibbonian aversion to Byzantium which the controversial rediscovery of Byzantium in the new Greek state itself in the nineteenth century did nothing to counteract'. Here, the picture of Byzantium is constructed by a scholarship – that is, historians – that complies with a very specific reading of Byzantium, the Gibbonian. And the Gibbonian reading complies with the Enlightenment's reading of the Middle Ages in general, and not only of Byzantium. In the age of Enlightenment, the West was emerging from a long period in which religion was of central significance and the Middle Ages needed to be redefined, negatively, by enhancing the values of other historical eras. So, historians have a share – as do the organizers of Byzantine art exhibitions – in one specific historical construct that denigrates or elevates a period. In this case, historians do not merely participate in the public discourse on history; they construct it. As Cameron observes too, referring (p. 20) to a perspicacious statement by Paul Magdalino, we are dealing with a 'species of *neo-Fallmereyerism*', which was characteristic of (but is today outmoded) leading British and other English-speaking Byzantinists. Let us think for a little about the opposite; the fortunes, for example, of Paparrigopoulian Byzantine history. The question that is asked today is to what extent this 'history' has a meaning other than that of being an index of historical education in the historian's time. Gibbon is the 'history of Byzantium' of his time (and indeed of a social group of his time), and by the same token, Paparrigopoulos is the 'history of Byzantium' of his time. Approaches of great historical value, but now outdated. Unless the contemporary reader of history insists on making them into tools, as we saw the pope make Palaiologos into a tool, and B. Johnson make Rome into a tool. But in this case, we do not move away from public history, the history that which supplies the public with ideology, in other words, purposely undermined representations. Consequently, Britain was acquainted with Byzantium, in both its public discourse and its scientific (the scholarship to which Cameron refers), but it was acquainted with it in accordance with British constructs. And these constructs, in their turn, were serving the images Britain already had of itself or of its foreign policy: the 'neo-Fallmerayerism' to which we have referred above. Or, in the best case, its present was telescoping the past and together with this Byzantium. How else can we understand the fascination that the spirituality of Byzantium exerted on W.B. Yeats, if not as an inquiry, in counterpart, of English society itself? Since it concerns events of our time, it would be worth looking at how Balkan history is used in the Anglo-Saxon domain when it comes to interpreting or to justifying policies in the Balkans, and specifically in Kosovo, as well as how Byzantine history is used in the Balkans for exactly the same reasons.

This brings us to the other use of Byzantium which Averil Cameron detects. The use of Byzantium as spirituality, as allure of the icons and the luxury objects. We have referred already, following Cameron, to W.B. Yeats. In Cameron's words (p. 20): 'It depends also on the works of a few much more sympathetic modern historians, headed by Steven Runciman ...'. And she comments, a little further on, that 'Dimitri Obolensky's classic book, *The Byzantine Commonwealth. Eastern Europe 500–1453*, published in 1971, also represents this sympathetic and pro-Orthodox view of Byzantium disposed and phil-Orthodox view of Byzantium ...'. Consequently, we have here yet another use of Byzantium, as well as of Medieval history in general. Its use as a specific spirituality. A use that is, after all, not unrelated to the geopolitical. A use we saw as living on through Byzantine art and the exhibitions dedicated to it, as well as through the pope's quoting of the passage from Palaiologos, analysed so well by Cameron. Byzantium in this case, in contradistinction to the interpretation of the Enlightenment (the Gibbonian interpretation for the British), becomes spirituality, that is, religion, and is therefore turned into 'sympathetic', serving other needs (we understand which) for its users. We should remember that this change in attitude towards a historical period, with emphasis now on the spirituality of an age, is observed already in Chateaubriand, when he discovers the 'Martyrs' and, together with them, the spirituality of Christianity, and therefore of the Middle Ages, having himself lived through – we have to admit – the mayhem of the Reign of Terror. This attitude is explicable and understandable and sympathetic, but it is again a use of history with many potential ramifications into ideology and even into politics. And certainly it emanates from a particular proclivity, regardless of where it leads each time: from the religious sentiment, or at least from a sentiment of religiosity. As Cameron herself says (p. 20), 'In England moreover, there has traditionally been a distinct warmth towards Orthodoxy in some parts of the Anglican Church ...'. Byzantium here ceases to be a historical reality in its dynamic fullness (social and political hegemonies, economy and exploitation, ideology and social reproduction) and is transformed into 'spirituality', which is implicitly religious. A shift that is absolutely understandable, as in the case of Chateaubriand, but here we are not dealing with history, but with a selection from history. Or, at least, one more use of Byzantium (or of the Middle Ages, or of history in general) in the public discourse.

So, Byzantium is always there, regardless of whether Cameron writes (p. 22), 'But there is still an absence'. And this time she means the difficult place it holds in 'Anglo-Saxon and western european scholarship', '[...] Byzantium occupies an uncertain place in current historiography [...], no one knows what to do with it'. 'Was it part of Europe? Or does it belong rather to the East?' And she aptly refers to an earlier position of hers, 'I have argued earlier for western attitudes to Byzantium as a form of Orientalism'. Here the issue is not some place for Byzantium in public discourse, but the place of Byzantium in scientific historical studies. We have spoken already about historical scientific studies being part of the public discourse, if they do not in fact construct it. We have spoken about the 'neo-Fallmerayerism' expressed, according to Magdalino, by many Byzantinists, mainly British ones. This raises the question of the wellspring of this uncertain relationship between current – and usually Western – historiography of the Middle Ages and Byzantium, and indeed to what degree this uncertainty is related to a difficulty in defining its own object. A difficulty that is by no means innocent but subverted by ideological influences. First of all, by the long-suffering concept of Europe, so elusive and vague from every viewpoint, which certainly cannot be used as a serious conceptual tool. As Cameron points out, many Medievalists present a trend of retrenchment when it comes to defining Europe. It goes without saying that they tend to limit it to what we call traditionally the West (an equally problematical concept, if we really think about it). In our opinion, this is a totally restrictive concept of Europe, since it is Eurocentric (American thought participates in this Eurocentric concept, possibly because it considers American history as the continuation of yesterday's European hegemony). In other words, it starts off by considering as given that which it is trying to define, Europe. A dispassionate analysis of the Medieval world would have shown that the West, with its numerous centres and its fragmentations, Byzantium with its centre but also its own fragmentations that brought new centres to the forestage, and, last, Islam (including the Ottoman Empire) with its centres and its own fragmentations, are always interdependent worlds, developing competitively and dynamically, the one always taking from the other. Sometimes they are close, sometimes they move apart, but never does one of them constitute an independent history. If now history is written, usually, much later and starting from the world that prevailed, in part, at the expense of the others, that is the Western world, this inevitably influences the historiography. The historiography, which we have seen above also as public discourse, papal, political (neo-Fallmereyerism), ideological (Christian spirituality). If behind each of these three is hidden a claim, behind one particular historiography of the Middle Ages is hidden one other claim. Consequently, this is not so much about a scientific historiography as about a genealogy of dominance, which we would readily compare with the genealogical genres of antiquity and the Middle Ages, that is, with a claim to the past (we shall see at once which past). Medieval historiography – that is, the historiography of the Medieval West – is accountable to its Christian (papal) roots and to the flowering of European hegemony in the nineteenth century. The history of the modern world and of modernity is accountable to the history of Protestantism. And Byzantine Studies are frequently their counter-paradigm. The tools available to the first were, until recently, totally inadequate for understanding both the Western 'Middle Ages' and the other 'Middle Ages'. Moreover, as has been demonstrated, the very concept of the Middle Ages, as used by Medievalists until recently – if not to this day – is totally unsuitable and has very little meaning. The same holds for the concept of antiquity, as shown by the debate on Late Antiquity, to which Cameron has contributed so much. Mainly, one thing has been demonstrated: That behind the periodizations and the definitions of the scientific objects are hidden emotional or ideological criteria (associated with the present and the claiming of the past in relation to this) and a need to enhance the origin laid claim to. Consequently, historical studies which have been organized around a need to enhance origin are closed with regard to their communication vis-à-vis other specialities which too respond to similar needs: the historical studies of the Medieval West vis-à-vis Byzantine studies. As far as this point is concerned, however, Byzantine studies too appear frequently to be closed to western ones. Starting always from a point of ideological differentiation. If we follow the development of Byzantine studies in Greece, for example, as well as in Russia, from the late nineteenth century, we ascertain that they were used as a tool of identity and of differentiation from the West, more than as a tool for understanding the Byzantine and Medieval world.

Now, as far as the problem of the periodization of Late Antiquity is concerned, which Cameron analyses so penetratingly in pages 25–33 of her article, this should not be, in our opinion, a major problem impeding communication between specialities. The main question (p. 25) that Cameron asks, 'to whether it ended (the late antiquity) some time not long after the fall of the Roman empire in the west, or whether it actually extended to include the emergence of Islam, and even as late as the eighth century'; and her observation that 'This has much to do with cultural history, and inclusion of the eastern part of the empire, where archaeology and other evidence show that life was flourishing later than in the west is crucial for the argument' must, in our view, be confronted with greater relativity than they are confronted by their specialists. First of all, drawing on the history of the West, so as to determine the slow and relative transition, leaving aside the concept of decline (charged with the ideology of classical purity), and then in continuance, to separate, as for the West too, cultural expression from other expressions of social and political life. Duration in cultural expression is much greater than in other expressions, where accelerations may function incrementally in the direction of a reorganization of the society as well as of the hegemony of one class. We believe, taking into consideration the above, that also the problem posed by Polymnia Athanassiadi – and discussed by Cameron (pp. 32–33) – as an *interval between two entities, Antiquity and the Middle Ages, during which an society centred on Man was mutated into one constituted to the greater glory of God*, would have much to gain. It would allow us specifically to see how the one entity is diffused into the other, without their separation into all the social groups, into all the 'nations', ever being absolutely clear, but how the entities obey always specific social hegemonies and one mode of production. On this point we would agree with Cameron when she writes (p. 33) that, 'cries not only for a fresh and more realistic political and economic assessment of the Byzantine State, but also for an investigation of its supposed religiosity as a the defining factor …'.

We have said above that the very concept of the West, and the historical studies that have been constructed around this, are subject to the criticism of the reliability of the very concept West and, by extension, of the concept 'Byzantium'. We could say also of the concept Middle Ages (this unbearable, that is for the most part incomprehensible, intermediate period between antiquity and modernity, the latter a constituent myth of Western civilization). In other words, the question of the reliability of the basic concepts which historians use for their constructs is raised. To what extent their conceptual tools stand up to an epistemological analysis or constitute pseudo-concepts borrowed from the current representations. Here, we reverse Cameron's question concerning the place of Byzantium in public discourse, by posing the question of public discourse in Byzantine history and in history in general. The pseudo-concepts (from a scientific viewpoint) that derive from the first and are mixed up in the scientific analysis needed by the second. The question is important more than ever today, when, despite the achievements of the social sciences, analyses continue to be produced, such as that of Samuel Huntington in his well-known book, in which all the ideological stereotypes of a specific culture reappear as given concepts: Renaissance, Reformation, Enlightenment, overseas colonialism.

(Not for one moment does it occur to him that all these were discoveries, already, of the Middle Ages). A vicious circle of the instrumentalization of history, with the latter serving ideology. It is worth asking whether it is Byzantium that is absent from public discourse or whether the right to critical discourse, and along with it history, is absent altogether? Or, in the best case, whether we are dealing with a history that serves the current ideology (imperial in Huntington's case, semi-imperial in the case of the ideologues of Europe, oriental-imperial in the mythology of the Russians. Soon, an instrumentalization of the Chinese Empire will be added, in order to serve the enhancement of the giant, and already a neo-Ottoman instrumentalization has been added to modern Turkey). As Cameron puts it (p.50), 'but it is important to realize the modern political imperatives that lie behind such judgements, [...] the underlying assumptions about the Soviet and the post-Soviet regimes which a western neo-liberal agenda all to well'. We could say that we have progressed little from the use that certain German historians made of the Middle Ages, so as to discover the great German nation. They, we recall, passed from a supposed single Germanic civilization to the history of one German State, and, together with it, to the history of the German blood.

Cameron very rightly includes (p. 38) among 'the easy answers' to the absence of Byzantium from public and political discourse, the fact that Byzantium is not taught in British schools; the fact that its religious tradition is different from that of Britain and the United States, and of the greater part of Europe. Although with regard to the last point, we have seen the invention of the appropriate uses of Byzantine spirituality, when one religious community needs it. One more 'easy answer' (p. 38) to the absence of Byzantium from public discourse is that the 'language of the Byzantine State was Greek', but not the 'Greek taught in our Classical courses' (this too another major ideological choice). Of the above reasons, the first refers, of course, to the quality of teaching history in secondary education, and there is no reason to analyse it here. The second refers to religion and shows how much history and perceptions of history are captive to it. The third reason refers to the importance of language for the study of Byzantine history. We hasten to add its importance also for the history of the Medieval West, as a reminder that this issue is not unrelated to the ideological domination of Classical antiquity in Western culture – a domination totally relevant to the secondary place of both Byzantine and Medieval studies. Cameron herself writes (p. 38): 'because while the language of the *Byzantine State* was Greek' (our italics). Thus, she excludes, *a priori*, the other Greek languages of Byzantium, the non-state ones, in other words the vernacular. As Stylianos

Alexiou has pointed out,[4] many Byzantinists are ignorant of vernacular Greek, if not of Greek in general. We can understand what is hidden behind such ignorance. The 'holy war' of claiming antiquity, Christianity and their language. The rest are considered decadence, and together with them the vernacular Greek of the Middle Ages. The phrase 'language of the Byzantine State' conceals again a particular conception of Byzantium, the conception that identifies Byzantium with its State. That is, Byzantine civilization with certain of its dominant classes. From this point onwards comes an avalanche of stereotypes, to which Cameron refers (p. 38): Byzantium 'is absent ... because "we" are not East Europeans; because Byzantium defines itself both against the classical world and against the medieval west; because it is seen as obscurantist or rigid rather than as foreshadowing civil society and liberal values; because it is associated both with the idea of decline from the classical world and the Roman empire, and with passing on authoritarian values to Russia'. And, just imagine, these views are espoused by established historians and not chance orators of public discourse.

In other words, one more use – not only by public opinion and public discourse, but also the scientific and the academic community – of history as a tool, to the advantage of identities and of ideological constructs. We are fully aware that in this situation the responsibility falls not only on public opinion but also on its historians and its thinkers, who continue to operate in the framework of producing an identity (national, cultural, political, religious) and not as meditators of time and societies. The examples that Cameron cites, on pages 41–45, point to a great lack of historical thought in many historians and academics in universities in the West, an inability to comprehend the Medieval world outside the 'western perspective', that is, the perspective constructed by the narration of hegemonic Western European (and American) history. In our opinion, this lack is due on the one hand to the withdrawal of history in general from the fields of social science to the fields of empiricism and of pseudo-political science, which in its turn uses empirical categories to understand complex phenomena, and on the other to the inability of historians (indeed, in the age of globalization), to think of history as an articulation of cultures and as durations, and not as history of individual worlds and individual cultures, and, in the worst case, as history of powers and empires (we suspect the ideological distortions of historians who discuss the history of empires).

However, this question has yet to be asked also of Byzantinists. How do they perceive their Byzantine world? How do they communicate with other civilizations and the historians of these? And, primarily, to what degree do they condone, in contradistinction to these other historians, similar stereotypes as well as the same stereotypes of public discourse. In short, it is worth asking whether we are dealing with a history of man (which is legitimized only for this reason) or with a historicism that enhances unique cases and ends up reading the others through its current conceptual tools; in the end enhancing the uniqueness of today's civilization? In this way, we understand that this is not a problem about Byzantine studies but about the place that societies reserve for historical studies in general, and what answers they await from these. Since the study of history continues to be posed with quasi-anachronistic terms, that is, as metaphor of today's world (and its concepts) in the medieval or the ancient, and we come to questions of the type 'Europe between Brussels and Byzantium', it is certain that the historical discipline has not made particular progress and is trapped, simply, in a succession of rise and falls of empires. That is a tautology (the rise and the fall), with only nuance the narrations and the rhetorical development. Even more dangerous are the reductionist constructs of the type 'Byzantium-absolutism', but the same does not happen so often in Medieval history in general, in which the Middle Ages equal theocracy (without explanation of what the Middle Ages and theocracy mean), just as there is rarely an explanation of what exactly we mean when we say Byzantium.

It would have been interesting to have proposed an *a priori* examination of the actual terms we use and their historicity, that is, when they begin to be used and by whom, in order to see whether they have any scientific value. Thus, for example, it would be quickly revealed that the terms Byzantium and Middle Ages are pseudo-terms, fabricated in order to serve or to describe situations invented *post hoc*. Just as the inability of the terms state, empire, taxation, power, etc., would be revealed when they are used of ages that had a completely different conception and lived experience of these. The same applies to the terms Church, God, absolutism, and many more. And things are still difficult if we ask what precisely is meant by historical source. And things are even more difficult since historians carry on without asking themselves whether they understand the words in the sources they are reading. Usually, they suffice with the translation given by a dictionary, whether the sources they are reading are Greek or Latin (to stay in the Middle Ages). If it is assumed that a person today has a clear idea of what the words mean in his own age. It would be very interesting for someone to explain what state, empire, economy, social class, religion, mean today. But this is another issue, what we understand from our own era, and mainly what the historians understand, so as to dare to write the history of other ages.

If history wants to make a serious intervention in public discourse it must find perhaps the strength to remind it of its ephemeral relativity and not to emphasize its narcissism and its tendency to consider the present omnivorous; its tendency to start off from itself, in order to understand other ages and other men. But also to find the strength to question its object and its methods. Judging by Averil Cameron's splendid article, the Anglo-Saxon world, to which it mainly refers, and taking into consideration that the place this reserves for Byzantium is committed – fortunately there are exceptions – to its ideological and religious stereotypes, to its assessment of hegemony and to its uniqueness, the more difficult it is for it to communicate with differences, as well as to see itself clearly. There is a future for historical studies if they want to oppose this and, of course, provided they are allowed to do so by those who fund them.

Notes

1 First published as 'Η 'απουσία του Βυζαντίου' ή η απουσία της ιστορίας, γενικότερα;' (The 'absence of Byzantium' or the absence of history in general?) in *Nea Estia* 164/1807 (October 2008), pp. 626–41.

2 Cameron, Averil, 'Η απουσία του Βυζαντίου' (The absence of Byzantium), *Nea Estia* 163/1807 (January 2008), pp. 4-59.

3 Nissim, Liana and Silvia Riva (eds), *Sauver Byzance de la barbarie du monde,* Università degli studi di Milano. Facoltà di Lettere e Filosofia (Milano, 2004) (Quaderni di Acme, 65).

4 Alexiou, Stylianos, 'Το άγνωστο Βυζάντιο' (The Unknown Byzantium), *Nea Estia* 163/1812 (June, 2008), pp. 1011–12.

Bibliography

Alexiou, Stylianos, 'Το άγνωστο Βυζάντιο' (The Unknown Byzantium), *Nea Estia* 163/1812 (June, 2008), pp. 1011–12.

Cameron, Averil, 'Η απουσία του Βυζαντίου' (The Absence of Byzantium), *Nea Estia* 163/1807 (January 2008), pp. 4–59.

Nissim, Liana and Silvia Riva (eds), *Sauver Byzance de la barbarie du monde,* Università degli studi di Milano. Facoltà di Lettere e Filosofia (Milano, 2004) (Quaderni di Acme, 65).

7

Aspects of Renaissance Studies, 1985–2005: A Survey of Three Periodicals and Some General Remarks

Benjamin Arbel

Despite the use of this term in other contexts, the Renaissance as a historical phenomenon is essentially a Western European development that has also become a chronological definition. Obviously, it is interpreted and considered in different ways, and accorded different degrees of importance, depending on national historical developments and various historiographical traditions. So, to survey 20 years of scholarly activity in a field marked by a very intensive and variegated scientific production is a well-nigh impossible assignment for a short paper. Consequently, I have chosen to follow the developments in this field by focusing on three well-established periodicals dedicated to Renaissance studies, and published in three different countries and languages.

Focusing on periodicals has the disadvantage of leaving aside books, which generally have a stronger effect or resonance among historians. Even so, a survey of periodicals is not only a more realizable assignment for a short presentation, it is also justifiable, considering that many subjects and theses that ultimately appear in book form are first launched into the scholarly arena in the form of articles. For the present survey, we shall focus on thee periodicals that can be considered as leading ones in this field: one Italian, one French and one American.

The Italian journal *Rinascimento*, which is, as far as I know, the earliest historical periodical dedicated to the Renaissance (it was published under the name *La Rinascita*, between 1938 and 1944, and has continued in its present form since 1950), is published once a year by the *Istituto Nazionale di studi sul Rinascimento* in Florence, and includes articles in Italian, English, French, and occasionally in other languages. It does not have a book review section, but includes a list of recent publications received, which gives the reader a broad spectrum of historical production both in Italy and abroad.

The articles published in *Rianscimento* over the past 20 years can be described as conservative in their approach, largely focusing on the works of famous Renaissance writers, such as Petrarch, Boccaccio, Leonardo Bruni, Leon Battista Alberti, Angelo Poliziano, Lorenzo the Magnificent, Niccolo Machiavelli, and Francesco Guicciardini. Another specific trait of this journal is its penchant for philosophical issues, probably reflecting the preferences of Eugenio Garin, who served as its chief editor until 1992. This tendency continues under the present editors, with no shortage of articles dealing with the works of Marsilio Ficino, Giovanni Pico Della Mirandola and Giordano Bruno.

For a few years, between 1986 and 1989, the journal produced a bibliography of works on the Renaissance period, which had been published in Italy during the year previous to the respective volume. These lists offer an impressive vista of a very intensive historiographical activity, reaching at one point over 1,400 publications, the majority of which are articles. Most of the listed articles appeared in periodicals not dedicated exclusively to the Renaissance, which indicates how partial a presentation based merely on studies published in a specialized journal can be.

Examination of the section of *Rinascimento* listing Renaissance publications yields an impression of the subjects in which Italian scholars have been mostly interested. A preliminary examination, focusing on one year – 1987 – and involving the sorting into several categories of all books listed as published in Italy and relating in some way to the Renaissance, produced the following results: of a total of 342 books listed for that year, 54 (15.7 per cent) are on Church history and religious subjects; 45 (13.1 per cent) on art history; 43 (12.5 per cent) on various literary subjects; 39 (11.4 per cent) are annotated editions of Renaissance writings; 24 (7 per cent) are on social and economic history; 18 (5.2 per cent) on local or regional issues; 16 (4.6 per cent) are biographies; 15 (4.3 per cent) deal with documentation, archives etc.; 13 (3.8 per cent) are on philosophical issues; 12 (3.5 per cent) on political and institutional history; 10 (2.9 per cent) can be defined as broad syntheses; 8 (2.3 per cent) deal with the history of books; 7 (2 per cent) philological subjects; 6 (1.7 per cent) the history of Renaissance women; 6 (1.7 per cent) science and magic; 4 (1.1 per cent) Renaissance music; and 4 (1.1 per cent) Jewish issues.[1]

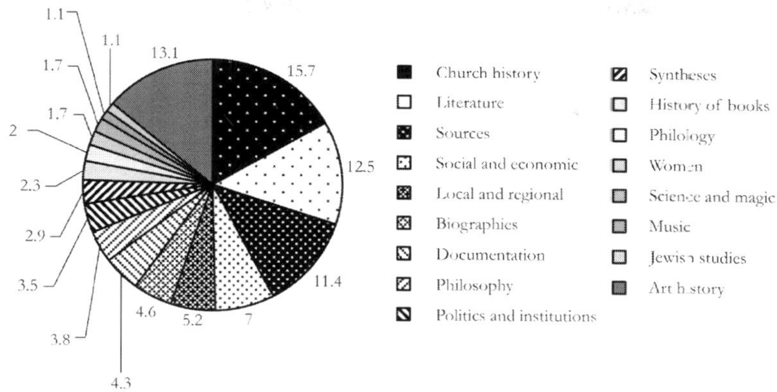

Figure 7.1 Italian books concerning the Renaissance period, 1987

The second journal chosen for this survey, the *Bibliothèque d' Humanisme et Renaissance* (organ of the International Association 'Humanisme et Renaissance'), is mainly, though not exclusively, concerned with the French Renaissance, and it too publishes articles in different European languages. Predictably, many of its articles are dedicated to central figures of the French Renaissance (which, according to French historiographical tradition, begins only with the Cinquecento). Even so, our survey of the last 20 years has revealed a somewhat unexpected bias in favour of certain authors, whereas others have been relatively neglected. Thus, Erasmus of Rotterdam, who, of course, cannot be considered French, and Michel de Montaigne, lead the gallery of prominent Renaissance authors, with 21 articles dedicated to each, followed by Pierre de Ronsard (13 articles), Agrippa d' Aubigné (13 articles), Marguerite de Navarre (11 articles) and Clément Marot (nine articles). Other authors have attracted less attention in this journal. For example, it is surprising that, in the period under review, only one article was dedicated to the great author François Rabelais. Whether this rather restricted statistical sample reflects editorial policies, sheer chance, or more general trends among French Renaissance scholars is an open question.

A not insignificant number of articles in this periodical deal with subjects relating to Italy, Spain and other areas outside France, while a regular section surveying recent publications on Elizabethan England and related fields is also included. However, generally speaking, as in its Italian counterpart, the tendency of the articles in this journal is not to digress from the traditional and more limited conception of the Renaissance as a literary, humanistic and artistic phenomenon, and there are hardly any studies touching upon social, economic or wider cultural issues.

Nonetheless, it should be noted that this journal's book-reviews section covers a wider cultural and geographical spectrum. Although concentrating mainly on literary aspects, it does include numerous discussions of other themes, such as religion, institutions, patronage, classical humanism, travelogues, women's studies, political writings, historiography, the history of books, and so on. Special attention is paid to publications of new editions of sources.

The American journal *Renaissance Quarterly* can be considered as a sounding board of recent trends in Renaissance historiography, considering the leading role that the American academic world occupies today in this field, and also the relative freedom from national or nationalistic biases that are still influential in European Renaissance scholarship.[2] Though sharing the traditional concept of European Renaissance scholarship, which considers literary and cultural themes as the core of Renaissance studies, the 20 volumes of *Renaissance Quarterly* that have been surveyed (1985–2005) reflect, at the same time, a conviction that literature, humanism, philosophy, the arts, education and religion cannot be separated from other aspects of Renaissance life. Consequently, over these years a growing number of articles have been devoted to social history, with particular emphasis on the family, marriage, and the role of women in society and culture. Another laudable trend is the journal's effort to offer a wide panorama of recent scholarship in the field, by dedicating special surveys to recent Renaissance studies in Spain, Germany, France and Italy, in addition to the ever-growing section of book reviews.[3]

Interestingly, although *Renaissance Quarterly* is an organ of an English-speaking country, the English Renaissance is not its major subject. Of the 400 or so articles published between 1985 and 2005, about 41 per cent deal with various aspects of the Italian Renaissance, which is the favoured area in this American periodical; only 24 per cent discuss issues related to the English Renaissance, 12 per cent to the French and a mere 3 per cent to the German Renaissance; while 13 per cent deal with issues transcending the boundaries of a single country.

The volumes of this journal that have been reviewed for this study offer a continuous reflection on the classical issues that have been preoccupying Renaissance studies since the mid-nineteenth century, such as the role

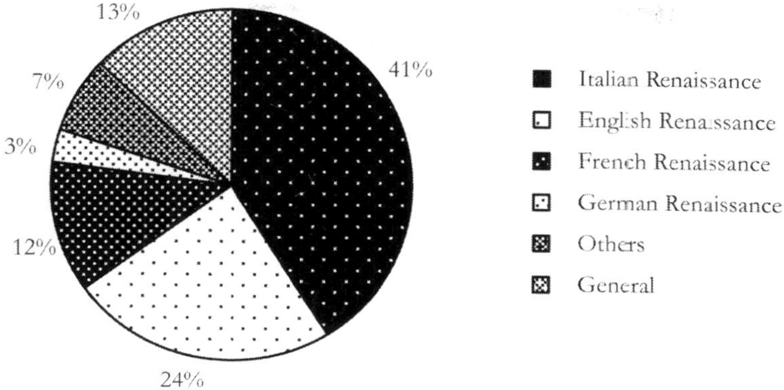

Figure 7.2 Articles in *Renaissance Quarterly*, 1985–2005

of Classical scholarship in cultural renewal, the question of Renaissance individualism, the significance of Renaissance humanism, aesthetics, the relation of art and literature, literary criticism, as well as various forms and functions of rhetoric. However, these themes appear alongside other topics, such as the representation of power, the role of confraternities, religious sensibilities, the role of charity, the family, marriage, sexuality, and the role of women in Renaissance culture and society. An increasing focus on subjects relating to these topics is the most conspicuous characteristic of American Renaissance scholarship during these years.

My impression from the book-reviews section of all three journals is that recent Renaissance scholarship seems to avoid grand syntheses, preferring to address more specific questions. In the Anglo-Saxon scholarly world, Italy continues to be the centre of interest, with an increasing number of studies focusing on the Venetian world, as opposed to the more traditional interest in Florence.

Needless to say, the three aforementioned periodicals, though probably the most prestigious in the field, are not the only ones dedicated to Renaissance studies. There are now about 30 periodicals dealing either exclusively or partly with this area of study. Most of them have book-reviews sections and lists of publications received, attesting to a huge scholarly production, including monographs, articles, conference proceedings, publication of sources, etc.[4]

Four of the periodicals devoted exclusively to the Renaissance – one German, two British and one American – have appeared over of the past

23 years.[5] Thus, among the larger Western countries in which Renaissance culture was an important historical phenomenon, only Spain remains without its proper journal, a deficiency undoubtedly due to developments specific to Spanish modern historiography, recently analysed in two articles by Ottavio Di Camillo.[6]

For the general public, the term 'Renaissance' is associated, first and foremost, with art, and with the names of the great painters, sculptures and architects of that period. It is therefore striking that there is no significant periodical devoted exclusively to Renaissance art. Consequently, art historians specializing in this period have to choose between publishing in periodicals dealing with the Renaissance in general, where technical problems often limit the possibilities of including colour plates and high-quality illustrations, or in periodicals dedicated to art history in general. However, it seems that this situation is not peculiar to the Renaissance, since, contrary to that in other historical areas, there are very few professional periodicals focused on one period of the history of art.

A final word about Renaissance studies on the Web. In addition to the electronic periodical dedicated to the English Renaissance, and to the *Renaissance Quarterly*, which is also accessible and searchable via the Internet, various data bases can be found on the Web, among them *Iter*, the useful bibliographical database of Medieval and Renaissance studies launched and developed at the University of Toronto. The fact that it also covers the Middle Ages has some advantages, considering the fluid dividing line between the two periods, but it also constitutes a handicap, since it is much more difficult to cover the huge amount of material related to both the Middle Ages and the Renaissance. Consequently, Renaissance studies are far from being covered sufficiently and satisfactorily in this database, which, nevertheless, is being expanded continuously. A very good bibliographical resource for Renaissance studies remains the periodical *Bibliographie internationale de l'Humanisme et de la Renaissance*, published annually in Geneva, an indispensable research tool, which, unfortunately, does not yet have an electronic version.

Notes

1 Lunetta, Loredana and Anna Laura Puliafito, 'Bibliografia italiana di studi sull'umanesimo ed il Rinascimento: 1987', appended to *Rinascimento* 28 (1988), pp. 1–104 (separate pagination); Lunetta, Loredana and Anna Laura Puliafito, 'Bibliografia italiana di studi sull'umanesimo ed il Rinascimento: 1988', *Rinascimento* 49 (1989), pp. 1-95 (separate pagination); *Rinascimento* 30

(1990), pp. 367–80 ('Libri ricevuti'); *Rinascimento* 31 (1991), pp. 343–67 ('Nuove accessioni').

2 Between 1995 and 2002, the size of *Renaissance Quarterly* (henceforth: *RQ*) has increased considerably, reaching the highest point in 2001, with no less than 36 articles per volume, not including book reviews.

3 See *RQ* 1987: 'Recent trends in Renaissance studies: the family, marriage and sex'; *RQ* 43 (1990): 'Education in the Renaissance and Reformation'; 1991: 'Renaissance psychology'; *RQ* 47 (1994): 'Recent French works on the Renaissance'; 'Recent Italian works on the Renaissance'; 'Renaissance studies in Germany'; *RQ* 48 (1995): 'Recent French works'; 'Recent Italian scholarship on the Renaissance'; *RQ* 49 (1996): 'Recent French works'; *RQ* 50 (1997): 'Recent French and German works'; *RQ* 52 (1999): 'Recent studies on women and religion in Spain'.

4 Special mention should be made of the *Sixteenth Century Journal*, which has a very rich book-review section.

5 *I Tatti Studies. Essays in the Renaissance*, published by the Harvard University Center for Italian Renaissance Studies (Florence), started appearing in 1965, with one volume every two years; *Pirkheimer Jahrbuch für Renaissance u. Humanismus Forschung*, published by the Willibald Pirkheimer Gesellschaft zur Erforschung von Renaissance u. Humanismus, started appearing in 1986, thus filling a gap in German Renaissance scholarship; *Renaissance Studies*, published by the British Society for Renaissance Studies, which began appearing in 1987; and *Renaissance Forum*, an Electronic Journal dedicated to the English Renaissance, published twice yearly as from 1996.

6 Di Camillo, Ottavio, 'Interpreting the Renaissance in Spanish historical thought', *RQ* 48 (1995), pp. 352-65; idem, 'Interpreting the Renaissance in Spanish historical thought: the last thirty years', *RQ* 49 (1996), pp. 360–83.

Bibliography

Bernstein, Eckhard (ed.), 'Of Scholars, Knights and Table Manners: Recent German Scholarship', *Renaissance Quarterly* 50/3 (1997), pp. 850–64.

Chojnacki, Stanley (ed.), 'Recent Trends in Renaissance Studies: The Family, Marriage and Sex', *Renaissance Quarterly* 40/4 (1987), pp. 660–761.

Conley, Tom (ed.), 'A Smorgasbord of Champions: Recent French Books on the Renaissance', *Renaissance Quarterly* 50/1 (1997), pp. 251–60.

Di Camillo, Ottavio, 'Interpreting the Renaissance in Spanish Historical Thought', *Renaissance Quarterly* 48 (1995), pp. 352–65.

—, 'Interpreting the Renaissance in Spanish Historical Thought: The Last Thirty Years', *Renaissance Quarterly* 49 (1996), pp. 360–83.

Chojnacki, Stanley (ed.), 'Recent Trends in Renaissance Studies: The Family, Marriage and Sex', *Renaissance Quarterly* 40/4 (1987), pp. 660–761.

I Tatti Studies. Essays in the Renaissance, published by the Harvard University Center for Italian Renaissance 'Libri ricevuti', *Rinascimento* 30 (1990), pp. 367–80.

Karant-Nunn, Susan C. (ed.), 'Humanism to the Fore: Renaissance Studies in Germany Today', *Renaissance Quarterly* 47/4 (1994), pp. 930-41.

Lunetta, Loredana and Anna Laura Puliafito, 'Bibliografia italiana di studi sull'umanesimo ed il Rinascimento: 1987', appended to *Rinascimento* 28 (1988), pp. 1–104.

—, 'Bibliografia italiana di studi sull'umanesimo ed il Rinascimento: 1988', *Rinascimento* 49 (1989), pp. 1–95.

Marin, John (ed.), 'Recent Italian Scholarship on the Renaissance. Aspects of Christianity in Late Medieval and Early Modern Italy', *Renaissance Quarterly* 48/3 (1995), pp. 593–610.

Neely, Carol Thomas (ed.), 'Recent Works in Renaissance Studies: Psychology. Did Madness Have a Renaissance?', *Renaissance Quarterly* 44/4 (1991), pp. 776–91.

'Nuove accessioni', *Rinascimento* 31 (1991), pp. 343–67.

Pirkheimer Jahrbuch für Renaissance u. Humanismus Forschung, published by the Willibald Pirkheimer Gesellschaft zur Erforschung von Renaissance u. Humanismus.

Renaissance Studies, published by the British Society for Renaissance Studies.

Renaissance Forum, an electronic journal dedicated to the English Renaissance, published twice yearly as from 1996.

Schiffman, Zachary Sayre (ed.), 'Education in the Renaissance and Reformation', *Renaissance Quarterly* 43/4 (1990), pp. 774–824.

—, 'Recent French Works on the Renaissance', *Renaissance Quarterly* 47/2 (1994), pp. 379–89.

—, 'Rabelais, Renaissance and Reformation: Recent French Works on the Renaissance', *Renaissance Quarterly* 48/1 (1995), pp. 129–40.

—, 'Dimensions of Individuality: Recent French Works on the Renaissance', *Renaissance Quarterly* 49/1 (1996), pp. 114–23.

Weber, Alison (ed.), 'Recent Studies on Religion and Women in Spain', *Renaissance Quarterly* 52/1 (1999), pp. 197–206.

8

On Economic History: The Progress of a Discipline Living with its Neighbours

Peter Mathias

Reading this text in retrospect, with emotion recollected in tranquillity, it seems to have become almost exclusively Anglo-Saxon in content and orientation. Doubtless, this reflects, in large measure, my own commitments in economic history and the trajectory of my own career. Had the main focus of the text been that of social and cultural history – demographic studies, *histoire des mentalités*, integrated regional studies in society and economy, and so on – then European scholarship and the *Annales*, as the leading French journal capturing many of these trends, would have loomed larger. But I would argue that in economic history, after the era of Labrousse's quantification and Braudel's *la longue durée*, most methodological and conceptual innovations have come from North America to Europe – with the United Kingdom serving as the main bridgehead. In this respect, as in others, the Atlantic has proved to be narrower than the Channel.

Any subject with intellectual life in it advances and differentiates in a normal academic process of progressive nucleation. Advances come from new knowledge, as research proliferates and ideas multiply, giving an intrinsic internal dynamic. But much change is responsive to external stimuli. In some cases, new ranges of awareness are derived from contemporary issues which focus attention (economic historians following in the wagon-train of other observers): ecological problems, the limits of non-renewable resources, energy are current categories. For economic history, most infusions of new blood – it seems to me – have come from adjacent social sciences: economics above all, sociology, anthropology, political science, legal studies, and so on, both directly and indirectly. Economic theory – in particular development economics – so much concerned with the analysis of present-day, long-run economic growth, has much in common with the concerns of economic historians exploring comparable relationships, if in different contexts (which can require differences in the explanatory apparatus). Further common ground has been established in the unending search for quantification of economic change in all its variables. National income accounting for most national economies, in particular, has now produced a comparative record of rates of growth, levels of income, distribution of wealth, demographic trends and the like, which have been pushed back as far as historical data allow (and in some cases much further). Despite ferocious, and often irresolvable, issues of comparability over time and context, the analysis of longer-term economic growth has proved to be the most important focus for economic historians since the 1950s, at the level of local, regional, sectoral, national and international analysis. I once described the role of economic history as 'Living with the Neighbours', a fate which has not disappeared.[1] Recent trends, widening the explanatory apparatus in the analysis of long-term growth, cited below, have developed this further.

Cliometrics and after

In formal terms, judging by such criteria as the number of departments of economic history in the UK (where the great expansion of the subject in British universities in the 1950s and 1960s was embodied primarily in the establishment of new departments offering honours degrees), the number of honours degrees in economic history (as distinct from individual papers in economic history, as constituents in honours degrees in history or in economics), the recruitment of students for economic history degrees and the courses, economic history has been declining as a subject in British universities since the 1970s. The decline of individual membership (i.e. non-library subscriptions) of the Economic History Society can be seen as representative of the trend. Membership numbers grew rapidly in the 1950s and the 1960s (being 1,900 in 1966), to reach a maximum of 2,460 in 1974. This peak has been followed by a gradual but steady decline: to 2,160 in 1981, to 1,767 in 1991, down to 1,274 in 2005. This has been the case where economic history had a formal presence in departments of economics (where the subject was not regarded as so 'useful' vocationally as other branches of the subject). One principal reason for this shrinkage of the subject was the general trend towards sophisticated quantification and the use of more elaborate statistical methods for processing and interpreting data.

Then, as a 'double whammy', came the impact of the 'new economic history' from the United States, beginning in the 1950s.[2] Never was a label better fashioned: by implication 'new' equalled good and 'old' equalled bad. Econometric history, to use the more specific term, was a major methodological innovation in the subject, born and bred for the most part in American departments of economics. The methodology was based on quantification, a universal trend in the social sciences, but, more significantly, its claim to more 'scientific status' lay in the statistical testing of specific variables in a formal model, which allowed causation to be identified, by correlation analysis of the variables, and therefore 'real' explanations of historical change to be determined. A major claim indeed! All other potential – but unspecified – variables in the explanation of change were outside the model and therefore unanalysable in comparable terms. Eclectic explanations might be interesting, like stamp collecting, but they had no claim to scientific status.

This may be a caricature, but not much more so than the necessary assumptions behind the most dramatic exercises, and the greatest claims, in 'cliometrics': that the economy was in a state of competitive equilibrium, with perfect information, and that prices could be accepted as valid proxies from costs. On the basis of the new methodology, elaborate 'counterfactuals' could be construed, with a quantified reconstruction of a mythical economy, against which what actually happened could be tested against the 'reality' of what could have happened. These exercises were forged particularly on the economics of slavery and the contributions of railroads to the growth of the American economy.[3] Full-blooded 'cliometrics' might be important exercises in the methodology for economic history, but most economic historians asked whether one could hope to understand the process of historical change excluding, by definition, all institutions, legal, political, societal and cultural relationships. For understanding wider processes of change, at least precision was being bought at too high a price.

For some years, 'cliometrics' was hailed as the new dawn of economic history, with missionaries arriving by the planeload from North America to spread the gospel. I feared that economic history was panting itself into a corner, being defined against itself ever more narrowly. The identifications of what 'economic history' was were, in essence, being challenged. This was not an argument *per se* against quantification, with the techniques-tide flowing in all the social sciences, but against the methodological reductionism of 'cliometrics', which was soon challenged from within by advances in economic theory itself.

The excesses of 'cliometrics' were restricting enough conceptually but, more practically, access to economic history in this mode was only possible for those having the necessary technical expertise, which put it beyond the pale for most students in Britain, who came to the subject with a background in history (perhaps with some elementary economics), whereas most in the United States were in departments of economics. This was particularly the case for modern economic history, and still is. Hence, where the price of citizenship in the new republic was a formidable apprenticeship in theory, methodology and statistical techniques, students abandoned economic history on a large scale for social history and cultural history, widely seen as 'softer' disciplines and more accessible, even if techniques there were becoming more rigorous (as demographic and family history, for example, were demonstrating). Social history and cultural history were flourishing on their own terms, so there was a strong pull as well as a push to this trend.

One consequence has been that the radical tradition in British historiography, centred in economic history from the first generation of academic economic historians in the late nineteenth and early twentieth century, flourishing in the interwar years and after, when mainstream economic history, which guarded the historical flank for the eternal truths of Fabian socialism, was challenged and left the field of battle. There were wider reasons for this, of course. When, in the long run, the progress of industrialization was seen to be the greatest creator of wealth the world had ever seen, and also, in the long run, the basis of rising standards of living, and where every state, new or old, had as a policy imperative the promoting of industrial growth, it was seen increasingly as anomalous – perverse – to categorize the British Industrial Revolution as an economic and social disaster. This did not deny the acute social problems which were intensified by the process of industrialization.

The essential truth of the 'optimistic' interpretation was demonstrated by systematic quantification of the historical record, provided by the reconstruction of national income statistics. In British economic historiography, I believe, the most widely acknowledged turning point in this interpretation came with T.S. Ashton's influential little textbook *The Industrial Revolution*, published by Oxford University Press in 1948. A key quotation from the book bears repetition: 'There are today on the plains of India and China men and women, plague-ridden and hungry, living lives little better, to outward appearance, than those of the cattle that toil with them by day and share their places of sleep by night. Such Asiatic standards, and such unmechanized horrors, are the lot of those who increase their numbers without passing through an industrial revolution'.[4]

Driven out by quantification, protesting that the 'new economic history' offered only quantified expressions of bourgeois ideology, the radical tradition in British historiography found a congenial home in social history, led in Britain by Edward Thompson, Raphael Samuel and the 'Social History Workshop', et al. Their banner read: 'Thou shalt not judge by real-wage indexes alone'.[5]

Other trends, much more conceptually congenial to good old economic history, as it has seemed to me, then came on the scene, with further advances in economic theory. Indeed, the implications of one such had lain largely hidden since the 1950s. All the exercises in 'accounting for growth' had revealed a large, if unidentified, residual when growth over time was measured in relation to quantified inputs of capital, labour and resources at constant levels of productivity over the period of scrutiny.[6]

This residual, by definition, lay outside the terms of the equations – being literally a residual part of the higher mysteries of growth. Technological change and 'improvements in human capital' (i.e. education, training, skills) were assumed to be the main components of the residual but, equally, institutional change, improvements in organization and other changes in the context of the economy were also potentially relevant. Even entrepreneurship, which could be rejected by definition under neo-classical assumptions of perfect competition, could be an activating force for improving the performances of other variables. Schumpeterian theorizing about entrepreneurship being the principal means of an economy breaking out of the 'circular flow' of imitative decision-making through innovation enjoyed a sustained revival, particularly being embodied in the great expansion of business history. This has become a new sub-species of economic history and has owed much to the magisterial work of Alfred D. Chandler, in charting the evolution and the progressive importance of the large-scale business organization in the process of 'globalization'.[7]

And then came Douglass North and others, with the 'new institutional economics', which opened doors wide enough for all of us to re-enter the temple.[8] The momentum for economic change (or the sources of inertia holding back the process) were to be found deeply embedded in the fundamental institutions of society and the state, or in the socio-cultural matrices of a country, together with the political process and the legal system, which embodied in large measure underlying social and cultural determinants. The 'incentive structure' within which an economy operated was identified as being all-important, and this depended on the development of private-property rights, economic and tax policies, finding the appropriate balance between freedom of action and the regulatory framework that conditions the operation of all markets. 'Agency relations', the fostering of personal trust and confidence, which underlie on-going commercial dealings and contractual relations, formed another dimension of the reality of how an economy actually worked. All these issues recognized that economic action and institutions were socio-cultural constructs embedded in a wider society and its values. They also offered new insights into the roles of minority groups. The balance between incentive and inertia could be analysed conceptually, if not always measured, through the concept of 'transaction costs', which set the terms for the interplay of these relationships governing changes.[9] But 'transaction costs', which imposed inertia upon the operation of the market, could arise from a multitude of things – climate and resources, transport, the political and legal system, the efficiency of communications and information flows in a market economy, the business system, the level of risk (itself arising from many aspects of the context) and other issues.

With such diverse variables – some 'real' and others arising from 'perceptions of reality' – collectively mobilized into the concept of 'transaction costs', it was impossible to construe them into a single, all-embracing operational model with quantified variables. Attempting to do so simply introduced an arbitrary and subjective allocation of degrees of significance by the back door, while the ostensible objective of such modelling was to exclude subjectivity from its front door.

All this comes as no surprise to economic historians accustomed to investigate aspects of the empirical context through primary sources and contemporary commentaries. They did not need a sophisticated conceptual apparatus to tell them how complex matters were in practice. But it has broken through constraints in formal economic theorizing and dramatically widened the agenda for analysing economic growth, which had been operational in the other social sciences, such as sociology, political theory and anthropology, for a long time. The range of relationships which the new conceptual apparatus in economic history brings to the analysis of economic change included many neo-economic variables, as described, and although many of these may invite quantification on their own terms they cannot be captured within a single general model, being too numerous and too heterogeneous, although organically part of the process of change. This has opened up the discipline conceptually again, as the methodology of cliometrics had narrowed it, providing a basis for reconciliation, if not a symbiosis, between the older and newer traditions of the historiography, and bringing the conceptual and the empirical into relationships in new ways.

Proto-industrialization

One methodological innovation, also hailed as a new dawn in the 1970s and later, but now absorbed into the much-diversified mainstream, was antithetical in many ways to 'economist's economic history'. This was 'proto-industrialization', brought into the canon of social history as much as economic history, and rightly so, because its basic assumption was integrative between economy and society.[10] Proto-industrialization was identified by some as a new universal 'stage' in the evolution of society and economy, between 'feudalism' and 'industrialization', as the lead-in to the 'industrial revolution'. Handicraft manufacturing industry in a rural context, mainly textiles of all sorts and small metal wares, commercially orientated to non-local markets, was identified as a new dynamic. Proto-industrial growth generated crucial non-agricultural skills, developed a (largely seasonal) industrial labour force, accumulated profits and capital, produced a commercial infrastructure led by merchants and, in general, paved the way for later factory technology.

While accepting the significance of these developments empirically – on the ground –, as a supposed general historical process proto-industrialization bristled with problems: rural-based industries were known from the thirteenth century in England (so where did that place the chronology of 'stages'?); some leading proto-industrial districts flourished, others faded and disappeared (what were the criteria?). Some major industrial districts did not pass through a 'proto-industrial' apprenticeship; much 'proto-industry' was urban-based, rather than rural … Nevertheless, this new mode of historical analysis yielded important perceptions in the complex inter-linkages between social and economic change. The focus was that local communities were studied 'in the round', exploring all the relationships in life and work – communal, familial, technical, commercial – in intricate interplay. Perhaps the most fruitful enquiries linked the development of proto-industry with its demographic dynamic. The offer of more non-agricultural employment allowed families to be supported on smaller holdings, encouraged marriage at a younger age and enhanced the rate of marriage; breaking older constraints on demographic advance and the level of population that a rural locality or region could sustain with traditional agriculture.

Mega-economic history

An exception to the new 'eclecticism' in theorizing about causation in long-term economic change – the retreat from pursuit of an integrative general theory, a single integrative, all-embracing explanatory variable – is the spate of studies of 'mega' economic history, that is, of economic history seen as a world process in the very long run. This carries the Braudelian tradition of *la longue durée* to an ultimate destination and can be seen as being in the long tradition of interpretations of world evolution in terms of the working out of a particular philosophy of history. It is one dimension of the study of economic growth in historical perspective. This has been led by economists and economic historians in the West, capitalizing in their own way upon the unprecedented success story of western economies since the Middle Ages, with the United States in the van more recently, leading the process of globalization.[11] The titles of some leading examples of this genre send the message: 'The European Miracle', 'Growth Recurring: Economic Change in World History', 'World Economic Primacy, 1500–1900', 'The Rise of the Western World: a New Economic History', 'How it all Began: Origin of the Modern Economy', 'How the West Grew Rich; the Economic Transformation of the Industrial World', 'The Lever of Riches: Technological Creativity and Economic Progress', 'The Wealth and Poverty of Nations: why some are so rich and some are so poor', 'The Rise and Decline of Nations', 'The Great Divergence: China, Europe and the Making of the Modern World', 'The World Economy: History and Prospects'. There are many others in similar vein.

With some latter-day recognition of the more recent transformations of Japan, Southeast Asia and China now *in via*, this world process has been dubbed 'the West and the Rest'. The main tide of interpretation of the global process of development has moved away from single-cause explanations, such as a favourable indigenous natural-resource endowment or abundant capital with a low interest rate, to more eclectic formulations, as current empirical or historical evidence casts doubt on the explanatory force of single variables. Favoured explanations of European dominance, apparent in quantitative data by the end of the eighteenth century but with roots going back to the sixteenth, encompass European expansion to the New World (to North America and the West Indies in particular), with colonial settlements, commercial and maritime strength, superior firepower and naval technology. These were consequential, in large measure, on the scale of resources which effective national states could mobilize, in itself evidence of multifaceted modernization. A progressive scientific culture, advances in intellectual secularization, with motivations to discover, measure and control the forces of nature, were also characteristic of 'Westernization', impacting upon the dynamic of long-term growth.

At the level of analysis of national economies, the focus of explanation for sustained economic growth has seen growing recognition of the importance of political and legal processes, aided by the methodological influence of the 'new institutional economics'. Much advance, it is argued, has come from the dynamics of free markets, which has concentrated attention on the necessary attributes of a progressive market economy. The physical security of persons and property, an assured legal system with secure private-property rights, procedures for enforceability of contracts, accepted procedures for the transferability of assets (including financial assets) at their proper market prices, and other aspects of the political-legal-cultural matrix within which an economy operates, are seen as essential foundations – even if the 'autonomous' operations of a market are always comprised in various degrees. A market – operating with a balance of freedom and constraint – is inevitably embedded in the legal and political process. Beyond formally enforceable procedures, but embodying them, lie socio-behavioural norms of ethical standards, reliability and honesty in personal dealings, the maintenance of trust and the like, which are also integral with continuous dealings in a market context. This widens the analysis still further into cultural and religious as well as societal and legal relationships.

This strong tide of interpretation of historical processes of development in terms of market-economy relationships has had a countercurrent of alternative radical hypothesizing in terms of 'core-periphery' relationships and the exploitation of the primary producers on the periphery in successive modes from the sixteenth century, as they have been drawn into the international economy under the initiative (and largely the control) of shippers, merchants and financiers of the modernizing/industrializing economies.[12] Formal colonialism and imperialism in particular contexts form one dimension of this wider process. A. Gunder Frank and Immanuel Wallerstein are identified with this mainly Marxist interpretation. This accepts the thesis of invasive market relationships but (in parallel with the earlier interpretations of the Industrial Revolution as a social disaster) sees the results as inimical. This trend has also been on the defensive against the 'optimists', who see the process of historical and ongoing globalization as inevitable and – in aggregate, long-run terms – beneficial, while acknowledging the problems of finite resource depletion, ecological deterioration and inequality of income distribution. A process that has produced unprecedented increases in wealth, rising productivity and progressive technologies will be able to mitigate, if not resolve, these offsets, it is argued, as it has done in large measure for the internal dynamics of economic, political and social change within the industrial economies. This is clearly an ongoing debate for interpretations in 'mega-economic' history.

Diversification and social history

Sometimes, it seems that 'economic history' as a defined entity in Britain is disappearing beneath a welter of specializations, increasing in number and sub-dividing exponentially. Social history was always integral to economic history as a subject in Britain, despite the nomenclature. The contents of the *Economic History Review* from its foundation in 1927, for example, bear testimony to that reality. The radical tradition in British economic history, which saw the Industrial Revolution as disaster, was primarily concerned with the adverse social consequences of industrial and agricultural capitalism. Demographic history, social history in many manifestations (for example, the social history of medicine, family history and the history of childhood), urban history, financial and banking history, business history, transport history, the history of technology and so many other specialisms have spun off. They become institutionalized on their own terms, growing up as independent adults from a mainly common childhood in economic and social history, with separate journals and societies, conferences and colloquia at regional, national and international forums. The International Economic History Association (formally established at Munich in 1965) has shown the same fissiparous imperative.

This may be regarded as the standard path of evolution of a subject, whether in the sciences, social sciences or the humanities, a momentum of expansion coupled with progressive specialization, differentiation and 'hybridization'. New research adds new knowledge; wider ranges of perception bring new insights, new perspectives, new linkages. In this sense, economic history continues to explore new frontiers and makes settlements in territories which formerly belonged to others, while itself being subject to incursions from without.

A brief text of this nature cannot attempt to do justice to the extraordinary growth and diversification of social history and cultural history since the 1970s. They prosper from the shrinkage of 'hard' economic history, being widely seen (especially by students) as 'softer' options, even if the reality is more complex. One trend, out of many, which has become prominent, is that of a new style of socio-cultural history.[13] Economic historians have had a long tradition of concentrating on production rather than consumption: their consciousness has been focused on the spectrum of themes centring on production. The main themes of the 'new' social history reverse this priority: the study of consumption in many aspects covers a different spectrum, and puts relationships in a new perspective. It brings to the fore the study of markets and marketing, with retailing at the fulcrum of supply and demand. Consumption trends have to be explicable in terms of such diverse considerations as disposable incomes, the distribution of income, channels of information about worldly goods for households and persons, family relationships, fashion and aesthetics, the cultural norms of social groups, the demands of emulation and 'respectability' in different social contexts, concepts and the operational embodiment of 'luxury', how taste is led, and a host of other relationships. Not all these trends originated in the progressive commercialization of relationships or were expressed in a commercialized nexus.[14]

Identifying perceived needs (helping to lead, encourage and persuade, if not actually creating such trends) was becoming a progressive influence in shaping the path of growth in consumer-goods industries from the seventeenth century, if not before. This new focus for explaining the basis of material life in the social and cultural matrix of family relations, social groups, class and culture, has also integrated fields of study that were previously professionally isolated in the fine and the applied arts and 'connoisseurship', with professional standards as high as, and sometimes higher than, those of social historians. In the latter case, too, in contrast to the labours of most academic social and cultural historians, great potential gains in wealth (or the reverse) rested upon the professional identification of artifacts.

As yet ...

With the old-style economic history being invaded by successive waves of new-style theorizing, losing students and fragmenting progressively into new hybrids, many have assumed that the subject has been forced onto the defensive and, indeed, that it has lost the battle. Yet, from a broader academic viewpoint, it can also be argued that the economic and social dimensions of change have now penetrated all other aspects of history – military history, the history of science and medicine, political and diplomatic history, technological history, the history of art, etc. – previously almost hermetically sealed within their own methodological conventions, utilizing just their own internal criteria. As an optimist for the future of the subject, I am tempted to claim that, even if economic history was in danger of losing its own battle, it has now recovered and, on the wider scene, has been winning the war.

Notes

1 The references cited are no more than initial bridgeheads into the different topics featured in the text. Most contain further bibliographies. For a pedigree of this text see Mathias, Peter, *Living with the Neighbours* (Oxford, 1971), p.

3; Harte, N.B. (ed.), *The Study of Economic History: Collected Inaugural Lectures* (London, 1971), pp. 367–83; Mathias, Peter, 'Still Living with the Neighbours', in P. Hudson (ed.), *Living Economic and Social History* (Economic History Society, 2001), pp. 232–5; *Journal of European Economic History* XXXV/1 (2006). The text and almost all the references here are as they were presented at the Corfu conference in 2005, which helps account for the impression of being a period piece.

2 McCloskey, D.N., *Econometric History* (London, 1987), p. 3; McCelland, P.D., *Casual Explanation and Model Building in History, Economics and the New Economic History* (Ithaca, 1975); Parker, W.N., *Economic History and the Modern Economist* (Oxford, 1986).

3 Fogel, R.W., *Railroads and American Economic Growth: Essays in Econometric History* (Baltimore, 1964), p. 4; Fogel, R.W. and S.L. Engerman, *Time on the Cross: The Economics of American Negro Slavery* (Boston, 1974).

4 Ashton, T.S., *The Industrial Revolution* (Oxford, 1948), p. 161.

5 In the radical Fabian tradition were: R.H. Tawney, Sidney and Beatrice Webb, G.D.H. Cole, J.L. and Barbara Hammond, Raymond Postgate and others. For examples of more recent radical social history see Thompson, E.P., *The Making of the British Working Class* (Harmondsworth, 1963), p. 6; Hobsbawm, E.J., *Labouring Men: Studies in the History of Labour* (London, 1964); Samuel, Raphael (ed.), *History of Workshop* series; Kaye, H.J., *The British Marxist Historians* (Basingstoke, 1955).

6 Abramovitz, M., 'Resources and Output trends in the United States since 1870', *American Economic Review* XLVI (1956), p. 6; idem, 'The Search for the Sources of Growth', *Journal of Economic History* LIII (1993); Solow, R.M. and P. Temin, 'The Inputs for Growth', in P. Mathias and M.M. Postan (eds), *Cambridge Economic History of Europe*, vol. VII (1), (Cambridge, 1978); Denison, E.F., *The Sources of Economic Growth in the United States* (Committee for Economic Development, New York, 1962).

7 Schumpeter, J., *The Theory of Economic Development* (published in German 1911), *Harvard Economic Studies* XLVI (Cambridge, MA, 1934), p. 8; Casson, M., *The Entrepreneur: an Economic Theory* (Oxford, 1982; Cheltenham, 2005); Kilby, P. (ed.), *Entrerpreneurship and Economic Development* (New York, 1971); McClelland, D.C., *The Achieving Society* (Princeton University Press, 1961); Hagen, E.E., *On Theory of Social Change* (Homewood, IL, Dorsey Press, 1962).

8 North, D.C., *Institutions, Institutional Change and Economic Performance* (Cambridge, 1990), p. 8; idem, *Structure and Change in Economic History* (New York, 1981); Williamson, O., 'The New Institutional Economics', *Journal of Economic Literature* XXXVIII (2000); idem, *The Economic Institutions of Capitalism: Firms, Markets, Relational Contracting* (New York, 1985); Breziz, E.S. and Peter Temin (eds), *Elites, Minorities and Economic Growth* (Amsterdam, 1999); Harris, R., *Industrialising English Law: Entrepreneurship and Business Organisation* (Cambridge, 2000). For Chandler's main work see: *Strategy and structure: Chapters in the History of the Industrial Enterprise* (Cambridge, 1962); *Giant Enterprise* (New York, 1964);

The Visible Hand: the Managerial Revolution in American Business (Cambridge, MA, 1977); *Scale and Scope: the Dynamics of Industrial Capitalism* (Cambridge, MA, 1990).

9 Williamson, O. and S.E. Masten, *Transaction Cost Economics: Theory and Concepts* (Aldershot, 1995); Buchanan, J.M., R.D. Tollinson and G. Tullock, *Towards a Theory of the Rent-Seeking Society* (Austin, 1980).

10 Mendels, F., 'Proto-industrialisation: the first phase of the industrialisation process', *Journal of Economic History* XXXII (1972); Clarkson, L.A., *Proto-Industrialisation: the First Phase of Industrialisation?* (London, 1985); Coleman, D.C., 'Proto-Industrialisation: a concept too many', *Economic History Review* XXXVI (1983); Kriedte, P., H. Medick and J. Schlumbohm, *Industrialisation before Industrialisation* (Cambridge, 1981).

11 Jones, E.L., *The European Miracle* (Cambridge, 1981); idem, *Growth Recurring: Economic Change in World History* (Oxford, 1988); Kindlegerger, C.P., *World Economic Primacy, 1500-1990* (Oxford, 1996); North, D.C. and R.P. Thomas, *The Rise of the Western World: a New Economic History* (Cambridge, 1973); Rostow, W.W., *How it all Began: Origins of the Modern Economy* (London, 1975); idem, *The World Economy: History and Prospects* (London, 1978); Rosenberg, N. and L.E. Bridzell, *How the West Grew Rich: the Economic Transformation of the Industrial World* (New York, 1986); Mokyr, J., *The Lever of Riches: Technological Creativity and Economic Progress* (Oxford, 1990); Landes, D., *The Wealth and Poverty of Nations: Why Some are so Rich and Some so Poor* (London, 1998); Olson, Mancur, *The Rise and Decline of Nations* (London, 1982); Pomeranz, K., *The Great Divergence: China, Europe and the Making of the Modern World* (Princeton, 2000); Maddison, A., *Phases of Capitalist Development* (Oxford, 1982); Clark, G., *A Farewell to Alms: a Brief Economic History of the World* (Princeton, 2007); Diamond, J., *Guns, Germs and Steel: the Fate of Human Societies* (New York, 1997, 1999).

12 Wallderstein, I., *The Modern World System* (New York, 1974); Gunder Frank, A., *World Accumulation, 1492–1789* (London, 1978).

13 Erdmann, K.D., *Towards a Global Community of Historians: the International Historical Congresses and the International Committee of Historical Sciences, 1898–2000* (New York, Oxford, 2003).

14 Berg, M., *Luxury and Pleasure in Eighteenth Century Britain* (Oxford University Press, 2005); Berg, M. and H. Clifford (eds), *Consumers and Luxury: Consumer Culture in Europe, 1650–1850* (Manchester, 1999); Brewer, J. and R. Porter (eds), *Consumption and the World of Goods* (London, 1993); Plumb, J.H., *The Commercialisation of Leisure in Eighteenth Century England* (Reading, 1972); McKendrick, N., J. Brewer and J.H. Plumb (eds), *The Birth of a Consumer Society* (London, 1982); Jardine, L., *Worldly Goods: a New History of the Renaissance* (London 1996); Weatherill, L., *Consumer Behaviour and Material Culture in Britain, 1660–1760* (London, 1988); Smith, W.W., *Consumption and the Making of Respectability* (London, 2003); Lemire B., *Dress, Culture and Commerce: The English Clothing Trade before the Factory* (Basingstoke, 1997). For a general survey of these trends see White, J., 'A World of Goods? The Consumption Turn and Eighteenth-Century British History', *Cultural and Social History* 3 (2006), pp. 93–104.

Bibliography

Ashton, T.S., *The Industrial Revolution* (Oxford, Oxford University Press, 1948).

Abramovitz, M., 'Resources and Output Trends in the United States since 1870', *American Economic Review* 46 (1956).

—, 'The Search for the Sources of Growth', *Journal of Economic History* 53 (1993).

Berg, M., *Luxury and Pleasure in Eighteenth Century Britain* (Oxford, Oxford University Press, 2005).

— and H. Clifford (eds), *Consumers and Luxury: Consumer Culture in Europe, 1650–1850* (Manchester, Manchester University Press, 1999).

Brewer, J. and R. Porter (eds), *Consumption and the World of Goods* (London, Routledge, 1993).

Breziz, E.S. and Peter Temin (eds), *Elites, Minorities and Economic Growth* (Amsterdam, Elsevier, 1999).

Buchanan, J.M., R.D. Tollinson and G. Tullock, *Towards a Theory of the Rent-Seeking Society* (Austin, Texas University Press, 1980).

Casson, M., *The Entrepreneur: An Economic Theory* (Oxford, 1982; Cheltenham, Edward Elgar, 2005).

Chandler, Alfred D., *Strategy and Structure: Chapters in the History of the Industrial Enterprise* (Cambridge, MA, MIT Press, 1962).

Chandler, Alfred D., *Giant Enterprise* (New York, Harcourt Brace, 1964).

—, *The Visible Hand: The Managerial Revolution in American Business* (Cambridge, MA, Harvard University Press, 1977).

—, *Scale and Scope: The Dynamics of Industrial Capitalism* (Cambridge, MA, Harvard University Press, 1990).

Clark, G., *A Farewell to Alms: A Brief Economic History of the World* (Princeton, Princeton University Press, 2007).

Clarkson, L.A., *Proto-Industrialisation: The First Phase of Industrialisation?* (London, Macmillan, 1985).

Coleman, D.C., 'Proto-Industrialisation: A Concept too Many' *Economic History Review* XXXVI (1983).

Denison, E.F., *The Sources of Economic Growth in the United States* (New York, Committee for Economic Development, 1962).

Diamond, J., *Guns, Germs and Steel: The Fate of Human Societies* (New York, Norton, 1997, 1999).

Erdmann, K.D., *Towards a Global Community of Historians: The International Historical Congresses and the International Committee of Historical Sciences, 1898–2000* (New York and Oxford, Berghahn Books, 2003).

Fogel, R.W., *Railroads and American Economic Growth: Essays in Econometric History* (Baltimore, Johns Hopkins University Press, 1964).

— and S.L. Engerman, *Time on the Cross: The Economics of American Negro Slavery* (Boston, Little Brown, 1974).

Hagen, E.E., *On Theory of Social Change* (Homewood, IL, Dorsey Press, 1962).

Harris, R., *Industrialising English Law: Entrepreneurship and Business Organisation* (Cambridge, Cambridge University Press, 2000).

Harte, N.B. (ed.), *The Study of Economic History: Collected Inaugural Lectures* (London, Frank Cass, 1971).

Hobsbawm, E.J., *Labouring Men: Studies in the History of Labour* (London, Weidenfeld and Nicolson, 1964).

Gunder Frank, A., *World Accumulation, 1492–1789* (London, Macmillan, 1978).

Jardine, L., *Worldly Goods: A New History of the Renaissance* (London, Macmillan, 1996).

Jones, E.L., *The European Miracle* (Cambridge, Cambridge University Press, 1981).

—, *Growth Recurring: Economic Change in World History* (Oxford, Oxford University Press, 1988).

Kaye, H.J., *The British Marxist Historians* (Basingstoke, Macmillan, 1955).

Kilby, P. (ed.), *Entrerpreneurship and Economic Development* (New York, 1971).

Kindlegerger, C.P., *World Economic Primacy, 1500–1990* (Oxford, Oxford University Press, 1996).

Kriedte, P., H. Medick and J. Schlumbohm, *Industrialisation before Industrialisation* (Cambridge, Cambridge University Press, 1981).

Landes, D., *The Wealth and Poverty of Nations: Why Some are so Rich and Some so Poor* (London, Little Brown, 1998).

Lemire, B., *Dress, Culture and Commerce: The English Clothing Trade before the Factory* (Basingstoke, Macmillan, 1997).

Maddison, A., *Phases of Capitalist Development* (Oxford, Oxford University Press, 1982).

Mathias, Peter, *Living with the Neighbours* (Oxford, Clarendon Press, 1971).

—, 'Still Living with the Neighbours', in P. Hudson (ed.), *Living Economic and Social History* (Glasgow, Economic History Society, 2001), pp. 232–5.

McClelland, D.C., *The Achieving Society* (Princeton, Princeton University Press, 1961).

McCelland, P.D., *Casual Explanation and Model Building in History, Economics and the New Economic History* (Ithaca, Cornell University Press, 1975).

McCloskey, D.N., *Econometric History* (London, Macmillan, for the Economic History Society, 1987).

McKendrick, N., J. Brewer and J.H. Plumb (eds), *The Birth of a Consumer Society* (London, Taylor and Francis, 1982).

Mendels, F., 'Proto-industrialisation: The First Phase of the Industrialisation Process', *Journal of Economic History* 32 (1972).

Mokyr, J., *The Lever of Riches: Technological Creativity and Economic Progress* (Oxford, Oxford University Press, 1990).

North, D.C. and R.P. Thomas, *The Rise of the Western World: A New Economic History* (Cambridge, Cambridge University Press, 1973).

—, *Structure and Change in Economic History* (New York, Norton, 1981).

—, *Institutions, Institutional Change and Economic Performance* (Cambridge, Cambridge University Press, 1990).

Olson, Mancur, *The Rise and Decline of Nations* (London, Yale University Press, 1982).

Parker, W.N., *Economic History and the Modern Economist* (Oxford, Blackwell, 1986).

Plumb, J.H., *The Commercialisation of Leisure in Eighteenth Century England* (Reading, Reading University Press, 1972).

Pomeranz, K., *The Great Divergence: China, Europe and the Making of the Modern World* (Princeton, Princeton University Press, 2000).

Rosenberg, N., and L.E. Bridzell, *How the West Grew Rich: The Economic Transformation of the Industrial World* (New York, Basic Books, 1986).

Rostow, W.W., *How it all Began: Origins of the Modern Economy* (London, Methuen, 1975).

—, *The World Economy: History and Prospects* (London, Macmillan, 1978).

Schumpeter, J., *The Theory of Economic Development* (published in German 1911), *Harvard Economic Studies* 46 (Cambridge, MA, Harvard University Press, 1934).

Smith, W.W., *Consumption and the Making of Respectability* (London, W.W. Norton, 2003).

Solow, R.M. and P. Temin, 'The Inputs for Growth', in P. Mathias and M.M. Postan (eds), *Cambridge Economic History of Europe*, vol. 7 (1), (Cambridge, Cambridge University Press, 1978).

Thompson, E.P., *The Making of the British Working Class* (Harmondsworth, Penguin Books, 1963).

Wallderstein, I., *The Modern World System* (New York, Academic Press, 1974).

Weatherill, L., *Consumer Behaviour and Material Culture in Britain, 1660–1760* (London, Routledge, 1988).

White, J., 'A World of Goods? The Consumption Turn and Eighteenth-Century British History', *Cultural and Social History* 3 (2006), pp. 93–104.

Williamson, O., 'The New Institutional Economics', *Journal of Economic Literature* 38 (2000).

—, *The Economic Institutions of Capitalism: Firms, Markets, Relational Contracting* (New York, Free Press, 1985).

Williamson, O. and S.E. Masten, *Transaction Cost Economics: Theory and Concepts* (Aldershot, Edward Elgar, 1995).

9

Business History, Post-Chandler[1]

Walter A. Friedman

Today the field of business history appears to be flourishing. In 2008, 163 scholars presented papers at the Business History Conference in Sacramento, California, and 152 did the same at the European Business History Association in Geneva. The papers covered a great range of topics – private banking in Copenhagen; business leadership and environmental reform; Armani's clothing empire in Milan; the marketing of Nestlé under the Ottoman Empire; Hollywood studios and racial equality; corporate governance in Greece; Japanese foreign direct investment.[2] The conferences were multidisciplinary in nature. The largest group of presenters (33 per cent) came from business schools; the second largest, from history departments (28 per cent); just under one-quarter (24 per cent) were employed by economic and economic-history departments; and the remaining participants (15 per cent) were from political science or sociology departments, or else were independent scholars.[3]

Nonetheless, a deeper examination reveals reasons for concern. In some places – including India, most countries in Africa, and many in Latin America – the subject, as a scholarly discipline, hardly exists. The leading American and European journals in the field of business history receive lower 'impact ratings' than those in economic history.[4] History departments in the United States seldom offer courses in the subject to their undergraduates, while economics departments marginalize history in favour of theory. In business schools, the spread of social-science methods and quantification in management studies has led to a sharp decline in the number of business history courses offered over the last three decades. At the 2008 Business History Conference, conference president Pamela Laird urged the gathering to expand their connections with other disciplines and reach out to the public media to make a case for the subject's importance.[5]

But as the field grows in diverse directions, it is difficult to define just what 'business history' is. One recent occurrence, however, inspired ruminations on the state of business history and predictions of where it may be headed by several leading scholars: the death of Alfred D. Chandler Jr, in May 2007.

Chandler's death – in Cambridge, Massachusetts, not far from his home or the institution where he spent much of his career, Harvard Business School – brought notices in newspapers throughout the world. Obituaries appeared in papers ranging from *The New York Times*, *The Wall Street Journal*, *The Times* of London, *Le Monde*, *La Stampa* (Turin), and *El Pais* (Madrid), to name but a few. *The Economist* noted, 'Mr Chandler was the dean of American business historians, the man who more or less invented the history of the big corporation'.[6]

Economists, historians and other scholars also took up the question of how to assess Chandler's legacy in more detail. The academic journals *Business History Review* and *Enterprise and Society* solicited essays on his legacy and relevance. The Association of Business Historians hosted a conference on 'Business History after Chandler'. The *Journal of Management History* sent out a call for papers to be published in a special issue, 'Honoring the Life and Works of Alfred Chandler'.[7] Because Chandler's influence on the field spanned so many years, these academic considerations of his work constitute a *de facto* survey of the state of business history in the twenty-first century.

Business history before Chandler

Before turning to these scholarly observations, it is important to reflect on Chandler's contributions.[8] Despite the claims of *The Economist*, 'business history' had been around for a long time in the United States before Chandler began his professional career in 1952.[9] His *alma mater*, Harvard University, was a particularly fertile place for scholarly investigations of the topic. Harvard Business School had forged a connection with history since its founding in 1908, when Edwin Gay, an economic historian, became the first dean. In 1927, HBS created a chair in the field – the Isidor Straus Professorship in Business History, endowed by the family that had founded the Macy's department store (Chandler held the Straus chair from 1970 until his retirement in 1989). N.S.B. Gras, the first to be named to the position, assembled a casebook on business history, in 1939, with his colleague Henrietta Larson.[10] Gras also raised funds to start a monograph series at

Harvard University Press; the series was launched with a biography of John Jacob Astor, which appeared in 1931.[11] Subsequently, Larson wrote two volumes for the series: a biography of Jay Cooke (1936) and *Guide to Business History* (1948).[12] In 1926, Harvard Business School began to publish the *Bulletin of the Business Historical Society*, which, in 1954, became the *Business History Review*. While Gras's detailed but conceptually weak writings are seldom referenced today, he and his colleagues helped to initiate academic inquiry in the field long before Chandler earned his doctorate.

Also, shortly after the Second World War, Harvard founded the Research Center in Entrepreneurial History, which lasted from 1948 to 1958. The Center was funded by the Rockefeller Foundation and headed by the scholar and librarian Arthur Cole, who helped to assemble a multidisciplinary team of scholars to study and define the entrepreneurial function. The original group included economists Leland H. Jenks, Alexander Gerschenkron, and William Miller, economic historian Fritz Redlich, and business historians Ralph and Muriel Hidy, among others.[13] Writing in 1965, historian of technology Hugh Aitken recalled that the Center 'was unusually hospitable to interdisciplinary work and … people from a wide variety of specialties could find in it a reasonably comfortable intellectual home'.[14] The most illustrious figure was the economist Joseph Schumpeter, who was working on his *History of Economic Analysis* at the time.[15] Although, at first, most of the participant research focused on individual entrepreneurs, the emphasis shifted during the 1950s and, as historian Robert Cuff observed, took 'an organizational turn'. One example of the original biographical impulse was Chandler's own Harvard PhD dissertation (and first book) on his great-grandfather, Henry Varnum Poor, the longtime editor of the *American Railroad Journal* and *Poor's Manual of Railroads of the United States*. Chandler's book explained how Poor, through his detailed reports on individual railroad companies and their operations, helped to invent the role of the modern business analyst and investment advisor. But Chandler, along with several others at the Center, began to study large organizations and top management.[16] His work in this area changed the field of business history.

Chandler's body of work

Chandler was the sole author of six books and co-author or editor of more than thirty others; he also wrote over sixty articles.[17] His most famous work appeared in three books about the rise of big business and the coming of a managerial class: *Strategy and Structure: Chapters in the History of Industrial Enterprise* (1962); *The Visible Hand: The Managerial Revolution in American Business* (1977); and *Scale and Scope: The Dynamics of Industrial Capitalism* (1990).[18] As many commentators acknowledged, these works were so original in their approach and so impressive in their depth of research that they set the agenda for the field of business history for many years afterward.

The first of these, *Strategy and Structure,* analysed DuPont, General Motors, Sears, and Standard Oil, and showed how each of these four companies came to adopt a multidivisional structure, or M-Form, by the 1920s. No previous historian had provided such a rich account of the work of corporate middle managers and the challenges they faced. Chandler's investigations of these four corporations were the basis for his influential argument that a company's strategy must shape its structure, not the other way around.

In *The Visible Hand*, Chandler sought to explain the rise of big business in the United States in the decades from 1840 to 1920, and to answer the question of why large firms arose in some industries and not in others. Chandler argued that in industries whose firms were able to benefit from economies of scale and scope, the 'visible hand' of management came to replace the 'invisible hand' of the market in co-ordinating the production and distribution of goods. This was to become his most famous book, winning not only the Pulitzer Prize, but also the Bancroft Prize and the Thomas Newcomen Book Award.

In *Scale and Scope,* Chandler branched out into international history, comparing his story of the ascendancy of capitalism in the United States, from the late nineteenth to the mid-twentieth century, with the histories of Britain and Germany. He argued that success in steel, chemicals, automobiles, and other industries that emerged during the second industrial revolution was achieved through three-pronged investment: in mass-production facilities, in international marketing and distribution networks, and in proper management of resource allocation. While Chandler praised German industry, which had developed strong capacities in research engineering, banking and the production of producer goods, he believed that Britain's tradition of 'personal capitalism' had prevented that country from making progress in developing large-scale industries.

Late in his career, he wrote of the triumph of Japanese industry over US competitors in the electronics industries in the final third of the twentieth century. In the 1990s, Chandler became fascinated with the question of why some industries failed and others rose in their place. He completed his final two books, both touching on these themes, while in his eighties: *Inventing the Electronic Century: The Epic Story of the Consumer Electronics and Computer Industries* (2001); and *Shaping the Industrial Century: The Remarkable Story of the Modern Chemical and Pharmaceutical Industries* (2005).[19]

Characteristics of these works

Chandler's scholarship can be characterized in a number of ways. In several of his books, he took for his main subject firms as important historical actors, especially large firms, arguing that these corporations (DuPont, General Motors, US Steel) had brought about the tremendous growth of the US economy during the second industrial revolution.[20]

In terms of methodology, Chandler believed in the importance of comparative analysis, a technique he embraced first in *Strategy and Structure*. The British economist Barry Supple remarked on this aspect of the book: '*Strategy and Structure* was novel because, as Chandler pointed out, it concentrated on a comparison of the ways in which different enterprises carried out the same activity – administration – rather than studying how a single firm undertook all its functions'.[21] Chandler took this methodology further in his internationally comparative book *Scale and Scope* (1990).

As a trained historian, Chandler argued for the necessity of collecting large amounts of empirical facts about the operation of firms – and then using these facts to formulate conceptual conclusions. This was the methodology he espoused in *Strategy and Structure*. Chandler's introduction to that book contains a vivid description of the type of history he was writing:

> Each case study [in this book] presents the events from the point of view of the busy men responsible for the destiny of their enterprise. Only by showing these executives as they handled what appeared to them to be unique problems and issues can the process of innovation and change be meaningfully presented. Only in this way can the trials of harassed executives faced with novel and extremely complex problems be clearly pictured, and the impact of specific personalities and of historical or accidental situations on over-all change be adequately presented. Moreover, if the chronological development of the story is kept intact and if it can be presented as it appeared to the actors in the story, the data should have more value to businessmen and scholars interested in the growth and government of the great industrial corporation than if they were selected and arranged to develop or illustrate one particular historian's thesis.[22]

The phrases 'process of innovation and change', 'novel and extremely complex problems', and 'specific personalities and of historical or accidental situations' are especially important. Chandler made it clear that he wanted to avoid being present-minded in his assessment of the behaviour of individual executives, and that his goal was to capture the ambiguity and complexity of the problems they faced. Chandler's approach was not merely descriptive, nor was it hostile to economic theory. He was arguing for a history in which data are not gathered to illustrate theoretical generalizations, but in which generalizations are derived from data. The 'complex decisions, actions, and events are not taken out of context and presented merely to be illustrative, as they would have to be in a general history of American business or of the American economy'.[23] Instead, they are analysed in order to develop theoretical propositions.

Finally, Chandler asked broad and ambitious questions: What role did the emergence of large corporations have in the American economy?[24] Why did large firms appear in certain industries and not in others? What was the relation between a firm's strategy and its structure? What happened when industries 'died' – as the electronics industry did in the United States: did the knowledge accumulated simply disappear, or did it find its way into newer industries?[25] These questions were of a nature that appealed to scholars in a variety of disciplines, including history, economics, business administration, and sociology.

His influence on the field

These characteristics of Chandler's work – important themes, empirically based arguments, comparative methodology, firm-centred studies – were inspiring to many scholars who read his work. His writings served as a point of origin for scholars in many fields, including those interested in business management (see, for instance, the work of Richard Whittington), organizational sociology (Neil Fligstein), international business history (Geoffrey Jones), institutional economics (Oliver Williamson), and national business histories (Franco Amatori in Italy, Leslie Hannah in Britain, Albert Carreras in Spain).

Richard Rumelt, Dan Schendel, and David Teece noted that the types of questions and issues that Chandler explored helped to inspire the scholarly study of business strategy.[26] Mira Wilkins, the renowned scholar of international business, met Alfred Chandler in 1962 at Columbia University's Graduate School of Business, where Chandler was giving a seminar on his new book *Strategy and Structure*. Wilkins felt that Chandler's 'narrative on the rise of the large US industrial corporation made remarkable sense'. She wrote, 'While economists looked at inputs and outputs and historians looked at business leadership, Chandler pushed his reader to get inside the business enterprise and observe more closely the realities of business goals and how they could be effectively achieved'.[27]

The sociologist Neil Fligstein, who later became a critic of Chandler's work, recalled his first encounter with Chandler's writings, in graduate school in the 1970s:

> I was taking a class on the sociology of organisations and finding that many of the assigned books and articles did not interest me. Corporations are clearly one of the dominant forces in our society, yet none of what I read seemed to capture what they do and how they do it. Reading the first eighteen pages of *Strategy and Structure* was like having the scales fall from my eyes. Here was a historical view of the largest corporations that placed them in their context and, most important, showed that real people with real purposes undertook to make these organisations work.[28]

Chandler's scholarship quickly attracted attention and inspired similar studies in other countries. In 1973, Derek F. Channon published *Strategy and Structure of British Enterprise*; this was followed three years later by Gareth P. Dyas's and Heinz T. Thanheiser's *The Emerging European Enterprise: Strategy and Structure in French and German Industry*. The First Fuji Conference, held in Japan in January 1974, was devoted to the 'Strategy and Structure of Big Business'.

Chandler's work also became central to curricula developed by business-history units from the early 1960s onward, forming the basis of course material taught by the group at the London School of Economics (in the late 1970s) and, in the following decades, by the faculty of the universities of Glasgow, Leeds, and Reading.

Critics and changing interests

Of course, Chandler also attracted his share of critics over the years, especially in the 1990s. Many objected to Chandler's seemingly relentless emphasis on business management, technology, organization and operation. There were subjects that Chandler wrote relatively little about, such as regulation, finance, business culture, and entrepreneurship. Chandler's longtime colleague at Harvard Business School, Pulitzer Prize-winning historian Thomas K. McCraw, commented, 'Many scholars are put off not only by [Chandler's] emphasis on big business but also by big business itself'.[29]

Some critics, especially historian Philip Scranton, law professor Charles F. Sabel, and economist Michael Piore, argued that Chandler downplayed the contribution of small- and medium-sized firms, and overlooked the ways in which the supplanting of independent artisans and flexible manufacturers by middle managers created problems for the American economy.

Chandler's most controversial book was *Scale and Scope*. British writers, in particular, bristled at his view that the preponderance of family-owned firms in the United Kingdom had contributed to that country's relative decline – and they collected detailed evidence showing the innovativeness and importance of this sector of the economy.[30] Barry Supple, writing in *Economic History Review* (August 1991), took exception to Chandler's assumption that the American model should be the 'standard against which to assess the structural characteristics and achievements of the business systems of other countries' (p. 514).

Other critics, particularly in the late 1990s and afterward, disagreed with the grand sweep of Chandler's narrative of the American economy's ascendancy. Fligstein commented that Chandler was 'wrong' in emphasizing the role of efficiency and technology in explaining the rise of large-scale corporations in the United States. He and other sociologists, including Robert Freeland and William G. Roy, argued that the story of the rise of large corporations during America's second industrial revolution was about a search for control and corporate political power, rather than a desire to improve efficiency and expedite the delivery of products.[31] Writing from an economics perspective, Naomi Lamoreaux, Daniel Raff and Peter Temin maintained that Chandler's account of the ascent of large corporations was overly 'Whiggish'. They offered a 'new synthesis of American business history' in the *American Historical Review*, which criticized Chandler's work as overly descriptive and provided an alternative survey of US business history, making use of Oliver Williamson's transaction-cost theory.[32]

Critics raised interesting challenges to Chandler's arguments and pointed out things that they felt he had undervalued or neglected, though some also misrepresented what Chandler had said. He was not, as some alleged, simply a champion of American industry.[33] Chandler objected to many trends that were taking place in American management practice during the 1960s, including the conglomerate movement. In the last decade of his life, he wrote extensively on the failure of the US electronics industry and the triumph of Japanese industry in that sector.

More than anything else, criticism kept Chandler's work at the centre of vital debates among business historians and pushed the field to grow. Mira Wilkins noted, 'I never joined the storm of critics of Chandler's contributions that mounted in the 1990s. I saw the criticisms as reflections of the success of Chandler's arguments. Strong arguments will and should stimulate responses'.[34]

Youssef Cassis, Professor of Economic History at the University of Geneva, remarked that the 'Chandlerian period' in the field of business history came to an end in the 1990s. But the reason for this had only partially to do with critical appraisals of Chandler's work. Rather, it came about, at least in the United States, because of changing trends within history departments. Cassis noted that just as Chandler was reaching his peak with the publication of *Scale and Scope*, mainstream historians were turning to other topics, including social, political and, especially, cultural history.[35] The rising interest among general historians in these subjects had two effects on the field of business history: not only were economics and business less likely to be taught in US history departments, but scholars were also beginning to examine business in new ways that focused on ethnicity, class, gender, popular culture, race, and other aspects of society, and that had seemingly little bearing on Chandler's perspective.

To look at only one of these areas in more detail: Some scholars were drawn to the intertwined history of gender and business, and wrote monographs on the subject. Notable among these were Angel Kwolek-Folland's *Engendering Business: Men and Women of the Corporate Office, 1870–1930* (1994); Wendy Gamber's *The Female Economy: The Millinery and Dressmaking Trades, 1860–1930* (1997); and Kathy Peiss's *Hope in a Jar: The Making of America's Beauty Culture* (1998). At the end of the 1990s, Kwolek-Folland published an initial survey of the subject, *Incorporating Women: A History of Woman and Business in the United States* (1998), and Mary A. Yeager produced a three-volume collection of articles and documents, *Women in Business* (1999).

In Europe, meanwhile, business history remained more focused on the operation of firms. Many of the European centres for the study of business history, built after 1990, were located in economic history departments or business schools. Bocconi University formed a business-history group in 1994, the University of Reading established the Centre for International Business History in 1997, and the Grupo de Investigación Complutense de Historia Empresarial was founded in Madrid in 2004. Many of these centres reflected Chandler's influence to a considerable degree, even if some scholars in them questioned or rejected parts of his findings. The Danish economic historian Ole Lange became enthusiastic about business history after hearing Chandler give a talk in the early 1990s. He persuaded the dean of the Copenhagen Business School to allow him to establish a course using *Scale and Scope* as a text, and he then recruited other business historians. When Kurt Jacobson came to the school, in 1997, he joined with Lange to found the Center for Business History in 1999. But while some scholars were inspired by Chandler's works, others turned to different theorists, such as Oliver Williamson and Douglass North. The theme of the 2004 business-history conference in Le Creusot, France, for instance, was 'networks', which drew on the work of sociologist Mark Granovetter.

The 'umbrella' of business history expanded in the 1990s, as manifested in the growing size of annual meetings sponsored by the Business History Conference, the European Business History Association, and the Association of Business Historians (UK). The field grew in ways that prevented any one scholar from dominating it.[36]

After Chandler

Despite his advanced years, Chandler's death at age eighty-nine came unexpectedly, the result of cardiac arrest following surgery. In the months that followed, scholars struggled to make sense of his achievement within the context of the field of business history as it existed in the early twenty-first century. Journal editors (including me) and conference organizers began commissioning more formal essays on his legacy and relevance.[37] Several authors suggested ways they thought the field would move forward:

1 Some business historians, especially critics of Chandler's work, maintain that the strength of Chandler's narratives, emphasizing rationality and managerial efficiencies, have made it harder to explain recent episodes of economic decline. The financial crisis of 2008 and the series of business scandals and bankruptcies that emerged prior to this downturn (including WorldCom, Parmalat, and Tyco) have raised new questions about the workings of capitalism.

For Christopher McKenna, at Oxford University's Saïd Business School, the series of corporate crises that began with the collapse of Enron in 2001 highlighted the need to rethink the ethical and moral dimensions of corporations. In traditional narratives of capitalist success, he wrote, business historians have focused on 'administrative capacity', rather than on ethics, as a guidepost to the past. Such a framework, which stressed profits, products and organizational shape, left no room for discussions of 'fraud, corporate corruption, or business ethics'. Business historians, thought McKenna, needed to 're-engage' with the 'implicit moral frameworks that have so long under-girded scholarship produced by the leading historians of labour, politics, and diplomacy', as scholars had once done.[38]

Similarly, Rutgers-based historian Philip Scranton remarked on the 'disconnect' between the historical portraits of large firms and the realities of business in the early twenty-first century. 'Our surroundings are sharply different, I would aver, from those in the high Chandlerian period, perhaps from the early 1950s to the mid-1970s, after which stagflation and deregulation, among other phenomena, emerged to derail a century-long trajectory', he wrote. 'Of what value to managers immersed in the challenges and incentives of currency arbitrage or financial derivatives … is the business history Chandler has bequeathed us'?[39]

Scranton is not simply calling on business historians to address the new themes that have emerged, but is also asking them to re-evaluate the works of Chandler (and other business historians, including himself) produced in the 1980s and 1990s in the light of theoretical critiques of modernism by sociologist Zygmunt Bauman, the Polish-born author of *Liquid Modernity* (2000), and other postmodernist scholars.[40] Business historians have to confront a story in which 'rational and rationalizing enterprises' are portrayed as natural and essential organizations for progress. To keep the discipline vital and relevant, business historians must 'explore business history's unvoiced assumptions, un-interrogated concepts, obvious units of analysis, and taken-for-granted modes of explanation (such as rationality, strategy, or the firm)'. The immediate task for business historians, according to Scranton, is to reconsider the ideological building blocks of traditional business history narratives, to 'restock its conceptual imagery' and vocabulary, and especially to critique the idea that the rise of big business, due to improved efficiency or organization, was self-evidently true or universal.[41]

2 Other historians, especially those working at business schools, believe that Chandler's focus on the firm and his multidisciplinary approach to research is vital to understanding economic growth and wealth creation. In their view, business historian must not be isolated, but must engage with the theory of other social sciences. Richard Whittington, Professor of Strategic Management at the Saïd Business School, wrote, 'Chandler's model of business history as a trans-disciplinary enterprise has much to inspire contemporary business historians'.[42] He proposes that business historians cooperate with psychologists, economists, sociologists, and business-management scholars. For one thing, the kind of detailed primary-source research engaged in by business historians could be used to test the accuracy of the theoretical constructs of scholars in other disciplines. (Whittington noted, for instance, that Chandler's detailed

empirical observations helped reveal the hard work and human effort that went into creating business strategy – in a way that more theoretical approaches did not.) But more critically, he states, business historians must become 'exporters of theory' themselves, in order to keep the field relevant. 'If new theory is typically generated by empirical anomaly, then immersion in the rich complexity of historical processes gives business historians a platform for theory-building altogether superior to the desiccated statistics of the econometrician.'[43] Whittington argues that primary research must precede theorizing, pointing out that theories will emerge from comparative (often international) studies. Of what conceptual value are a hundred monographs of individual corporations, if no comparisons are offered?

Geoffrey Jones, the current Straus Professor at Harvard Business School, similarly asserts that business historians must form theoretical concepts based on historical research; they must offer 'answers and not [just] details'. Moreover, he points out, Chandler 'asked the big questions'. Jones wrote, 'I aspire to follow his [Chandler's] path in trying to understand why some entrepreneurs, firms, networks, and business systems create more wealth than others, and to use that knowledge to better understand the historical causes of the wealth and poverty of nations'.[44] From this standpoint, the defining characteristic of capitalism is innovative enterprise – as practised by corporations, partnerships, start-ups, and multinationals. In this view, national economies are not formed by market impulses, but rather are dominated by commercial enterprises; and multinational enterprises, in particular, have built the global economy. Thus, it is important to understand the operation of these firms, which can have powerful real consequences, both positive and negative, on the well-being of individuals and of nations.[45]

3 Finally, another group of business historians, including many who work in history departments, see the need for business historians to broaden the scope of the topics they study, to move beyond the idea that business history must be wedded to the firm, and to produce works for a wide audience that reveal the interconnectedness of business and society. (At the 2008 Business History Conference, Stanford historian Richard White noted that 'business' is the 'elephant in the room', too long ignored by many mainstream historians.)[46]

In the remarks he published about Chandler for the journal *Enterprise and Society*, Kenneth J. Lipartito, Professor of History at Florida International University, argued that the goal of business historians should not be simply to add more details to the existing historical narratives – including Chandler's. He suggested that the task of the historian is to extrapolate, both from Chandler's writings and from those of his critics, the central place of businesses (broadly defined to include self-employed entrepreneurs as well as large corporations) in economies and in societies – not only through their part in building wealth, but also through their contributions to culture, politics, gender relations, and the environment. Lipartito describes the possibilities of going 'back to [Chandler's] work and seeing it in a new light':

> Starting in the 1990s, other scholars began looking at the history of business with their own agendas. William Cronon, in *Nature's Metropolis*, takes the very sources that Chandler used … to weave a tale of environmental history. Richard White writes about railroads – the starting point of modern enterprise for Chandler – but wants to know how railroad management and railway economics reshaped experiences of time and space.[47]

But Lipartito was not only encouraging business historians to think of historical narratives beyond the firm. He was also urging them to explore the complex social and cultural realities *within* firms, as Jeffrey Fear did in his study of the German steel magnate August Thyssen, and as Robert Freeland did in his history of Alfred Sloan's years at General Motors.[48] Lipartito concluded, 'We might find that business history is interesting not just for what it tells us about innovation, strategy, and management, but [also for] what it shows us about how people make and understand their world through the practices we call "business".[49] These comments suggest that business history is not simply a part of mainstream history, but that rather it *is* mainstream history.

And …

It is interesting to note how many of the goals of these business historians are the same ones that Chandler set out to accomplish in his own time: making use of contemporary sociological theory; creating new conceptualizations from the study of primary research; writing broad narratives that address issues important to general historians; and connecting with a multidisciplinary audience. These were the elements that once enabled the field of business history to grow, and, in different ways and to different ends, they remain necessary to keep the field moving forward.

Notes

1 The author would like to thank Geoffrey Jones, Pamela Laird and Ken Lipartito for their comments on this essay.

2 See papers from the Business History Conference and European Business History Association for 2008: Møller, Michael, Niels-Henrik Topp, 'Carl Frederik Tietgen and Privatbanken in Copenhagen, 1857–1896'; Rosner, Christine Meisner, 'Business Leadership and Environmental Reform: Connecting the nineteenth and twenty-First centuries'; Merlo, Elisabetta, '"Suiting Up for Easy Street": Armani and the emergence of Milan as the capital of ready-to-wear'; Koese, Yavuz, 'Doing Business in a Fractioned Market: Nestlé in the Ottoman Empire, 1870-1923'; Dawson, Andrew, 'Hollywood Studios and the Demand for Racial Equality in the Motion Picture Industry, 1963–1974'; Minoglou Pepelasis, Ioanna and Konstantinos Aivalis, 'A Preliminary Analysis of Early Corporate Governance in Greece, 1830–1909'; Shimpo, Hirohiko, 'Overseas Business Activities of Japanese Companies in the Prewar Period: The Japanese style foreign investment in the prewar period'.

3 Of those from economic and economic history departments, 11 per cent were from the former and 13 per cent the latter. Some regional differences are evident: At the US conference, historians predominated: 35 per cent of the presenters came from history departments, 28 per cent from business schools, and 17 per cent from economics departments. At the European conference, 39 per cent, the largest group, came from business schools, 32 per cent from economic and economic history departments, and 20 per cent from history departments.

4 Among business history journals, *Business History Review* has the highest 2007 impact factor (0.679), followed by the British journal *Business History* (0.62) and *Enterprise and Society* (0.475). The *Journal of Economic History* (1.015) and *Economic History Review* (1.171) are higher.

5 Laird, Pamela Walker, 'Looking Toward the Future: Expanding connections for business historians', *Enterprise and Society* 9/4 (December 2008), pp. 575–90.

6 'Alfred Chandler', *The Economist*, 19 May 2007, p. 91.

7 The University of London also hosted a conference, 'Beyond Chandler: Intellectual impulses for business and management history tomorrow', in June 2009.

8 For the best overall assessments, see McCraw, Thomas K. (ed.), *The Essential Alfred Chandler: Essays Toward a Historical Theory of Big Business* (Boston, 1988); idem, 'Alfred Chandler: His vision and achievement', *Business History Review* 82/2 (Summer 2008), pp. 207-26; and John, Richard R., 'Elaborations, revisions, dissents: Alfred D. Chandler, Jr's, The Visible Hand after Twenty Years', *Business History Review* 71/2 (Summer 1997), pp. 151–200.

9 This was a time when popular business historians had generally discredited firms and seen them just as swindlers and financial manipulators (as Matthew Josephson did in *The Robber Barons: The Great American Capitalists, 1861–1901* (New York, 1934)).

10 Gras, N.S.B. and Henrietta M. Larson, *Casebook in American Business History* (New York, 1939).

11 Kenneth Wiggins Porter's *John Jacob Astor, Business Man* (Cambridge, MA, 1931).

12 Larson, Henrietta, *Jay Cooke: Private Banker* (Cambridge, MA, 1936) and eadem, *Guide to Business History: Materials for the Study of American Business History and Suggestions for Their Use* (Cambridge, MA, 1948). See Cuff, 'Notes for a Panel on Entrepreneurship in Business History', *Business History Review* 76/1 (Spring 2002), pp. 123–32.

13 Cochran, Thomas C., 'Arthur Harrison Cole, 1889–1974', *Business History Review* 49/1 (Spring 1975), pp. 3–4.

14 Aitken, Hugh G.J. (ed.), *Explorations in Enterprise* (Cambridge, MA, 1965), p. 8.

15 Schumpeter's ideas were used in the writing of business histories by people like the German-born historian Fritz Redlich, and others, including Harold Passer. See, for instance, Redlich's *Molding of American Banking: Men and Ideas*, (New York, 1947–51), 2 vols and Passer's book on electricity *The Electrical Manufacturers, 1875–1900; A Study in Competition, Entrepreneurship, Technical Change, and Economic Growth* (Cambridge, MA, 1953).

16 See Cuff, 'Notes for a Panel on Entrepreneurship in Business History', *Business History Review* 76/1 (Spring 2002), pp. 123–32.

17 See McCraw, Thomas K., 'Alfred Chandler: His Vision and Achievement', *Business History Review* 82/2 (Summer 2008), pp. 207–26.

18 *Strategy and Structure: Chapters in the History of Industrial Enterprise* (Cambridge, MIT Press, 1962); *The Visible Hand: The Managerial Revolution in American Business* (Cambridge, MA, 1977); and *Scale and Scope: The Dynamics of Industrial Capitalism* (Cambridge, MA, 1990).

19 While most historians have focused on these core books, Chandler's other works should not be neglected. He co-wrote (with Stephen Salsbury) *Pierre S. du Pont and the Making of the Modern Corporation* (1971). Chandler also edited, or co-edited, many volumes, including, with Franco Amatori and Takashi Hikino, *Big Business and the Wealth of Nations* (1997); with James W. Cortada, *A Nation Transformed by Information: How Information has Shaped the United States from Colonial Times to the Present* (2000). For a list of many of his articles, see the bibliography of Thomas K. McCraw's edited collection, *The Essential Alfred Chandler: Essays Toward a Historical Theory of Big Business* (1988). One other article, published in 1994, and hence not mentioned in McCraw's volume, is his seventy-two-page, internationally comparative study, published in *Business History Review*, 'The Competitive Performance of US Industrial Enterprises since the Second World War'.

20 McCraw, 'Alfred Chandler: His Vision and Achievement', p 215.

21 Supple, Barry, 'Scale and Scope: Alfred Chandler and the Dynamics of Industrial Capitalism', *Economic History Review* XLIV/3 (1991), pp. 500–14.

22 Chandler, Alfred D., *Strategy and Structure: Chapters in the History of the American Industrial Enterprise* (Cambridge, MA, 1962; edition used, 1995), p. 7.

23 Chandler, *Strategy and Structure*, p. 7.

24 Fligstein, Neil, 'Chandler and the Sociology of Organizations', *Business History Review* 82/2 (Summer 2008), p. 241.

25 See Chandler Jr, Alfred D., *Inventing the Electronic Century: The Epic Story of the Consumer Electronics and Computer Industries* (New York, Free Press, 2001); and *Shaping the Industrial Century: The Remarkable Story of the Modern Chemical and Pharmaceutical Industries* (Cambridge, MA, 2005).

26 'The foundation of strategic management as a field may very well be traced to the 1962 publication of Chandler's *Strategy and Structure*', they wrote. Rumelt, Richard P., Dan E. Schendel and David J. Teece, 'Fundamental Issues in Strategy', in Richard P. Rumelt, Dan E. Schendel and David J. Teece (eds), *Fundamental Issues in Strategy: a Research Agenda* (Cambridge, MA, 1994), p. 17. Quoted in Whittington, Richard, 'Alfred D. Chandler, Founder of Strategy: A Lost Tradition and Renewed Inspiration', *Business History Review*.

27 Wilkins, Mira, 'Chandler: A Retrospect', *Enterprise and Society* 9/3 (September 2008).

28 Fligstein, 'Chandler and the Sociology of Organizations', *Business History Review*, p. 241.

29 See McCraw, 'Alfred Chandler: His Vision and Achievement', for an overview of central critiques of Chandler's work.

30 See Jones, Geoffrey, 'Great Britain: Big Business, Management, and Competitiveness in Twentieth-Century Britain', in Alfred D. Chandler Jr, Franco Amatori, and Takashi Hikino (eds), *Big Business and the Wealth of Nations* (Cambridge, 1997).

31 Fligstein, Neil, *The Transformation of Corporate Control* (Cambridge, MA, 1990); Roy, William G., *Socializing Capital: The Rise of the Large Industrial Corporation in America* (Princeton, 1997); Freeland, Robert F., *The Struggle for Control of the Modern Corporation: Organizational Change at General Motors, 1924–1970* (New York, 2001).

32 Lamoreaux, Naomi R., Daniel M.G. Raff, and Peter Temin, 'Beyond Markets and Hierarchies: Toward a New Synthesis of American Business History', *American Historical Review* 108/2 (Apr. 2003), p. 406.

33 As in Leslie Hannah's remarks at the 2008 Association of Business Historians.

34 Wilkins, Mira, 'Chandler: A Retrospect', *Enterprise and Society* 9/3 (September 2008), p. 414.

35 'Alfred Chandler, 'The Historian', *Business History News: The Newsletter of the Association of Business Historians* 36 (Autumn 2008).

36 But remarkably, Chandler's work continued to be quoted – as evidenced by the citations in books by authors who won the Hagley Prize for best book in the field. The following list cited Chandler at least once: in 1999, Roland Marchand's *Creating the Corporate Soul*; in 2001, Regina Lee Blaszczyk's *Imagining Consumers: Design and Innovation from Wedgwood to Corning*; in 2002, Gerald D. Feldman's *Allianz and the German Insurance Business, 1933–1945*; in 2005, Mira Wilkins' *The History of Foreign Investment in the United States, 1914–1945*; in 2006, Pamela Walker Laird's *Pull: Networking and Success since Benjamin Franklin*; in 2007,

Christopher McKenna's, *The World's Newest Profession: Management Consulting in the Twentieth Century*; and in 2008, Thomas K. McCraw's *Prophet of Innovation: Joseph Schumpeter and Creative Destruction*.

37 See articles in special issue of *Business History Review*, 'A Special Issue on Alfred D. Chandler Jr', vol. 82/2 (Summer 2008) and special section of *Enterprise and Society*, 'Alfred Chandler Tribute', vol. 9/3 (Sept. 2008).

38 McKenna, Christopher D., 'In Memoriam: Alfred D. Chandler and the Soul of Business History', *Enterprise and Society*.

39 Scranton, 'Beyond Chandler?', *Enterprise and Society* 9/3 (Sept. 2008), p. 428. Richard R. John, writing in *Business History Review*, sees Chandler as a student of the Progressive School, see 'Turner, Beard, Chandler: Progressive Historians', *Business History Review* 82/2 (Summer 2009), pp. 227–40.

40 Scranton also mentions Michel Foucault, Manuel Castells, Bruno Latour, and Richard Sennett.

41 Scranton, 'Beyond Chandler?', *Enterprise and Society* 9/3 (Sept. 2008), p. 429.

42 Whittington, Richard, 'Alfred Chandler, Founder of Strategy: Lost Tradition and Renewed Inspiration', *Business History Review* 82 (Summer 2008), pp. 267–8.

43 Whittington, Richard, 'Alfred Chandler, Founder of Strategy: Lost Tradition and Renewed Inspiration', *Business History Review* 82 (Summer 2008), pp. 267–77.

44 See Jones remarks in *Enterprise and Society* 9/3 (Sept. 2008), p. 421.

45 On this, see Lazonick, William, 'Varieties of Capitalism and Innovative Enterprise', *Comparative Social Research* 24 (2007), pp. 21–69.

46 See Pamela Walker Laird's presidential speech for the Business History Conference, 'Looking Toward the Future: Expanding Connections for Business History', *Enterprise and Society*, p. 578

47 Lipartito, Kenneth J., 'The Future of Alfred Chandler', *Enterprise and Society*.

48 Fear, Jeffrey, *Organizing Control: August Thyssen and the Construction of German Corporate Management* (Cambridge, MA, 2005); Freeland, Robert, *The Struggle for Control of the Modern Corporation* (Cambridge, 2001).

49 Lipartito, 'The Future of Alfred Chandler', p. 432.

Bibliography

Aitken, Hugh G.J. (ed.), *Explorations in Enterprise* (Cambridge, MA, Harvard University Press, 1965).

Business History Review, 'A Special Issue on Alfred D. Chandler Jr', vol. 82/2 (Summer 2008).

Cassis, Youssef, 'Alfred Chandler, 'The Historian', *Business History News: The Newsletter of the Association of Business Historians* 36 (Autumn 2008).

Chandler Jr, Alfred D., *Strategy and Structure: Chapters in the History of Industrial Enterprise* (Cambridge, MIT Press, 1962).

—, *Strategy and Structure: Chapters in the History of the American Industrial Enterprise* (MIT, 1962; edition used, 1995).

—, *The Visible Hand: The Managerial Revolution in American Business* (Cambridge, MA, Harvard University Press, 1977).

—, *Scale and Scope: The Dynamics of Industrial Capitalism* (Cambridge, MA, Harvard University Press, 1990).

—, 'The Competitive Performance of US Industrial Enterprises since the Second World War', *Business History Review* 68/1 (Spring 1994), pp. 1–72.

—, *Inventing the Electronic Century: The Epic Story of the Consumer Electronics and Computer Industries* (New York, Free Press, 2001).

—, *Shaping the Industrial Century: The Remarkable Story of the Modern Chemical and Pharmaceutical Industries* (Cambridge, MA, Harvard University Press, 2005).

— with Franco Amatori and Takashi Hikino, *Big Business and the Wealth of Nations* (1997).

— with James W. Cortada, *A Nation Transformed by Information: How Information has Shaped the United States from Colonial Times to the Present* (2000).

— with Stephen Salsbury, *Pierre S. du Pont and the Making of the Modern Corporation* (1971).

Cochran, Thomas C., 'Arthur Harrison Cole, 1889–1974', *Business History Review* 49/1 (Spring 1975), pp. 3–4.

Cuff, Robert, 'Notes for a Panel on Entrepreneurship in Business History', *Business History Review* 76/1 (Spring 2002), pp. 123–32.

Dawson, Andrew, 'Hollywood Studios and the Demand for Racial Equality in the Motion Picture Industry, 1963–1974', papers from the Business History Conference and European Business History Association for 2008.

The Economist, 'Alfred Chandler', 19 May 2007, p. 91.

Enterprise and Society, 'Alfred Chandler Tribute', vol. 9/3 (Sept. 2008).

Fear, Jeffrey, *Organizing Control: August Thyssen and the Construction of German Corporate Management* (Cambridge, MA, Harvard University Press, 2005).

Feldman, Gerald D., *Allianz and the German Insurance Business, 1933–1945* (Cambridge, Cambridge University Press, 2001).

Fligstein, Neil, *The Transformation of Corporate Control* (Cambridge, MA, Harvard University Press, 1990).

—, 'Chandler and the Sociology of Organizations', *Business History Review* 82/2 (Summer 2008).

Freeland, Robert F., *The Struggle for Control of the Modern Corporation: Organizational Change at General Motors, 1924–1970* (Cambridge, Cambridge University Press, 2001).

Gras, N.S.B. and Henrietta M. Larson, *Casebook in American Business History* (New York, F.S. Crofts, 1939).

John, Richard R., 'Elaborations, Revisions, Dissents: Alfred D. Chandler, Jr.'s, *The Visible Hand* after Twenty Years', *Business History Review* 71/2 (Summer 1997), pp. 151–200.

—, 'Turner, Beard, Chandler: Progressive Historians', *Business History Review* 82/2 (summer 2009), pp. 227–40.

Jones, Geoffrey, 'Great Britain: Big Business, Management, and Competitiveness in Twentieth-Century Britain', in Chandler Jr., Alfred D., Franco Amatori, and Takashi Hikino (eds), *Big Business and the Wealth of Nations* (Cambridge, Cambridge University Press, 1997).

—, 'Alfred Chandler and the Importance of Organization', *Enterprise and Society* 9/3 (Sept. 2008), pp. 419–21.

Josephson, Matthew, *The Robber Barons: The Great American Capitalists, 1861-1901* (New York, 1934).

Koese, Yavuz, 'Doing Business in a Fractioned Market: Nestlé in the Ottoman Empire, 1870–1923', papers from the Business History Conference and European Business History Association for 2008.

Laird, Pamela Walker, *Pull: Networking and Success since Benjamin Franklin* (Cambridge, MA, Harvard University Press, 2006).

—, 'Looking Toward the Future: Expanding Connections for Business History', presidential speech for the Business History Conference, *Enterprise and Society* 9/4 (December 2008), pp. 575–90.

—, 'Looking Toward the Future: Expanding Connections for Business Historians', *Enterprise and Society* 9/4 (December 2008), pp. 575–90.

Lamoreaux, Naomi R., Daniel M.G. Raff and Peter Temin, 'Beyond Markets and Hierarchies: Toward a New Synthesis of American Business History', *American Historical Review* 108/2 (Apr. 2003).

Larson, Henrietta, *Jay Cooke: Private Banker* (Cambridge, MA, Harvard University Press, 1936).

—, *Guide to Business History: Materials for the Study of American Business History and Suggestions for Their Use* (Cambridge, MA, Harvard University Press, 1948).

Lazonick, William, 'Varieties of Capitalism and Innovative Enterprise', *Comparative Social Research* 24 (2007), pp. 21–69.

Lee Blaszczyk, Regina, *Imagining Consumers: Design and Innovation from Wedgwood to Corning* (Baltimore, Johns Hopkins University Press, 2000).

Lipartito, Kenneth J., 'The Future of Alfred Chandler', *Enterprise and Society* 9/3 (Sept. 2008), pp. 430–32.

Marchand, Roland, *Creating the Corporate Soul: The Rise of Public Relations and Corporate Imagery in American Big Business* (Berkeley, University of California Press, 1998).

McKenna, Christopher D., *The World's Newest Profession: Management Consulting in the Twentieth Century* (Cambridge, Cambridge University Press, 2006).

—, 'In Memoriam: Alfred D. Chandler and the Soul of Business History', *Enterprise and Society* 9/3, 'Alfred Chandler Tribute' (September 2008), pp. 422–5.

McCraw, Thomas K. (ed.), *The Essential Alfred Chandler: Essays Toward a Historical Theory of Big Business* (Boston, Harvard Business School Press, 1988).

—, *Prophet of Innovation: Joseph Schumpeter and Creative Destruction* (Cambridge, MA, Harvard University Press, 2008).

—, 'Alfred Chandler: His Vision and Achievement', *Business History Review* 82/2 (Summer 2008), pp. 207–26.

Merlo, Elisabetta, '"Suiting Up for Easy Street": Armani and the Emergence of Milan as the Capital of Ready-to-wear', papers from the Business History Conference and European Business History Association for 2008.

Minoglou, Ioanna Pepelasis and Konstantinos Aivalis, 'A Preliminary Analysis of Early Corporate Governance in Greece, 1830–1909', papers from the Business History Conference and European Business History Association for 2008.

Møller, Michael, Niels-Henrik Topp, 'Carl Frederik Tietgen and Privatbanken in Copenhagen, 1857–1896', papers from the Business History Conference and European Business History Association for 2008.

Passer, Harold, *The Electrical Manufacturers, 1875–1900; A Study in Competition, Entrepreneurship, Technical Change, and Economic Growth* (Cambridge, MA, Harvard University Press, 1953).

Porter, Kenneth Wiggins, *John Jacob Astor, Business Man* (Cambridge, MA, Harvard University Press, 1931).

Redlich, Fritz, *Molding of American Banking: Men and Ideas* (New York, 1947–51), 2 vols.

Rosner, Christine Meisner, 'Business Leadership and Environmental Reform: Connecting the Nineteenth and Twenty-First centuries', papers from the Business History Conference and European Business History Association for 2008.

Roy, William G., *Socializing Capital: The Rise of the Large Industrial Corporation in America* (Princeton, Princeton University Press, 1997).

Rumelt, Richard P., Dan E. Schendel and David J. Teece, 'Fundamental Issues in Strategy', in Richard P. Rumelt, Dan E. Schendel and David J. Teece (eds), *Fundamental Issues in Strategy: a Research Agenda* (Cambridge, MA, Harvard Business School Press, 1994).

Scranton, Philip, 'Beyond Chandler?', *Enterprise and Society* 9/3 (September 2008).

Shimpo, Hirohiko, 'Overseas Business Activities of Japanese Companies in the Prewar Period: The Japanese Style Foreign Investment in the Prewar Period', papers from the Business History Conference and European Business History Association for 2008.

Supple, Barry, 'Scale and Scope: Alfred Chandler and the Dynamics of Industrial Capitalism', *Economic History Review* 44/3 (1991), pp. 500–14.

Whittington, Richard, 'Alfred Chandler, Founder of Strategy: Lost Tradition and Renewed Inspiration', *Business History Review* 82 (Summer 2008), pp. 267–77.

Wilkins, Mira, *The History of Foreign Investment in the United States, 1914–1945* (Cambridge, MA, Harvard University Press, 2004).

—, 'Chandler: A Retrospect', *Enterprise and Society* 9/3 (September 2008), pp. 411–44.

10

The Encounter of History with the Social Sciences

Paschalis Kitromilides

I

A distinctive feature of the intellectual history of the twentieth century has been the encounter of history with the social sciences. This encounter could be considered, without risking a very serious exaggeration, one of the great developments in the intellectual history of a century that has been catastrophic in so many other respects. It has been a fertile meeting, adding meaning and depth to research in the various branches of the social sciences. As for history, the encounter has added conceptual richness and motivation in breaking new grounds of research.

Let me illustrate these claims with a few examples. Few will disagree that the classic case of the encounter I am talking about is provided by *Annales* historiography in France: a meeting of historical research with economic thought, demography, geography, anthropology, which has produced the inspired and imposing works of Marc Bloch, Lucien Febvre, Fernand Braudel – a veritable '*defi Latin*' for historiography, as it has been described by an American reviewer of Braudel's *Mediterranean*.[1] The encounter of history and the social sciences in *Annales* historiography has been appraised as a major development in intellectual history by a leading American historian, H. Stuart Hughes.[2] Many other examples could be cited:

a) The encounter of history with sociology has produced impressive works in historical sociology, with the emblematic writings of Barrington Moore Jr serving as models for a whole school of historical sociology in America. The focus of this tradition of research on the state has profoundly influenced the field of political sociology as well.

b) History has also had a very happy encounter with anthropology, as attested by the school of symbolic anthropology initiated by Clifford Geertz: the refinement and perceptiveness of his writings on cultures and symbolic expression in historical settings acted as an excellent corrective to anthropology's earlier ahistorical tendencies and found a very fertile response in the work of historians such as Natalie Zemon Davis and Carlo Ginsburg.[3] It is to be regretted that the total capitulation of anthropology to the paroxysms of postmodernism, more recently, has really destroyed the creative dynamic released by Cliff Geertz's work in this field.

c) The encounter of history with political theory has brought about a major revolution in the study of the canon of political philosophy and political science. This has been the achievement especially of the Cambridge School of the history of political thought and of its offshoots in the USA, Canada, Australia and elsewhere. In a sustained effort since the 1960s, the Cambridge historians of political thought have brought about a veritable new substantive understanding of political ideas and their trajectories in historical time, and have considerably expanded the canon of political thought.

What can be achieved by the encounter of history with the social sciences and what is missed by the absence of the salutary contribution of history could be illustrated more concretely by a brief look at the study of nationalism, the ubiquitous motive force of modernity.

All social sciences, political science, sociology, anthropology and literary criticism, even psychology – although somewhat earlier on in this case – are keen to pronounce on nationalism, proffering what their practitioners think are causal explanations, interpretations and critical judgements. Yet, if one considers the final products of such initiatives what one is left with in most cases is just a sense of belabouring the obvious. The explanation of the futility of such exercises has to do, I believe, with the cavalier use of history and historical evidence: most social scientists working on nationalism fail to look at primary sources, they often ignore specialized secondary literature and tend to base their observations on textbook materials. The consequence of this is a serious pathology – misinformation, misunderstanding, arbitrariness and partial explanation – a pathology that often just confirms the myths of nationalism and plagues a good deal of contemporary writing in this field of research, including a considerable part of the recent literature – mostly produced by anthropologists or literary critics – on Greece.

What can be retorted to this tendency? I do not think that a historicist or a theoretically agnostic empiricist history could provide the answer. Such a history could not even raise the questions in the first place. What is needed is the reasoned but professional use of history to test, control and modify theoretical approaches, and turn then from Procrustean beds into sources not of all-encompassing explanations but of illuminating insights into regional or particular manifestations of broader phenomena. I dare to suggest that this is where the challenge and the promise lie for the future of scholarship in the human sciences.

II

Turning to a consideration of the case of Greece and of historical writing on modern and contemporary Greece, one might ask what can be said about the fruits of the encounter of history and the social sciences in contemporary scholarship?

A point of departure for exploring this question could be provided by the proceedings of the Historiography Congress organized in the autumn of 2002 by the Institute for Neohellenic Research at the National Hellenic Research Foundation. The Congress lasted just under a week and included over 70 papers and interventions in the concluding Round Table discussion. The contents of the two imposing volumes of proceedings, running to over 1,300 pages, provide a good basis, I think, for a first attempt at stock-taking on the condition of historical writing on Greece today and in particular on the question of the encounter of history and the social sciences.[4] At the Congress we even had a special session on history and the social sciences. With the exception of the paper on history and anthropology, by Peter Loizos, this session turned out to be quite different from what I, at least, as convener of the Congress, expected. In it, nevertheless, in an interesting although very short paper, George Dertilis, in order to voice his criticism of the tradition of academic historiography in Greece – its ossification, its ideologically preordained character, its penchant for rhetoric rather than criticism – reminded us of the seminal contributions of professionals from other disciplines, mostly economists and lawyers, to breaking new ground and opening new fields of research in historical writing on modern Greece, especially in the first half of the twentieth century.

Let me just share with you a few impressions that force themselves upon the reader who reflects seriously on these proceedings but also on the broader picture of academic practice in the field of history in today's Greece, by considering three encounters:

a) history and economics;
b) history and anthropology;
c) history and political science.

(a) History and economics

The encounter of history with economics in contemporary Greek historiography has produced a field of economic history that is multifarious and quite active in scholarly output. Although one of the participants in the historiography congress was rather critical, suggesting that the field – especially banking history – has been marked by a low degree of professionalization, there can be little doubt that the field of economic history as a whole has been well ploughed in the last quarter century[5] and some of its subfields in particular have been producing interesting results with a wider relevance for international scholarship.[6]

One special feature of the field has been the presence of personalities with a broader sense of the historian's task, who bring a more comprehensive historical culture to the definition of economic history. Such has been the distinctive character of the contribution of Spyros Asdrachas to the definition and growth of this field of research. He has been the inspiring teacher of a whole generation of Greek economic historians and is one of the founding fathers of the History Department of the Ionian University.

(b) History and anthropology

The story of the encounter of history with anthropology in scholarly writing about Greece has been marked by paradox. It had very auspicious beginnings, especially in the work of John Campbell, a great scholar who really brought together history and anthropology in a most serious manner in his work in the 1960s. Yet Campbell has been more successful subsequently in training at Oxford historians rather than anthropologists.[7] We were privileged in this meeting to have among us some of his prominent students. Anthropology in later decades, especially since the 1980s, has taken the strange and convoluted ways of postmodernism, producing work marked by arbitrariness and subjectivism. The most catastrophic results in this direction have been produced by the special curiosity anthropologists have shown in nationalism in Greek society. In considering this subject they tend to generalize from the partial impressions of ethnographic research, and draw conclusions without having read the literature, let alone primary sources. What we witness, therefore, is precisely a divorce between history and anthropology, which is not at all reassuring, at least from the perspective from which I have been discussing the subject.

I cannot resist the temptation to add here that the same pathology marks other branches of postmodernism as well, especially literary criticism and so-called cultural studies. If anything, in these fields, as practised mostly in America, things are worse. Scholars read texts in a total historical vacuum and write about nationalism only through secondary literature – if that – they despise chronology, prosopography and, of course, bibliography, with the inevitable qualitative consequences. It is disheartening to note that the pathology is spreading to Greece, through the local emulators of postmodernism's glories.

(c) History and political science

The meeting of history with political science in writing on modern Greece is a mixed one, also marked by paradox and inconsistencies. When political scientists read and use history seriously they can produce important and interesting work – in some cases even seminal works. The same is true of historians: when they use concepts drawn from political science to organize their historical analysis they can produce real classics, such as the work of the late John Petropulos, who in his book on political parties in the Othonian period[8] has left us a unique model of scholarship – a model and a source of inspiration for us all.

At the same time, the preoccupation with the possibilities offered by the social sciences for organizing conceptually historical materials and narratives has led to a desertion of political history. Thus, one of the marks of contemporary historical writing on Greece is the paucity of political history. An exception has been the writing of diplomatic history, in the sense of the history of the foreign relations of Greece. In this domain important work has been and continues to be produced by the most eminent practitioner of the genre, Professor Constantine Svolopoulos, who carries on the distinguished tradition of Driault and Lheretier, enriching it with insights from the approach of Renouvin and Duroselle. In this field too, developments have been marked by division and paradox: when the subject is negotiated by scholars with international-relations backgrounds the results are qualitatively poor, and this has marked most of the writing on Greece's European trajectories or on Greece's Balkan entanglements. But there are exceptions, the most reassuring provided by the work of younger scholars with history backgrounds, who, using international relations approaches, have managed to develop a critical perspective on the history of Greek foreign relations, mostly in the twentieth century.

III

Let me conclude by making explicit just a few thoughts. After all that has been said, I do not think I have to repeat, in closing, my conviction that the way forward for historical writing on Greece has to be a continuing dialogue with the social sciences. The reverse is also true, especially in the case of my own field, political science, in which the serious dialogue with history, and also with philosophy, is not just essential for qualitative work but its abandonment could be lethal for a field which is besieged, to an extraordinary degree, by the temptations of many sirens pointing to the slippery way of superficiality and current-affairs commentary. My main worry comes precisely from the attraction such sirens exert upon historians as well, including many of the younger generation, who seem keen to imitate their gurus' bad example. We witness too much of that today, as some historians try to gain visibility not through serious work but through power games, projects of hegemony, manipulation of intellectual values and total submission to the logic of the mass media. On the altar of such pursuits, the first sacrificial victims are, of course, professional ethics and the rules of scholarship. This is what really puts the future of serious scholarship at stake. But I assure you that some of us, at least, will resist and will persist in serving and promoting the critical agenda of scholarship. I put my hopes in this and in the younger generations who will choose to follow this difficult path.

Notes

1 Armstrong, John A., 'Braudel's Mediterranean: Un defi Latin', *World Politics* 29 (1977), pp. 626–36.

2 Stuart Hughes, H., *The Obstructed Path. French Social Thought in the Years of Desperation 1930–1960* (New York, 1966), pp. 29–64.

3 See Molho, Tony, 'Carlo Ginzburg: Reflections on the intellectual cosmos of a 20th century historian', *History of European Ideas* 30 (2004), pp. 121–48.

4 Kitromilides, P.M. and T. Sklavenitis (eds), *The Historiography of Modern and Contemporary Greece* (Athens, 2004), vols 1–11. The Congress and its proceedings provoked an extensive debate. For appraisals see Livanios, D., *Southeast European and Black Sea Studies* 8 (2008), pp. 75–7; Arvanitakis, D., *O Politis* 135 (July–August 2005), pp. 139–41; Augustinos, G., *Journal of Modern Greek Studies* 26 (2008), pp. 227–30.

5 See e.g. Asdrachas, Spyros I. and collaborators, *Greek Economic History 15th-19th Centuries*, transl. by Doolie Sloman (Athens, 2007), accompanied by Vol. II: *Sources*, ed. by Efthychia D. Liata, transl. by John Davis (Athens, 2007).

6 An example of this is the work of Gelina Harlaftis in the field of maritime history.

7 The collection *Networks of Power in Modern Greece*, edited by Mark Mazower (London, 2008) brings together studies by John Campbell's students in their teacher's honour.

8 Petropulos, John A., *Politics and Statecraft in the Kingdom of Greece 1833–1843* (Princeton, 1968).

Bibliography

Armstrong, John A., 'Braudel's Mediterranean: Un defi Latin', *World Politics* 29 (1977), pp. 626–36.

Asdrachas, Spyros I., Nikos E. Karapidakis, Eutychia Liata, Olga Katsiardi-Hering, *Greek Economic History 15th-19th Centuries*, transl. by Doolie Sloman (Athens, 2007), accompanied by Vol. II: *Sources*, ed. by Efthychia D. Liata, transl. by John Davis (Athens, 2007).

Kitromilides, Pascalis M. and Triandafyllos Sklavenitis (eds), *The Historiography of Modern and Contemporary Greece* (Athens, 2004), vols 1–11.

Livanios, Dimitrios, *Southeast European and Black Sea Studies* 8 (2008), pp. 75–7.

Mazower, Mark (ed.), *Networks of Power in Modern Greece* (London, C. Hurst and Co., 2008).

Molho, Tony, 'Carlo Ginzburg: Reflections on the Intellectual Cosmos of a 20th Century Historian', *History of European Ideas* 30 (2004), pp. 121–48.

Petropulos, John A., *Politics and Statecraft in the Kingdom of Greece 1833–1843* (Princeton, Princeton University Press, 1968).

Stuart Hughes, H., *The Obstructed Path. French Social Thought in the Years of Desperation 1930–1960* (New York, Harper 7 Row, 1966), pp. 29–64.

11

Trends in the History Writing of the Late Ottoman Empire

Donald Quataert

Introduction

This is an exciting and promising moment in Ottoman history writing. The cohort of Ottoman historians is both numerically greater and methodologically more-sophisticated than ever before. Moreover, the body of available materials is exploding exponentially. On the one hand, the ongoing cataloguing of materials in the Prime Ministry Archives in Istanbul has been producing amazing results. Documents are now available from the very lowest levels of the Ottoman bureaucracy, providing intimate details of everyday Ottoman life and making possible hitherto-nearly-impossible forms of social, cultural and labour history.[1] And, on the other hand, extraordinary masses of documents outside of this grand depository are reshaping the substance, form and focus of Ottoman history. Let me give three examples. First, central state documents that were produced and still rest in provincial locations, yielding an intimate picture of Ottoman life.[2] Second, private records resting, often, in the possession of families in the Arab provinces.[3] And third, the vast quantities of Greek-language business and family records that just now are opening up extraordinary perspectives, bringing into better focus a community that was an integral part of the imperial community.[4]

In the West, Ottoman history writing began as an offshoot of European history, usually the purview of historians interested in the 'Eastern Question'. Famously, William Langer's *Diplomacy of Imperialism*, a series of essays on various aspects of European diplomacy, gave prominent place to the Ottoman Empire.[5] Langer and other European specialists, well-trained historians, correctly treated the Ottoman past as an integral part of European history. But for all his disciplinary skills as historian, Langer and his contemporaries studied the Ottoman experience from the outside, using a rich array of European-language materials but not indigenous sources generated from within the Ottoman world.[6] The fact that Ottoman history writing is part of the larger discipline of history is a point worth stressing, since it was forgotten for too long, notably by those who insisted the Ottomans were *sui generis* and therefore, in a sense, outside of history.

The opening of the Ottoman archives and the quickening of the Cold War sparked a new interest in Ottoman studies.[7] A number of seminal works, based on Ottoman primary and secondary sources, began to appear in the 1960s, opening new paths for research into Ottoman history.[8] These studies are still important, especially for their often extensive use of the writings of the Ottoman chroniclers and contemporary observers. Bernard Lewis's *The Emergence of Modern Turkey* was particularly influential, expressing a paradigm that focused on westernization during the Ottoman nineteenth century, a process which, he argued inevitably led to the Turkish republican twentieth century.

These writings set the field of Ottoman history on a particular course, one that by and large it is still following, down to the present-day. Namely, they established an interpretative framework that has two main features. First (nearly) all of them worked from the presupposition that the Ottoman Empire and Turkey were synonymous entities; to speak of Turkey in the nineteenth century was not considered anachronistic[9] since the real goal in exploring the Ottoman past was to discuss the origins of the Turkish nation-state. In so doing, they dumped into the trash bin of history Ottoman experiences that were not directly related to the formation and history of the Turkish Republic, at least as they perceived that formation and history. And so, the histories of the Balkan and Arab provinces of the empire became largely irrelevant and off the agenda of these Ottoman historians. And second, as I already mentioned, they emphasized the westernizers in Ottoman political, cultural and social life. These westernizers, it turned out, also were the Ottoman elites, and so for the 1960s writers, Ottoman history by and large became the story of Ottoman elites who were effecting a process of change from the top down. Quite relatedly, since the republic patronized peasants and repressed workers, there was little place in the emerging historiography for an activist history from below. Instead, the new literature presented peasants as objects of state beneficence and ignored workers.

With this mindset in place, a pioneering generation of scholars began using the Prime Ministry Archives[10] in Istanbul, a repository for millions of the documents created by the recently-defunct Ottoman State. Researchers enthusiastically plunged into these archives, sources increasingly available from the 1960s onwards. And, they preached an infectious message that attracted me and my generation to this incredible trove of historical materials. The result was an explosion of historical scholarship and the accomplishments have been amazing. Since the 1970s, Ottoman history writing has grown from a minor field occupied by a handful into one with an annual bibliography numbering thousands of entries.[11] Ottoman history is now the largest subfield of Middle East history, and its practitioners are scattered in dozens of universities throughout the country where they often serve as the only Middle East specialist in their respective departments. Whole continents of former intellectual *terra incognita* have been mapped. The outlines of Ottoman economic and political change are now visible (if sometimes only faintly). Some themes in cultural and social history also have been explored, thanks in part to the discovery and use of the court records. Even the 'Dark Ages' of Ottoman history, the eighteenth century, have been researched and indeed this era is the subject of some of the most exciting work.

While the accomplishments have been amazing, many shortcomings remain. Overall, until the early 1990s, most of the dissertations and published work in Ottoman history shared a number of deficiencies.

1 They neglected sources outside of the Prime Ministry Archives.
2 Most researchers left theory at the door of the archives and, by design, too many works of scholarship were little more than annotated translations of their Ottoman originals.
3 Scholars forgot the lessons of the Langer school and treated the Ottoman Empire as *sui generis* and not part of a broader history. They treated Ottoman history in a vacuum, without connection to other histories, and too often presented the Ottoman experience as idiosyncratic and without parallel in world history.
4 They focused on the Anatolian lands of the empire and allowed these to stand for the empire as a whole.
5 They narrated state actions and reproduced the arguments and perspectives of the archival documents.

There are several corollaries to this last point. First, the state became the agent of change or stagnation. It so fully occupied the historical stage that there was scarcely any room for other actors. And second, elite groups overall were the focus of attention while the peasants, artisans (and to a lesser extent, merchants) remained absent from the narrative. Moreover, the discourse was heavily male-dominated; women were left to the margins of the Ottoman experience. Thus, Ottoman specialists created a formidable body of work that has provided a foundation of knowledge on which subsequent generations of historians can build. But that body of work, alas, has the structural weaknesses outlined above and was neither integrated into the discipline of history nor accessible to few but the cognoscenti.

Despite all the many improvements, Ottoman history writing still is powerfully-influenced by normative notions. These derive from (1) the state's vision of itself, of society and of the various social and economic groups and organizations; and (2) the perspectives of modernization theory and elite-driven, top-down change, whether that change be of the social, economic, political or cultural sort. Marginalized groups rarely have been able to capture the attention of Ottoman history writers.

Women's history, for example, has yet to mainstream and largely remains the preserve of women historians writing Ottoman history. Thanks to their efforts, we are now beginning to amass a core body of knowledge regarding women, both elite and non-elite. Zilfi's articles and edited book on *Women in the Ottoman Empire*[12] form an important milestone in the evolution of Ottoman history writing regarding marginalized groups. Artan's study of the consumption patterns of imperial women and the nature of female consumption as a tool of imperial power also is noteworthy.[13] At the non-elite level, Faroqhi's analysis of female workers who supplied guilds with processed materials – such as the mohair-spinners of Ankara in the eighteenth century – integrates women into mainstream economic history.[14] My own work demonstrates that, by the early decades of the nineteenth century, non-guild, female and rural labour had increased dramatically and is vital to understanding Ottoman manufacturers' successful adaptation to European competition. Elsewhere, studies by Micklewright and Frierson each centre women in their respective narratives.[15] Too often, however, women still are singled out for attention in the 'women's history article or book', rather than being normalized in discussions of larger issues, whether these be consumption patterns, politics or tax farming.

Labour history is another area of marginality still struggling for recognition.[16] Many Ottoman historians continue to see the study of workers, at the bottom of the political order, as ideological in nature, while their own studies of elites, at the top of the political structure, are seen as non-ideological. Labour history has been both ignored and mistreated in Ottoman historical writing. While the empire lived, writers (both residents of the empire and foreigners) came from the literate and upper strata of their societies, and were either disdainful of or outright hostile to workers and to labour history. These trends continued deep into the twentieth century. There are many causes for this pattern of scholarship. In the process of its formation during the 1920s–1950s, the emerging Turkish republic essentially excluded popular participation. It restricted political activity to a small elite, crushed labour movements and made them illegal, and kept peasants out of the political process. Government and elite suspicion of the popular classes was exacerbated because of the new Turkey's enmity towards the adjacent Soviet Union, self-proclaimed if flawed standard-bearer for the workers and peasants of the world.[17] Writing the history of workers and the working class (incorrectly) was seen to aid the enemies of the United States and its Turkish ally. Worker and peasant demands and activities inside Turkey too easily were labelled as communism and thus dismissed out of hand as dangerous and traitorous to the state. And so, an effective censorship and self-censorship regarding labour history came to prevail in Ottoman historical studies, and not only among scholars who were Turkish nationals. Around 1970, finally, writers in the Turkish and Arabic, and West European/US circles, began focusing some scholarly attention on workers.

Peasants were the backbone of Ottoman society and the mainstay of the economy, and yet, for all that, there have been virtually no studies of Ottoman cultivators for their own sake. Peasants remain as distant and shadowy figures in Ottoman history. A number of projects have discussed peasants as tax-payers and as quiescent or rebellious subjects, receptive or resistant to government reform agendas, that is, from the perspective of the state and in relation to the state. But few write of peasants' daily lives or depict village communities, despite an abundance of archival materials, especially during the post-1840 period.[18] For example, in a well-known work whose title promised an examination of both peasants and state, Ottoman cultivators were scarcely mentioned.[19]

In sum, the tendency towards history from below within Ottoman history mainly expressed itself in the form of studying economic history, itself an indirect means of learning about the non-elite groups who are so elusive in the historical record. Economic history became a major area of emphasis and produced fine studies about commerce, agriculture and, to a lesser extent, manufacturing and mining.[20] But actual history from below remains very unusual. There has been little concern for the individuals and groups working in those sectors. Merchants received some attention but peasants, artisans, miners and others have not. The narratives of Ottoman history even now are inhabited by few representatives of the popular classes but there are signs of hope.[21]

Among Ottoman specialists there is a widely shared view that most of the work in print regarding the Armenian community and its fate during the late Ottoman period is not based on scientific and systematic research. The work being done is largely dismissed *a priori* as ideological and without scientific merit. These sentiments are commonly held within our field. Moreover, colleagues in the history discipline outside of our field express astonishment at the apologetic nature of the work being generated by those with access to the Ottoman archives. Most historians within and outside Ottoman history believe that little light has been shed on what happened to the Armenians. These perceptions are important. Do they reflect the actual state of the scholarship? Is it actually biased and untrustworthy? Or do these perceptions tell us about ourselves, that we are unable to acknowledge work representing a different viewpoint? There may be some truth in the latter notion. After all, Ottoman historians as a group continue to demonstrate genuine reluctance to engage in intellectual debate, whether it be about the origins of the Ottoman State, that of Ottoman decline, or the destruction of the Armenian community.[22]

Egypt and its role in late Ottoman history have been receiving some reconsideration. Several recent works[23] remind us that there are impressive parallels in nineteenth-century Egyptian and Ottoman history that deserve fuller analysis. A number of issues could be explored for the light they shed on the connections between the empire and Egypt. Take these examples: the financial crises of the late 1870s; the passage of legislation regarding both land and guilds; the overlap between the Istanbul and Cairene elites. Clearly, the northern core and Egypt were functioning in the same (Ottoman) universe, but Egypt has been largely abandoned by those most comfortable in the Prime Ministry archives.

Ottoman history in the new millenium

The past few years generally have been kind to Ottoman history and a comparative plethora of works[24] have appeared. These works are important not only for their own sake but also for what their strengths and weaknesses can tell us about the current state of our craft. For purposes of discussion, I divide the works into three groups. The first are those focusing on the Arab provinces – overall, these are the best of the new studies and are playing a leadership role in the ongoing evolution of Ottoman history writing. In the second group are overviews of various aspects of Ottoman history, based exclusively, or nearly so, on western sources not Ottoman ones. And finally, there is the relative explosion of textbooks or broad-ranging surveys on Ottoman history, prepared by specialists versed in Ottoman language sources.

In the first group – books on the Arab provinces – are those by Ussama Makdisi on nineteenth-century Ottoman Lebanon; by Eugene Rogan on Transjordan, 1850–1921; and by James Grehan on eighteenth-century Damascus. These works, *inter alia*, serve as powerful reminders that the Arab provinces (and the Balkan ones as well) were integral parts of the Ottoman Empire and that focusing solely on the Anatolian portions powerfully distorts the Ottoman past. The studies by Makdisi, Rogan and Grehan exemplify the emergence of a new, more sophisticated and comprehensive approach to Ottoman history.[25] To varying degrees, each is based on a rich blend of wide-ranging sources, local and imperial, indigenous and foreign, private and official. In his study of Transjordan, 1850–1921, Rogan employs the court records of several towns, land-registration records, archives of a local Latin Church and of the Latin Patriarchate of Jerusalem, as well as manuscript materials held by notable families and religious organizations . Into this mix he skilfully blends significant amounts of archival materials from the imperial Ottoman capital and from Britain, France and the United States. The source base of Makdisi is no less impressive. He utilizes family papers, unpublished local histories from a number of locations, and missionary and patriarchate records. And, he effectively interweaves these with a considerable body of materials from the Ottoman central archives and from the foreign office holdings of the British and French governments. Both Rogan and Makdisi use their manifold source bases in the service of overarching arguments regarding their respective subjects of study. Grehan, for his part, relies heavily on 1,000 probate inventories from the period 1750–1763, to offer a stunningly new and original social history of everyday life.

Makdisi asserts that Lebanese sectarianism is indeed modernity. He argues forcefully that sectarianism was not an expression of primordial loyalties and identities which somehow failed to make the transition to nationalism. For him, sectarianism was a rupture in Lebanese life brought about by the interaction between Lebanese society as it had existed before *ca* 1840, the Tanzimat policies of the Ottoman State and Great Power intervention on behalf of local religious communities. As he puts it, the genealogical geography of local, non-religious elites gave way to a sectarian geography in which religious identity became the defining characteristic of the modern subject and citizen. He shows how local elites, the Ottoman State and the European powers worked together to block popular politics and re-install elite politics, now based on sectarian identities. More negatively, he over-stresses the gap between the imperial state and its subjects in the Eastern Mediterranean. And, he over-emphasizes the role of Europe in the creation of Lebanese sectarianism. Reservations aside, in Makdisi's work the agency of international forces combined with that of the distant Ottoman imperium, and of the local popular and elite groups, to give rise to the new form of identity. In his formulation, Ottoman history has moved a considerable distance from the westernization imposed from outside upon an inert Ottoman body politic. And, by historicizing sectarianism in one part of the empire, he invites us to re-examine its emergence elsewhere. He makes a powerful call for reassessing identity formation in the late Ottoman Balkans and Anatolia.

Rogan's work, for its part, provides a model for those who study the frontier and imperial rule, and not merely in the Ottoman world. His is often an amazing work, for it gives tangible meaning to the generalizations made by previous generations of Ottoman historians who have written extensively but often vaguely about imperial Ottoman reform legislation. Rogan illustrates the implementation of these reforms on the ground: for example, how the impact of the 1858 Land Law varied from tribe to tribe, depending on the nature of its livelihood – agriculture or stock raising. And he demonstrates the impact of central state policies of improved security, refugee settlement and land distribution on the frontier areas of northern Transjordan. There, merchants from nearby towns replaced the indigenous elites and linked Transjordan to the wider regional economy, just as new government officials tied the provincial administration to the larger Ottoman state. And yet, on the eve of the First World War, the southern districts were largely unassimilated into the larger Ottoman body and became the locale of a major revolt that erupted and defined the limits of Ottoman rule. Rogan's work on the Ottoman legacy of Transjordan and its dynamism stands in stark contrast to prevailing notions of the region as one without history until the formation of the Hashemite State in 1921.

Despite these many contributions, the Rogan book does not break with one of the characteristic shortcomings of Ottoman history writing. Notably, it does not deviate from the interpretative framework that presents the central state as the initiator of change. Thus, the Tanzimat derives from reforming sultans who sought to change the basic institutions of the state. The Land Law, in his view, owed its existence not to domestic demands but rather to the financial needs of the central administration. For all the excellence of his analysis, we are left with the impression of a process of change that remains one-way. There are no pressures from Ottoman society which trigger the Tanzimat and no changes in the agrarian sector which persuaded the state to change its land legislation.[26] In the end, in a real sense, social change remains trickle-down, from the elites above to society below.

Grehan offers a vivid picture of everyday life, likely the most successful effort yet in Ottoman studies. Perhaps the most impressive aspect of his achievement is his remarkable assimilation of the bulky and difficult probate inventories and his construction of a beautifully-written narrative that takes us back to these eighteenth-century lives. Thus, we learn not only about Damascenes' reliance on bread but also the role of oil and yoghurt in helping to create a nutritionally balanced diet. Moreover, his essay on water and water quality is masterfully done. On the negative side, his study is not of eighteenth-century Damascus but of one time period, 1750–1763, that of the inventories. Thus, his is not a narrative of change over time but rather a snapshot of one moment in time. And, he is too hasty in concluding that a consumer society had not yet emerged. Such a judgement, I believe, should await another study based on inventories of the early or the late eighteenth century.

A final word on these Arab provincial studies: for both Rogan and Makdisi, the Ottoman period is absolutely essential for understanding the history of modern Jordan and Lebanon. Both of them implicitly disregard the barrier of 1918 that previous generations had erected between the Ottoman world and that of the Ottoman successor states, not only in the Arab lands, but also in Turkey and the Balkan provinces.[27]

Our second group includes three works to be mentioned briefly here and consists of studies that focus on the Ottoman world but mainly or exclusively utilize western sources. The first of these – Mansel's overview of Ottoman history, published back in the mid 1990s – attracted considerable attention and was adopted in many college courses.[28] Mansel prepared his study in part by consulting with Ottoman specialists living in Turkey and he reflects the current continued emphasis in Ottoman history writing upon the upper strata of the Ottoman world. Mansel's *Constantinople* is inhabited only by elites, of the administrative, cultural as well as the military kind. But at least it has the merit of being grounded in Ottomanist scholarship.

The Efraim and Inari Karsh book[29] and David Fromkin's *Peace to End All Peace*[30] focus on the Ottoman world during the era of the First World War. The presence of such works reflects the increased popularity of Ottoman history among both academics and the general public. Popular Ottoman history surely is desirable. But works such as the Karshes' and Fromkin's, and on the shelves of bookstores across the country, is distressing and indicates the collective failure of Ottoman specialists to overcome persistent stereotypes about the Ottoman Empire. The Karsh work uses the entire Middle East as its canvas to present an Ottoman context to the remapping of the region during and after the First World War. It and Fromkin's earlier study each revisit the Eastern Question. The Fromkin book was lavishly praised in some circles; according to publicity on its cover, it was named a *New York Times* Book Review Editor's choice. Nonetheless, it suffers from some fundamental flaws – namely, it studies the complex diplomacy of the First World War era through external sources and is based solely on English-language materials. The Fromkin book centres its narrative about the Middle East not on an Ottoman leader or a leader of the Arab revolt, but instead on Winston Churchill! It narrates the creation of the modern Middle East and the actions of Young Turks, other Ottomans, loyalist and rebel Arabs through British eyes and English-language sources. Shockingly, Fromkin explicitly excludes Middle East agents from his narrative because, he says, they were not around the table when the decisions were made. This is bad history, a return to the days of imperial viceroys responsibly presiding over dusky restless peoples.

The Karsh book poses an important hypothesis, namely, that 'Middle Eastern actors were not hapless victims of predatory imperial powers but active participants in the restructuring of their region'.[31] This statement must be applauded, since it apparently offers agency to those who too often have been considered as the passive recipients of Western action. The book promises to offer the perspective of the Ottoman and Arab elites on the decisions they made before and during the First World War. These decisions, the authors argue, and not the policies of the Great Powers, brought about the partition and destruction of the Ottoman Empire. While controversial, such statements are legitimate interpretive positions that deserve to be argued. Indeed, they have exercised historians for decades. Could the Ottoman State have done anything to prevent its partition? Was Ottoman neutrality in the First World War an option? What caused the Ottoman entry into the war on the German and Austro-Hungarian side?

The book utterly fails to shed new light on these questions and does not deliver its promised internal perspective on Ottoman decision-making. It is doomed to fail because it completely depends on external, in fact, hostile sources. British government documents form the edifice upon which the authors build their inquiry.[32] The British Empire, let us remember, was the Ottoman State's mortal foe between 1914 and 1918. British insights into the behaviour of the central Ottoman and provincial Arab elites' behaviour indeed are valuable, but they cannot be used to provide an insider view of Ottoman thinking.[33]

Obviously, the use of indigenous primary sources does not automatically produce good history writing. An informed theoretical framework and a command of the secondary sources and other archival holdings, *inter alia*, also are required. But good history that seeks to determine the actions of agents cannot succeed if based only on sources external to those agents. The Karsh book's reliance on such exogenous materials and its virtually complete neglect of indigenous primary sources are unacceptable practices at this stage of Ottoman history writing.

Let us now turn to the third group. Broad surveys based on Ottoman sources have become almost commonplace in the past few years, a testimonial to the increasing popularity of the field. Finkel's broad survey[34] traces the history of the empire from beginning to end and does readers a great service in bringing together widely disparate sources and blending them into a coherent narrative. From my perspective, it is unfortunate that she emphasizes history from above and so continues a regrettable mainstream tradition of ignoring the vast bulk of Ottoman society and most of the society-state dynamic. Faroqhi's study[35] takes on the mid-sixteenth to the mid-eighteenth century and offers many important contributions. She persuasively argues for the porosity of the frontiers and the commonplace exchanges between the Ottomans and their neighbours. Moreover, in bringing together so many different sources, she offers readers a synthesis otherwise difficult to obtain. Viriginia Aksan[36] offers a fine overview of warfare from the second siege of Vienna in 1683 until the early nineteenth century. Strikingly, she argues that Ottoman soldiers were actually better fed and provided for than their Russian or Habsburg contemporaries and thus chips away at still-lingering notions of Ottoman decline. The study offers a helpful comparative perspective and nicely contextualizes the Ottoman experience. Hanioğlu[37] examines the final Ottoman century and presents many useful insights into both political and socio-cultural history; however, the absence of most of the scholarship written during the past 20 years and his insistence on an outdated centre-periphery dichotomy, mars his analysis.

The final work under review here, by Karen Barkey,[38] shares with Finkel a very broad view – that of the entire empire over time. Barkey focuses on the vital question – how to explain the incredible durability of an empire that reached from the late medieval era to that just out of living memory. Her emphasis on flexibility and adaptability are well-taken and quite helpful, and she argues for toleration as the key to Ottoman success and longevity. Less helpful is the confusion surrounding her discussion of why the empire disappeared after the First World War. Basically, she seems to blame the Europeans and Ottoman subjects. She argues that, unlike during the era of toleration, latter-day Ottoman subjects related to one another directly, instead of through the state as they once had. Precisely at the moment of direct subject interactions, Barkey seems to argue, intolerance began.

The above surveys treating the late Ottoman era – Finkel, Hanioğlu and Barkey – share one unfortunate characteristic. Namely, they fail to give due emphasis and discussion to the fate of the Armenians in 1915. Whatever their respective individual opinions, the several authors had the responsibility to discuss more fully these wartime events and their context. Their failure to do so is unfortunate for at least two reasons. First, it prevents readers from learning from the views of accomplished Ottomanists. Second, it gives the *appearance* that Ottomanists are still avoiding discussion of an issue that remains important even when ignored.

Conclusion

Both our geographical and subject areas of inquiry have been broadening. An over-emphasis on the Anatolian lands is giving way to a fuller discussion of some of the Arab provinces and an acceptance of Arab provincial history as an essential part of Ottoman history. Moreover, it also seems clear that the Balkan regions finally are beginning to receive some serious attention. The provinces have become important topics of research, a welcome balance to the previous over-stress on the central state. Moreover, much of the work shows the deep inter-penetration of social, economic, and cultural life in the capital and the provinces. Much work remains, for example, in reintegrating Egypt into late Ottoman history – it is clear that despite Muhammad Ali Pasha and his dynasty and the British, Egypt is many respects remained quite Ottoman. Still more desperate is our need for greater attention to the Balkan provinces. The linguistic barriers impeding such research are real but they can be overcome. After all, the use of both Ottoman and Arabic sources has become increasingly commonplace in recent years, and there is evidence for the rising use of Bulgarian, Greek and other languages. Moreover, state-centred studies are beginning to be complemented by those on marginalized groups such as women and workers.[39]

Notes

1 For example, there is a considerable potential around the so-called *istintaknameler* – investigations by officials that often involves a question and answer format with peasants and workers. Look for the ongoing research of Mr Can Nacar on

the tobacco workers in the late Ottoman Empire, PhD in progress, Binghamton University.

2 See my *Coal Miners and the State in the Ottoman Empire: the Zonguldak Coalfield, 1822–1920* (New York, 2006).

3 Doumani, Beshara, *Rediscovering Palestine: Merchants and Peasants in Jabal Nablus, 1700–1900* (Berkeley, 1995). For an account based on the family records of an Istanbul family, see Mataracı, Aliye F., *Trade Letters as Instances of Economy, Ideology and Subjectivity* (Istanbul, 2005).

4 For example: Harlaftis, Gelina, *A History of Greek-owned Shipping: the Making of an International Tramp Fleet, 1830 to the Present* (New York, 1996); Sifneos, Evridiki (ed.), *Soapmaking on Lesvos. A Momento* (Athens, 2002).

5 Langer, William, *Diplomacy of Imperialism, 1890-1902* (New York, 2nd edn, 1951); and, for example, Anderson, M.S., *The Eastern Question 1774–1923* (London, 1966).

6 Roderic Davison was a transitional figure who began in European history and over his career increasingly incorporated Ottoman sources into his work. Examine the source base for his *Reform in the Ottoman Empire, 1856–1876* (Princeton, 1963) and compare with that in the successive articles in his *Essays in Ottoman and Turkish History, 1774–1923. The Impact of the West* (Austin, 1990). Note in particular the increasing use of Turkish and then Ottoman sources.

7 Citino, Nathan J., 'The Ottoman Legacy in Cold War Modernization', *International Journal of Middle East Studies* 40/4 (November 2008), pp. 579–97.

8 For example, Lewis, Bernard, *The Emergence of Modern Turkey* (London, 1961); Niyazi Berkes, *The Development of Secularism in Turkey* (Montreal, 1964).

9 Note again the title of Bernard Lewis' book and contrast with the self-consciously titled *The Making of Modern Turkey*, by Feroz Ahmad (London, 1993). The triumphalist narrative of a linear progression from empire to republic is highlighted in the title of the Lewis book just cited and even more explicitly in: Shaw, Stanford J. and Ezel Kural Shaw, *History of the Ottoman Empire and Modern Turkey*, vol. II: *Reform, Revolution and Republic. The Rise of Modern Turkey, 1808–1975* (Cambridge, 1977).

10 Formerly the Başbakanlık Arsivi, now the Başbakanlık Osmanlı Arşivi.

11 See the *Turcology Annual/Turkologischer Anzeiger*, produced by an international team of bibliographers, published in Vienna. In successive issues, compare the growing number of citations and the ever-larger groupings of sub-categories.

12 Zilfi, Madeline (ed.), *Women in the Ottoman Empire: Middle Eastern Women in the Early Modern Era* (Leiden, 1997).

13 Artan, Tülay, 'Architecture as a Theatre of Life: Profile of the Eighteenth Century Bosphorus', PhD dissertation (Massachusetts Institute of Technology, 1989). Also eadem, 'Aspects of the Ottoman Elite's Food Consumption: Looking for "Staples", "Luxuries", and "Delicacies" in a Changing Century', in Donald Quataert (ed.), *Consumption Studies and the History of the Ottoman Empire, 1550–1922: An Introduction* (Albany, 2000), pp. 107–200.

14 Faroqhi, Suraiya, 'Labor Recruitment and Control in the Ottoman Empire (Sixteenth and Seventeenth Centuries)', in Donald Quataert (ed.), *Manufacturing in the Ottoman Empire and Turkey, 1500–1850* (Albany, 1994), pp. 13–57. See also, Zarinebaf-Shahr, Fariba, 'The Role of Women in the Urban Economy of Istanbul, 1700–1850', in Donald Quataert (ed.), 'Labor History in the Ottoman Middle East, 1700–1922', in *International Labor and Working Class History* (Fall 2001), pp. 141–52.

15 For example, Frierson, Elizabeth, 'Cheap and Easy: The Creation of Consumer Culture in Late Ottoman Society', in Quataert, *Consumption Studies*, pp. 243–60 and, in the same work, Micklewright, Nancy, 'Personal, Public and Political (Re) Constructions: Photographs and Consumption', pp. 261–87.

16 For a fuller discussion of this issue, with sources, see my 'Labor History and the Ottoman Middle East, 1700–1922', in Quataert (ed.), 'Labor History in the Ottoman Middle East, 1700–1922', pp. 93–109.

17 See Citino cited above.

18 Faroqhi, Suraiya, *Approaching Ottoman History. An Introduction to the Sources* (Cambridge, 1999), pp. 82–109.

19 Berktay, Halil and Suraiya Faroqhi (eds), 'New Approaches to State and Peasant in Ottoman History', *Journal of Peasant Studies* (April/July 1991).

20 See Inalcık, Halil with Donald Quataert (eds), *An Economic and Social History of the Ottoman Empire, 1300–1914* (Cambridge, 1994) for a summary of economic historiography.

21 For some recent inroads, see Cronin, Stephanie (ed.), *Subalterns and Social Protest* (London and New York, 2008); and Atabaki, Touraj (ed.), *The State and the Subaltern* (London and New York, 2007).

22 See Mazower, Mark, 'Review Essay: Violence and the State In the Twentieth Century', *American Historical Review* (October 2002), pp. 1158–78; also, Weitz, Eric D., 'From the Vienna to the Paris System: International Politics and the Entangled Histories of Human Rights, Forced Deportations, and Civilizing Missions', *American Historical Review* (December 2008), pp. 1312–43. And see my 'The Massacres of Ottoman Armenians and the Writing of Ottoman History', *Journal of Interdisciplinary History* (Autumn 2006), pp. 249–59.

23 Fahmy, Khaled, *All the Pasha's Men, Mehmed Ali, His Army and the Making of Modern Egypt* (Cambridge, 1998); Chalcraft, John, *The Striking Cabbies of Cairo and other Stories* (Albany, 2004).

24 Some recent and useful overviews of Ottoman history writing include: Woodhead, Christine, 'Consolidating the Empire: New Views on Ottoman History, 1453–1839', *English Historical Review* 123/503 (2008), pp. 973–87; Peirce, Leslie, 'Changing Perceptions of the Ottoman Empire: The Early Centuries', *Mediterranean Historical Review* 19/1 (June 2004), pp. 6–28; Hathaway, Jane, 'Rewriting Eighteenth-Century Ottoman History', *Mediterranean Historical Review* 19/1 (June 2004), pp. 29–53.

25 Makdisi, Ussama, *The Culture of Sectarianism. Community, History and Violence in Nineteenth Century Ottoman Lebanon* (Berkeley, 2000); Rogan, Eugene L., *Frontiers*

of the State in the Late Ottoman Empire. Transjordan, 1850–1921 (Cambridge, 1999); Grehan, James, *Everyday Life and Consumer Culture in 18th Century Damascus* (Seattle, 2007).

26 For these points I am indebted to the Ottoman history seminar, Fall 2002, Binghamton University and especially to Attila Aytekin.

27 The barrier of 1918 has been under assault and broken through earlier by a number of authors; an early example is Batatu, Hanna, *The Old Social Classes and the Revolutionary Movements in Iraq* (Princeton, 1978). More recently, see Gelvin, James, *Divided Loyalties: Nationalism and Mass Politics at the Close of Empire* (Berkeley, 1999).

28 Mansel, Philip, *Constantinople. City of the World's Desire, 1453–1924* (London, 1995 and New York, 1996).

29 Karsh, Efraim and Inari Karsh, *Empires of the Sand. The Struggle for Mastery in the Middle East, 1789-1923* (Cambridge, 1999).

30 Fromkin, David, *A Peace to End All Peace. The Fall of the Ottoman Empire and the Creation of the Modern Middle East* (New York, 1989).

31 This assertion is emphasized by its placement on the back cover of the book's dust jacket and so must be seen as the authors' own assessment of their contribution. See also Karsh, *Empires of the Sand*, p. 2.

32 Except for a smattering of Arabic and Turkish secondary sources, indigenous-language sources are absent from the book.

33 As Ottoman specialists are fully aware, the Ottoman perspective, and to a lesser extent that of the local Arab elite, has been available in Istanbul, in the Prime Ministry Archives, for many years. To the best of my knowledge, the first published catalogue of Ottoman archival holdings appeared in 1955 and consisted of 90 pages of archival inventory and commentary. A far more complete catalogue followed in 1979, comprising 171 pages of catalogue entries and other archival data. As the classifying and organizing of the archives continued, the catalogue grew accordingly and reached 634 pages in the 1992 edition. These catalogues are readily available and make clear the abundance of material available to scholars doing research on topics relating to Ottoman history. For the most recent editions, see *Başbakanlık Osmanlı Arşivi Katalogları Rehberi* (Ankara, 1995) and idem, *Başbakanlık Osmanlı Arşivi Rehberi* (Ankara, 2000).

34 Finkel, Caroline, *Osman's Dream: the Story of the Ottoman Empire, 1300–1923* (New York, 2005).

35 Faroqhi, Suraiya, *The Ottoman Empire and the World Around It* (London and New York, 2004).

36 Aksan, Virginia, *Ottoman Wars: An Empire Besieged* (London, 2007).

37 Hanioğlu, M. Şükrü, *A Brief History of the Late Ottoman Empire* (Princeton, 2008).

38 Barkey, Karen, *Empire of Difference: The Ottomans in Comparative Perspective* (New York, 2008).

39 The Fall 2002 H-Turk discussion on the state of Ottoman studies, has been productive. See, for example, Ehud Toledano's communication dated November 4, 2002.

Bibliography

Ahmad, Feroz, *The Making of Modern Turkey* (London, Routledge, 1993).

Aksan, Virginia, *Ottoman Wars: An Empire Besieged* (London, Longman, 2007).

Anderson, M.S., *The Eastern Question 1774–1923* (London, Macmillan, 1966).

Artan, Tülay, 'Architecture as a Theatre of Life: Profile of the Eighteenth Century Bosphorus', PhD dissertation (Massachusetts Institute of Technology, 1989).

—, 'Aspects of the Ottoman Elite's Food Consumption: Looking for "Staples", "Luxuries", and "Delicacies" in a Changing Century', in Donald Quataert (ed.), *Consumption Studies and the History of the Ottoman Empire, 1550–1922: An Introduction* (Albany, State University of New York Press, 2000), pp. 107–200.

Atabaki, Touraj (ed.), *The State and the Subaltern* (London and New York, I.B. Tauris, 2007).

Barkey, Karen, *Empire of Difference: The Ottomans in Comparative Perspective* (New York, Cambridge University Press, 2008).

Batatu, Hanna, *The Old Social Classes and the Revolutionary Movements in Iraq* (Princeton, Princeton University Press, 1978).

Berkes, Niyazi, *The Development of Secularism in Turkey* (Montreal, McGill University Press, 1964).

Berktay, Halil and Suraiya Faroqhi (eds), 'New Approaches to State and Peasant in Ottoman History', *Journal of Peasant Studies* (April/July 1991).

Chalcraft, John, *The Striking Cabbies of Cairo and other Stories* (Albany, State University of New York Press, 2004).

Citino, Nathan J., 'The Ottoman Legacy in Cold War Modernization', *International Journal of Middle East Studies* 40/4 (November 2008), pp. 579–97.

Cronin, Stephanie (ed.), *Subalterns and Social Protest* (London and New York, Routledge, 2008).

Davison, Roderic, *Reform in the Ottoman Empire, 1856–1876* (Princeton, Princeton University Press, 1963).

—, *Essays in Ottoman and Turkish History, 1774–1923. The Impact of the West* (Austin, Texas University Press, 1990).

Doumani, Beshara, *Rediscovering Palestine: Merchants and Peasants in Jabal Nablus, 1700–1900* (Berkeley, University of California Press, 1995).

Fahmy, Khaled, *All the Pasha's Men, Mehmed Ali, His Army and the Making of Modern Egypt* (Cambridge, Cambridge University Press, 1998).

Faroqhi, Suraiya, 'Labor Recruitment and Control in the Ottoman Empire (Sixteenth and Seventeenth Centuries', in Donald Quataert (ed.), *Manufacturing in the Ottoman Empire and Turkey, 1500–1850* (Albany, State University of New York Press, 1994), pp. 13–57.

—, *Approaching Ottoman History. An Introduction to the Sources* (Cambridge, Cambridge University Press, 1999).

—, *The Ottoman Empire and the World Around It* (London, I.B. Tauris, 2004).

Finkel, Caroline, *Osman's Dream: The Story of the Ottoman Empire, 1300–1923* (New York, John Murray, 2005).

Frierson, Elizabeth, 'Cheap and Easy: The Creation of Consumer Culture in Late Ottoman Society', in Donald Quataert (ed.), *Consumption Studies and the History of the Ottoman Empire, 1550–1922: An Introduction* (Albany, State University of New York Press, 2000), pp. 243–60.

Fromkin, David, *A Peace to End All Peace. The Fall of the Ottoman Empire and the Creation of the Modern Middle East* (New York, Henry Holt and Co., 1989).

Gelvin, James, *Divided Loyalties: Nationalism and Mass Politics at the Close of Empire* (Berkeley, University of California Press, 1999).

Grehan, James, *Everyday Life and Consumer Culture in 18th century Damascus* (Seattle, University of Washington Press, 2007).

Hanioğlu, M. Şükrü, *A Brief History of the Late Ottoman Empire* (Princeton, Princeton University Press, 2008).

Harlaftis, Gelina, *A History of Greek-owned Shipping: The Making of an International Tramp Fleet, 1830 to the Present* (London and New York, Routledge, 1996).

Hathaway, Jane, 'Rewriting Eighteenth-Century Ottoman History', *Mediterranean Historical Review* 19/1 (June 2004), pp. 29–53.

Inalcık, Halil with Donald Quataert (eds), *An Economic and Social History of the Ottoman Empire, 1300–1914* (Cambridge, Cambridge University Press, 1994).

Karsh, Efraim and Inari Karsh, *Empires of the Sand. The Struggle for Mastery in the Middle East, 1789–1923* (Cambridge, Cambridge University Press, 1999).

Langer, William, *Diplomacy of Imperialism, 1890–1902* (New York, Knopf, 2nd edn, 1951).

Lewis, Bernard, *The Emergence of Modern Turkey* (London, Oxford University Press, 1961).

Makdisi, Ussama, *The Culture of Sectarianism. Community, History and Violence in Nineteenth Century Ottoman Lebanon* (Berkeley, University of California Press, 2000).

Mansel, Philip, *Constantinople. City of the World's Desire, 1453–1924* (London, 1995 and New York, John Murray, 1996).

Mataracı, Aliye F., *Trade Letters as Instances of Economy, Ideology and Subjectivity* (Istanbul, Ottoman Bank Archives and Research Centre, 2005).

Mazower, Mark, 'Review Essay: Violence and the State In the Twentieth Century', *American Historical Review* (October 2002), pp. 1158–78.

Micklewright, Nancy, 'Personal, Public and Political (Re)Constructions: Photographs and Consumption', in Donald Quataert (ed.), *Consumption Studies and the History of the Ottoman Empire, 1550–1922: An Introduction* (Albany, State University of New York, 2000), pp. 261–87.

Peirce, Leslie, 'Changing Perceptions of the Ottoman Empire: The Early Centuries', *Mediterranean Historical Review* 19/1 (June 2004), pp. 6-28.

Quataert, Donald, 'Labor History and the Ottoman Middle East, 1700-1922', in Donald Quataert (ed.), 'Labor History in the Ottoman Middle East, 1700–1922', in *International Labor and Working Class History* (Fall 2001), pp. 93–109.

—, 'The Massacres of Ottoman Armenians and the Writing of Ottoman History', *Journal of Interdisciplinary History* (Autumn 2006), pp. 249–59.

—, *Coal Miners and the State in the Ottoman Empire: the Zonguldak Coalfield, 1822–1920* (New York, Berghahn, 2006).

Rogan, Eugene L., *Frontiers of the State in the Late Ottoman Empire. Transjordan, 1850–1921* (Cambridge, Cambridge University Press, 1999).

Shaw, Stanford J. and Ezel Kural Shaw, *History of the Ottoman Empire and Modern Turkey*, vol. II: *Reform, Revolution and Republic. The Rise of Modern Turkey, 1808–1975* (Cambridge, Cambridge University Press, 1977).

Sifneos, Evridiki (ed.), *Soapmaking on Lesvos. A Memento* (Athens, 2002).

Weitz, Eric D., 'From the Vienna to the Paris System: International Politics and the Entangled Histories of Human Rights, Forced Deportations, and Civilizing Missions', *American Historical Review* (December 2008), pp. 1312–43.

Woodhead, Christine, 'Consolidating the Empire: New Views on Ottoman History, 1453–1839', *English Historical Review* 123/503 (2008), pp. 973–87.

Zarinebaf-Shahr, Fariba, 'The Role of Women in the Urban Economy of Istanbul, 1700–1850', in Donald Quataert (ed.), 'Labor History in the Ottoman Middle East, 1700–1922', in *International Labor and Working Class History* (Fall 2001), pp. 141–52.

Zilfi, Madeline (ed.), *Women in the Ottoman Empire: Middle Eastern Women in the Early Modern Era* (Leiden, Brill, 1997).

12

On the Study of Diasporas

Ina Baghdiantz McCabe

'This is indeed India! The land of dreams and romance ... of tigers and elephants ...The country of a hundred nations and a hundred tongues. Cradle of the human race, birthplace of human speech, mother of history, grandmother of legends, great grandmother of tradition.' The words are Mark Twain's, used in a 1991 advertisement. A Hindu sect with headquarters in Queens New York, the BAP, had sponsored the 35-million dollar cultural festival and chosen a great American writer, Mark Twain, to represent India in their *New York Times* ad. So begins Sandya Shukla's book *India Abroad: Diasporic Cultures of Postwar America and England.*[1] In turn, I begin this article, a short overview of the study of diaspora by academics, by pointing out that in its most common usage the term diaspora is not an academic one. 'Diaspora' has now become a self-referential term for many groups. There is, however, a difference between an ethnic group abroad and a diaspora. That difference has been pointed out by a number of scholars across the globe, whose work on defining diasporas has in turn defined the field of diaspora studies.

In 1976, the American political scientist, John Armstrong, proposed a typology of 'diasporas', but it was only in 1986, with Gabriel Sheffer's book *Modern Diasporas in International Politics*, published in Israel, that a comparative approach seeking a contemporary definition emerged.[2] The book compared Jews, Armenians, Turks, Palestinians, Chinese and Indians, and many other groups, to reach a definition of the term diaspora in the social sciences. The BAP discussed above, would fall under John Armstrong's earliest definition: 'Any ethnic collectivity that lacks a territorial base with a given polity, i.e., a relatively small community throughout all portions of the community'. The Armstrong definition would include the gypsies, as it did not implicate any concept of return to or memory of the land of origin. Ten years later, Sheffer tightened the definition of the word diaspora and excluded nomadism, by putting two *sine qua non* conditions: a link to a homeland and a hope for return to the land of origin, be it an imaginary one.[3] As will be discussed below, Sheffer's definition was wider than what had been accepted initially. The three classical diasporas were, until then, the Jews, the Armenians and the Greeks.

French scholars also played a pioneering role in the new emerging field of diaspora studies in the 1970s. In France, the first journal in the field, *Les cahiers de diaspora*, was launched in 1979, and several prominent scholars work on diasporas. Geographers Michel Bruneau and George Prévélakis focus on the Greeks; geographer Emmanuel Ma Mung and historian Pierre Trolliet, as well as sociologist Live Yu Sion, on the Chinese; anthropologist Martine Hovanessian and historians Claire Mouradian and Anahide Ter Minassian on the Armenians; Christine Chevallon on the West Indians and the 'black diaspora'.[4] Apart from the scholars in the USA, Israel and France, mentioned above, scholars in Armenia, Australia, Belgium, Canada, England, Greece and Sweden have been working on diasporas. In a short article, such as this, is not possible to follow precisely the development of the field, which is, in any case, accomplished in Stéphane Dufoix's upcoming *Habilitation* thesis in France. Here, in the space allotted, I simply hope to cover a few major turning points. The issue of self-representation remains critical and beyond the field of scholarship. Khachig Tölöyan puts it well when he asks, 'Who represents diaspora – the community or scholars?', aware that both are an act of representation. He relies on Althusser and Machery to point out that the diasporic social domain exists only when there is emic self-representation by a community. A field of study would not exist without this self-representation. Representation takes a different shape when diasporas become an object of academic knowledge, as in the discourse produced by academics participating in diaspora studies.[5] It should be noted first, before we continue on the thorny terrain of definitions, that many, but certainly not all, scholars engaged in the field, who justly claim etic knowledge of the subject through their academic expertise, are more often than not part of the group they study and have emic knowledge of it too. These scholars have a broad theoretical interest in a growing field that goes well beyond the groups they may belong to by birth. Rey Chow may write about the Chinese, Khachig Tölöyan about the Armenians, but both have theoretical writings that transcend the study of a specific diaspora. The work of many scholars in different countries and within different disciplines has contributed to what most scholars define today as a diaspora. The 1990s mark a peak in the production of works on diasporas.

In North America, in 1991, Tölöyan founded the pioneering journal in the field in English: *Diaspora: A Journal of Transnational Studies*. The new journal was instrumental in acknowledging a new phenomenon, the wider use of the term diaspora in the 1990s, when one could read about Indians, Iranians, Russians, Lebanese, Nigerians and other groups living abroad, described as a diaspora in the media. The wider use of the term reflected a contemporary reality, when many groups were subject to displacement because of war, revolution, famine or labour issues. Was this displacement to be viewed as forcible or as voluntary migration? The issue of forcible scattering and displacement, implied by the biblical term diaspora, became an issue of controversy. Two seminal articles in the journal defined the term even more closely than Sheffer, the first was by William Safran,[6] the second by Tölöyan himself.[7] In this new wider definition, the term diaspora was used in the 1990s for any displaced group with a memory of its land of origin, a perceived cultural difference with its host country and a longing for return, be it an imaginary one. The definition stayed close to Sheffer's but avoided the biblical implication of forcible scattering. Yet, in the 1990s its looser usage in the media eroded the meaning of the term further It created confusion between ethnic groups and diasporas.

The difference between an ethnic group in a host country and a diaspora remains critical. The theoretical aspects of what ethnicity is in discourse have been best explored by a specialist in the Chinese diaspora, Rey Chow, in *The Protestant Ethnic and the Spirit of Capitalism*.[8] Chow, like many others, has been influenced by Etienne Balibar and Immanuel Wallerstein and their work on ambiguous identities.[9] The study of diasporas entered the strong trend for studying identities, which prevailed in American academia in the 1980s and 1990s. The study of race and gender became all-important in the social sciences and the humanities. There was also a strong trend for area studies and cultural studies. Diaspora studies straddled all of these established academic fields without having one of their own. As opposed to many of my colleagues in this book, who write about established historical fields, with traditional fields and chronologies, the study of diaspora not only transcends national boundaries, it transcends disciplines and often defies accepted chronologies. It is worth looking at the first fields that mark the inception of diaspora studies, before the work of Armstrong and Sheffer.

The study of diaspora commenced in the well-established field of Biblical and Jewish studies but has gone far beyond it. One can call some of the most famous pioneers in the field 'the three Cohens', because one constantly sees apologies in articles saying this article was cited as Joseph Cohen's, whereas it really belongs to Robin Cohen,[10] or you have the same errata all over footnotes with the third name, Abner Cohen, who in 1971, at a conference in Paris on merchant networks, objected to the over-use of the term diaspora for merchants abroad and argued for the term merchant networks rather than merchant diasporas. Historians have participated rather infrequently in the multidisciplinary (or interdisciplinary) field of diaspora studies, which has grown so rapidly since the 1990s. They work on merchant diasporas. Yet, some eminent historians, such as Jonathan Israel, have long argued that most existing historiography has an inherent bias towards emphasizing national achievement and has long tended to play down the positive contributions of ethnic and religious minorities of all sorts.[11] Diasporas – scattered peoples dispersed from their original homeland but not entirely cut off from it, and who then remain sharply and self-consciously different from their host societies, but united among themselves by strong ties of culture, religion, language and ethnicity – often have an elite that is a merchant elite. These elites, among them merchant 'princes', on whose wealth the community depends, were long invisible to historians, whose field was formed in the national mould dictated by the nation-state. They have undoubtedly played a major and remarkable role in many areas of social, cultural, intellectual and economic history. Most historians work on these elites, merchant diasporas, and not on diasporas.

Before the 1970s, the term diaspora had been much narrower and referred to three groups alone: the Jews, the Greeks and the Armenians. It is of some importance to retrace how these groups became labelled as classical diaspora. As mentioned above, biblical studies were at the inception of diaspora studies. Robin Cohen has argued, that the Old Testament word diaspora carried the message that the 'scattering to other lands' constituted punishment for breaking with tradition.[12] Soon, with approximately the same meaning but in a different context, it was applied to two more groups, the three classical diasporas being the Jewish, the Armenian and the Greek. The intensity of international migration, the phenomenon of globalization and the imminent demise of the nation-state have been crucial to the creation of the current debate about diaspora. The editor of *Diaspora* wrote, as he inaugurated the journal, that the term could now be extended to over twenty-eight groups. In its wider definition, studying diaspora became of interest to scholars of migration, transnationalism, cosmopolitanism and globalization. Today, the term is used for some 30 different groups.[13] The notion of diaspora, coined and first used many centuries ago for a specific group, the Jews, suddenly acquired great importance in the closing decades of the twentieth century, because of globalization, and it has become of interest to historians, anthropologists and sociologists.[14]

Prominent among those defining the field were Robin Cohen and Steve Vertovec, who ran a centre for the study of Migration, Diasporas and Transnationalism in England, in the 1990s.[15] The classical diasporas, as they were called, had been the object of study for some time and the extension of the term to so many groups did not go unnoticed, generating a debate with scholars who were proponents of the more classical definition.[16] Stéphane Dufoix has written the most sophisticated and accessible introduction to the concept of diaspora to date.[17] He is preparing a more detailed work on the usage of the term diaspora since the third century BC. If debates about the definition of the term are very recent, the term is very old. The term 'diaspora', first found in the Greek translation of the Bible, was initially reserved exclusively for one group, the Jews. It implied a forcible scattering, as it is described in the Old Testament, in Deuteronomy (28:25). It is fitting, therefore, that the pioneers in the field, if one can speak of a field, because there is certainly not a unified one, were devoted to the study of the Jewish Diaspora. Yet, it is a sociologist and not a historian, Robin Cohen, who attempted to situate diaspora within global history: he writes in his work *In Global Diasporas*:

> By the end of the twentieth century it is likely that the membership of the United Nations will comprise 200 states. However, the number of 'nations-peoples' (groups evincing a 'peoplehood' through the retention or expression of separate languages, customs, folkways and religion) is estimated at 2,000, ten times the number of recognized nation-states. Such peoples are only imperfectly, and sometimes violently held within the confines of the nation-state – as the multiplicity of secessionist movements, civil wars and the fragmentation of the Soviet Union and several of its allies testify.[18]

The demise of the Soviet Union, in the late 1980s, and the independencies of smaller states, such as Latvia or Armenia, in 1991, can be considered pivotal events. The journal *Diaspora* was launched in 1991. Tölöyan, as its editor, was well aware of its topical impact, as he wrote in the first volume that the world had entered a 'transnational moment'. It is paradoxical to note that this was during a year when many small groups acquired statehood by leaving the Soviet Union. The perennial phenomenon of parochial 'diaspora nationalism' was on the rise, a topic that is also of great interest to Tölöyan. There are different approaches. In his book on global diaspora, Robin Cohen adopts Sheffer's definition of diasporas, to theorize on global displacement, and any group maintaining a real or imagined tie to their homeland qualifies. He also defined new categories: the Armenians and the Africans are classed as victim diasporas, the English and the Indians are respectively labour and imperial diasporas, the Chinese and the Lebanese are trade diasporas, and so on. For Robin Cohen, the only classical diaspora remains the Jews. In 1994, James Clifford wrote that the Jewish, Greek and Armenian diasporas were a starting point for a discourse about more global travelling,[19] yet the Greeks are absent from his classification. Clearly, even after there was general acceptance of the three classical diasporas, not everyone held the same views. How did the Greeks and Armenians achieve their status as a classical diasporas? Both groups have known forcible scattering because of invasion and massacre several times in their history, not just once. In this respect they share a fate in part similar to that of the Jews, but this similarity does not seem to have been the defining issue.

For the Greeks, Michel Bruneau traces the first reference to the Greeks as a diaspora to a dictionary of Modern Greek (1659) that describes Greek presence through the world as one, and to Iosipos Moesiodax's *Moral Philosophy*, published in Venice in 1761, where one can read about ' all the diasporas of the Greeks'.[20] This is an emic self-definition within Greek literature. Stephane Dufoix argues that, until the 1950s, the term diaspora in scholarship had no other possible meaning except religious. He also clearly dates scholars' inclusion of the Greeks and Armenians in the classical diasporas to an American encyclopaedia article.[21] In the 1931 edition of the *American Encyclopedia of the Social Sciences*, historian Simon Dubnov, author of the entry 'Diaspora', defines it as follows:

> Diaspora is Greek term for nation or part of a nation separated from its own state or territory and dispersed among other nations but preserving its national culture. In a sense, *Magna Graecia* constituted a Greek diaspora in the ancient Roman Empire, and a typical case of diaspora is presented by the Armenians, many of whom have voluntarily lived outside their small national territory for centuries. Generally, however the term is used with reference to those parts of the Jewish people residing outside Palestine.[22]

To make the study of diasporas even more complicated, some groups feel territorial (no pun intended) about the term diaspora itself. This is true not only for the Jews, for whom the term was coined, but also for the African Americans. In the United States, when one uses the term diaspora it invokes none of the three classical diasporas, neither the Jews nor the Greeks nor the Armenians, but the African Americans displaced by the brutality of slavery. The emergence of the term Black diaspora is dated to the nineteenth century, in the writings of W.E. Dubois and Edward Blyden, who used the biblical episode of the Exodus to draw a parallel with the Jewish experience of forced displacement. This time, the similarity with the Jewish experience was an emic part of the self-definition. Furthermore, the idea of return to the homeland, so central to the concept of diaspora, had been espoused earlier by formal programmes: the British Government supported settlers from the USA and Britain in Sierra Leone as early as 1787. Edward Blyden 'returned' to Africa through an 1820 programme for the return of slaves, which led to the creation of Liberia, in 1850.[23]

The term Black/African diaspora emerges in American academia within the context of African American studies. At a conference at Yale, in 1969, the president of the Ford Foundation announced a policy of grants for the institutionalization of Black Studies, as they were then called. This was in the hope of integrating the demands of Black activists, who were set on challenging all-white academic institutions and their teachings. The first department for Black Studies was created in San Franciso, after a student strike. The Ford Foundation funding was transformative and effective: whereas there was only one programme in 1968, within four years, by 1972, there were 500.[24] The term African/Black diaspora emerged within African-American Studies in the 1980s.[25] One of the oldest centres for the study of the African/Black diaspora is the John L. Warfield Center for African and African American Studies at the University of Texas at Austin. Many centres combined the study of Africa with the African/Black diaspora. There are such centres in many universities, the Dubois Institute at Harvard being the most famous.

Merchant diaspora or networks

It is from African Studies that one of the most novel ways of studying diasporas emerged. In the late 1960s, the concept of the trading or commercial diaspora emerged among historians of Africa, notably Ivor Wilks, Abner Cohen and, later, Paul Lovejoy and Philip Curtin.[26] The Africanist Abner Cohen is the historian who coined the term merchant networks, as opposed to merchant diasporas, in 1971. It is specifically in the field of merchant diasporas that you will find historians working. Most of them are economic historians. The largest body of work has been produced on Jewish merchants and on the Indian merchant diaspora. The Greek maritime diaspora has been the object of some research in the past and is now being studied by Gelina Harlaftis and a team of nearly 20 researchers.

Gelina Harlaftis and I recently co-edited a first book of comparative studies on merchant/diaspora networks. Some of the initial common perspectives we share on merchant/diaspora networks can be found in our foreword, which we co-wrote in summer 2003. The book examines organized groups of merchant families and their extended regional networks of the same ethnic origin, whether Arabs, Armenians, Chinese, Greeks, Jews, Japanese, Maltese, Parsis, Scots or west-coast Indians. Within some groups we study regional sub-groups with organized networks, such as the Julfan Armenians, Bahgdadi Jews, Hadhrami Arabs. The merchant/diaspora networks of the three classical diasporas, the Jews, the Greeks and the Armenians, occupy a large part of the discussion. Among the groups examined, only the Sephardic Jews had any Atlantic trade. For the Arabs, the Baghdadi Jews, the Chinese, the Gujaratis, the Parsis and the Scots, in the Indian Ocean, it was the Muslim-Hindu-Chinese divide that was a main axis of activity. These 'trans-territorial', 'trans-ocean', 'trans-cultural', 'transnational', 'international', or 'multinational' networks conducted business beyond national and imperial boundaries, maintained an unfettered flow of information and communication that sustained a permanent competitive advantage for the service sector.[27]

Contrary to many a current belief, the integration of the world economy, the so-called globalization of modern economic life, does not owe its present character solely to the actions (and omissions) of the colonialism and imperialism of prominent Western or Eastern powers. Trade diasporas have played a major role in the process of globalization. If they have been noticed, their role has often been misunderstood. These trade diasporas, which lived in the Ottoman, Safavid, Indian and Chinese empires, and were involved with trade within the Western maritime empires, such as the Portuguese, the Spanish, the Dutch and the British, have sometimes been described erroneously as brokers of the West, as a service bourgeoisie, or as *compradors*. Or, on the contrary, it is often assumed that diaspora networks are a service bourgeoisie in their host societies, and therefore the competitors or the rivals of Western entrepreneurial or trading networks.[28]

The significant political role of merchant diasporas, as elites participating in empire- and state-building in the Muslim world, has often been minimized. Many contributors to the aforesaid book show the clear participation of several ethnic trade diasporas in national trading networks, including companies, such as the Sephardic Jews in the Dutch East Company (VOC), and the Armenians in the French East Indian Company. In order to build their own commercial empires, ethnic trade diasporas excelled at being on good terms with everybody. They were not merely cross-cultural brokers, they were building considerable political and economic spheres of influence for their own interests. The second period examined in the said book, the nineteenth and twentieth centuries, brings to the forefront the question of the participation of trade diasporas in the formation of nation-states and the importance of Western capitalism. The nineteenth century is the age of industrialization, technological achievements and quicker communications. Moreover, the multinational activities of trade diasporas in Eurasian trade in the nineteenth century retained characteristics of the early modern period, integrating the old with the new, adapting to the modern economic reality.[29]

To some extent, diaspora entrepreneurship and international networks preceded this Western European economic expansion. It appears that during the colonial and imperial expansion of Europe, in the nineteenth and the first half of the twentieth century, trade diasporas continued to play an important role in the services sector, namely trade, shipping and finance. The ethnic groups that interplayed between East and West became part of state building in European nations. For example, the Greek trade diaspora, dispersed from Odessa to Trieste, Amsterdam and London, was to be a fundamental element in the formation of the Greek State in 1830, as Gelina Harlaftis argues in her article. The contributors to the collective volume on diaspora entrepreneurial networks argue against traditional interpretations, certainly against Weber's view that diasporas are pariah communities, and attempt a comparative approach to a range of diasporas, including the Jewish, Arab, Chinese, Japanese, Indian, Maltese, Greek and Armenian diaspora networks.[30]

The issue of definition is also at the core of scholarship on diaspora networks. Philip Curtin argued for a clear dichotomy between host societies and outside trading groups: 'The traders were specialists in a single kind of economic enterprise, whereas the host society was a whole society, with many occupations, class stratification and political divisions between the rulers and the ruled'.[31] Curtin, who initiated the debate, makes clear in other passages that he saw trade diasporas as totally exempt from political participation in their host societies.[32] He uses the term trade network and trade diaspora interchangeably, and argues that these groups were only cross-cultural brokers, helping to encourage trade between the host society and their own. Based on the secondary scholarship available to him, Curtin has argued that the Armenian trading diaspora was a self-contained and self-regulating body, a commercial organization divorced from political participation in state formation.[33] The Julfan Armenians have served as his model. Sanjay Subrahmanyam follows this pattern for the Armenians; because of the secondary literature in English, the Julfan Armenians are seen as a service bourgeoisie even in his innovative study on the contribution of the Iranian merchant diaspora, a displaced elite, to early state formation in Golconda, the Deccan and Thailand. Although he finds them participating in state formation, Sanjay Subrahmanyam uses the Armenian case as a classical diaspora to conclude that he cannot make a model of what he finds for Iranian merchant networks abroad:

> … that this does not mean either that the 'Iranian model' can be used as paradigmatic, or that it is one that does away entirely with the concept of diaspora community. Clearly the functioning of the Armenian community--significantly also the one chosen by Curtin to illustrate his theory--does correspond far more closely to the self regulated body, largely divorced from the world of politics ….[34]

Subrahmanyam observes that an Asian trade diaspora, specifically the Iranians, participated politically and not simply financially in state building in their host societies. In my own findings on the Armenians of Julfa, there are at least two cases of clear political participation in state building. These findings demand an amendment of the definition of trade diasporas, as they stood in Curtin's work in 1984. The nation-state, once the ubiquitous model for historical thought, has masked many elements, perhaps not least the contribution of diasporas or outsiders to state formation.[35] I point specifically to the participation of groups labelled as outsiders, such as the Huguenots in seventeenth-century France, or as foreigners, such as the Armenians in Iran, in state formation during Early Modern times. Today, there is much preoccupation with globalization, global history, the 'new ' global history, yet, ironically, most of these early modern global networks remain to be studied, let alone integrated into general books on global history.

Philip Curtin is also a pioneer in a second problem. In his discussion of trade networks, in 1984, he includes the European militarized diaspora within the same category as the Armenians, the Banians and the Fukein Chinese. This remains a contentious issue, as the term diaspora has rarely been applied to Europeans abroad.

Diaspora and diaspora merchant networks

Most merchant diasporas, such as the Greeks and the Armenians, survived abroad as a different group from their host country, through their specific and distinct culture. Some remained stateless for centuries, as is true of the Jews, the Greeks and the Armenians, but managed to keep their language and culture alive without a state. Their cultural institutions depended on the wealth and success of their own merchant networks, which financed both cultural and religious institutions. Studying history beyond the state has not always been evident. Yet, book production and lay scholarship, such as geographies, were sponsored by merchants. Additionally, through diasporization, many books were printed for the first time, such as a 1666 Bible printed in Amsterdam, on an Armenian printing press in the Dutch Republic. Merchant money and their contacts in Europe financed Armenian printing presses in Europe, while most of the diasporas were still living in Asia.[36] The merchant diaries and archival material left by Armenians engaged in commerce are not the high literature that other periods of Armenian history have produced, but secular documents, some of them humble messy accounts in a code near impossible to decipher. These documents were scattered by a global network, and one could find things in a myriad of languages, from London to Shanghai and from Calcutta to Riga. It would take hundreds of scholars to reconstitute the real history of this Armenian merchant network, or many of the networks formed by Jewish and Greek or Chinese merchants, for that matter. Clearly, the history of diasporas could not have been possible within the old school of history, which prized State and Church documents alone. Studying diaspora became possible only with the trend in socio-economic history, which commenced in France, several decades ago and made the lives of merchants and peasants and shopkeepers a legitimate field of study. Nevertheless, within the study of diaspora, it is, more often than not, the elites that are studied and not the common people, because it is often the elite that involves itself in cultural production and the wealthier merchants who leave records.

As in the case of the Armenians, discussed above, most diasporas depend on funding from the wealthy merchants among them, their 'merchant princes', who in one way or another become rulers within the group. These are the most visible elements within diasporas, as they often engage in international trade. Within their diasporas, there is often an internal system of taxation, via the church, temple or mosque. The wealth of merchant princes supports a distinct religion or culture, within a larger and often hegemonic imperial or national culture. Therefore, the distinct culture that separates a diaspora from its host country is impossible without merchant wealth. Successful merchant activity is, in turn, based, among other things, on solidarity within a community, which is cemented by cultural communality. This solidarity it often both class-based and centred on provenance from a small town of origin for the Armenians and the Greeks. The larger donors being the merchants, it would be a mistake to divorce merchant diasporas as such from the larger diasporas *per se*. It would be perhaps best to look at merchant diasporas as the most active multi-local diasporic members of a diaspora.[37] They are often actively engaged both in their host country and elsewhere, not only in commerce but also in supporting the survival of their own distinct culture.[38] Although these two groups are seen as distinct, as the merchants are the exclusive domain of historians, they are in fact interdependent and would not exist otherwise.

Here I cannot resist paying homage to Fernand Braudel, who, half a century ago, highlighted the importance of Jewish and Armenian networks in the Mediterranean, by quoting a Huguenot merchant's comments on the importance of the competition between the Armenians and the Jews in the seventeenth century. A paragraph in Braudel's work, lifted from Jean-Baptiste Tavernier, inspired my own work on the Armenian silk trade. The famous Huguenot jeweller is best remembered for pulling the Hope diamond out of an Indian idol and making possible Louis XIV's diamond collection. In the gem trade, the Huguenot diaspora had their ties with the Armenians. Many trade diasporas collaborate or compete at different points, a chapter of history that still remains to be explored, as, just as with diasporas, trading diasporas have been studied on a national model, one by one. After Sheffer's pioneering volume in 1986, there have been several comparative works. Among others, Francesca Trivellato has done some comparative work on competition in the making of the gem trade. For competition between the Greek and Jewish networks, there is an article by Evridiki Sifneos, 'The Dark Side of the Moon', which highlights how competition for the grain trade and housing led to a nineteenth-century pogrom of the Odessa Jews, in which the Greek merchants of the city participated.[39] For the Armenians and the Greeks, a comparative conference was held at the Ecole Française d'Athènes, in 2001, and the papers were published.[40]

Historians have tried their hand at so many things since Braudel wrote about the Mediterranean in 1947. So much fashion has come and gone, the *Annales* School created by Braudel and his followers, the *histoire des mentalités*, histories of daily life, psycho-history, cultural relativism, the theoretical schools of feminism, postmodernism, chaos theory, micro-history, global history, 'total history', 'new historicism', the history of material culture, historical ecology, the history of landscape, cultural then transcultural history. All have contributed in some way to the study of diaspora History has been a very innovative and exciting field to work in. The study of diaspora merchant networks makes use of the tried and true methods of the *Annales* School, coupled with the aspirations of global history; it stays firmly grounded in historiography and historical methods when it is approached by historians. Not so when it comes to the study of diaspora proper. This is a multidisciplinary field, often called an interdisciplinary one, where there are sociologists and anthropologists and cultural theorists and professors of English; it is rich in theoretical concepts. Is there actually an academic field called Diaspora Studies?

Diaspora studies?

Diaspora Studies were non-existent as an academic programme in institutions until very recently. Happily, I can no longer argue that the field does not exist in its own right. There is now, as I write, a unique centre, the Centre for Diaspora and Transnational Studies, at the University of Toronto. It is directed by Ato Quayson, Professor of English, who previously directed the African American Studies Centre in the same institution. If Black/African American Studies in the USA were propelled by political forces and tense race relations that led to serious funding by the Ford Foundation in the late 1960s, if area studies in general have had government funding behind them since the 1970s, as well as a political *raison d'être*, as is the case for Middle Eastern Studies, Diaspora Studies are not backed by any specific groups or governments, making their funding a larger issue. Yet, the study of networks and diaspora networks might be of political interest today.

New funding was devoted to understanding virtual global diasporas, at the Nautilus Institute in 2002, in the wake of 9/11:

> Today information communication technologies bind transnational diaspora communities with their homeland, facilitate new and efficient economic networks in both the host and home countries, and increase identity and belonging to a greater transnational community. Yet other observers contend that virtual diaspora networks are an emerging source of global conflict, as they facilitate transnational terrorist and criminal activity, finance wars in 'home states', and, most importantly, cultivate divisive and fragmenting nationalism throughout the online diaspora community.[41]

The most important ones would be in conflicts such as Karabagh or the Israeli/Palestinian conflict. The Nautilus Institute stated that it is beginning a process of understanding these challenges with the Virtual Diasporas and Global Problem Solving Project; there was no follow up after 2002. The project, funded by the Rockefeller Foundation, examined the growing impact of global diasporas, and their use of information technologies, on international conflict and cooperation. It posed the question: ' How will this first ever funding for a "war against networks" impact transnational diaspora communities?' (www.nautilus.org/gps/virtual-diasporas/). In the twenty-first century the study of diasporas is sharing new territory with conflict resolution, national security and terrorism. Some of the new funding was devoted to research on how states work with these global diaspora networks within their own territories, to further their political aims.

This new security aspect only yielded sporadic funding and it might revive a suspicion of cosmopolitanism that is only too easy to provoke, lending a negative connotation to the word diaspora, such as that the once neutral term network is fast acquiring. On a more optimistic note, the study of networks, of cosmopolitanism and the view that history should be beyond transnational, transregional, is making great progress in history departments previously devoted to dividing the world through a purely national lens (itself implied, albeit in contradiction, by the word transnational). Diaspora Studies is an emerging field within the larger fields of transnationalism, global history, cultural studies, subaltern studies, post-colonial studies, and as such it will have a bright future should these fields continue to find favour in academic departments.

Notes

1 Shukla, Sandya, *India Abroad: Diasporic Cultures of Postwar America and England* (Princeton, 2003).
2 Sheffer, Gabriel (ed.), *Modern Diasporas in International Politics* (New York, 1986).
3 Dufoix, Stéphane, *Diasporas* (Berkeley, University of California Press, 2008), pp. 20–1.
4 Dufoix, *Diasporas*, pp. 25–6.
5 Tölölyan, Khachig, 'The Contemporary Discourse of Diaspora Studies', *Comparative Studies of South Asia, Africa and the Middle East* 27/3 (2007), p. 47.
6 Safran, W., 'Diasporas in Modern Societies: Myths of Homeland and Return', *Diaspora: A Journal of Transnational Studies* 1 (1991), pp. 63–97.
7 Tölölyan, Khachig, 'Rethinking Diaspora(s): Stateless Power in the Transnational Moment', *Diaspora: A Journal of Transnational Studies* 5/1 (1996), pp. 3–36.
8 Chow, Rey, *The Protestant Ethnic and the Spirit of Capitalism* (New York, 2002).

9 Balibar, Etienne, and Immanuel Wallerstein, *Race, Nation, Class: Ambiguous Identities* (London, 1992).
10 See *Diaspora*, 1/9 (2000), p. 160.
11 Israel, Jonathan I., *European Jewry in the Age of Mercantilism 1550–1750* (Oxford, 1998).
12 Vertovec, Steven and Robin Cohen, *Migration, Diasporas and Transnationalism* (Cheltenham, 1999), p. 267.
13 Vertovec and Cohen, *Migration, Diasporas and Transnationalism.*
14 Vertovec and Cohen, *Migration, Diasporas and Transnationalism*, p. 267.
15 See Vertovec and Cohen, *Migration, Diasporas and Transnationalism.*
16 Dufoix, *Diasporas*, p. 2.
17 Dufoix, *Diasporas*, p. 2.
18 Cohen, Robin, *Global Diasporas: An Introduction* (Baltimore, 1997), pp. ix–x.
19 Cohen, *Global Diasporas*, p. 2.
20 Bruneau, Michel, *Diasporas et Espaces Transnationaux* (Paris, 2004), p. 8.
21 Dufoix, *Diasporas*, pp. 16–17.
22 Dubnov, Simon, *American Encyclopedia of the Social Sciences* 1931, p. 126.
23 Dufoix, *Diasporas*, p. 10.
24 Rooks, Noliwe M., *White Money/Black Power: The Surprising History of African American Studies and the Crisis of Race and Higher Education* (Boston, 2006, 2007), pp. 93–4.
25 Rooks, *White Money/Black Power*, p. 151.
26 Dufoix, *Diasporas*, p. 19.
27 Baghdiantz-McCabe, Ina, Gelina Harlaftis and Ioanna Pepelasis Minoglou (eds), *Diaspora Entrepreneurial Networks: Four Centuries of History* (New York, 2005), foreword.
28 Baghdiantz-McCabe, Harlaftis and Minoglou, *Diaspora Entrepreneurial Networks*, foreword.
29 Baghdiantz-McCabe, Harlaftis and Minoglou, *Diaspora Entrepreneurial Networks*, foreword.
30 Gelina Harlaftis, 'Mapping the Greek Maritime Diaspora from the early 18th to the late 20th century', in Baghdiantz-McCabe, Harlaftis and Minoglou, *Diaspora Entrepreneurial Networks*, pp. 147–73.
31 Curtin, P., *Cross Cultural Trade in World History* (Cambridge, 1984), p. 5.
32 Curtin, *Cross Cultural Trade in World History.*
33 Curtin, *Cross Cultural Trade in World History*, pp. 179–207.
34 Subrahmanyam, S., 'Iranians abroad: Intra Asian Elite Migration and Early Modern State Formation', *The Journal of Asian Studies* LI/2 (1992), p. 359.
35 See also Reid, Anthony, 'Diaspora Networks in the Asian Maritime Context' in Baghdiantz-McCabe, Harlaftis and Minoglou, *Diaspora Entrepreneurial Networks.*
36 McCabe, Baghdiantz, Ina, 'Merchant Capital and Knowledge: the Financing of Early Armenian Printing Presses by the Eurasian Silk Trade', part of a symposium held in May 1994 at the Pierpont Morgan Library in conjunction

with the exhibition, published in *Treasures in Heaven. Armenian Art Religion and Society* (New York, 1998), pp. 58–73.

37 See Tölölyan, 'The Contemporary Discourse of Diaspora Studies'.

38 McCabe, 'Merchant Capital and Knowledge'.

39 Sifneos, Evridiki, 'The Dark Side of the Moon: Rivalry and Riots for Shelter and Occupation Between the Greek and Jewish Populations in Multi-ethnic Nineteenth-century Odessa', *The Historical Review/Revue Historique* 3 (2006), pp. 189–204.

40 Bruneau, Michel et Claire Mouradian (eds), *Arméniens et Grecs en diaspora: approches comparatives* (Athènes, 2007).

41 www.nautilus.org/gps/virtual-diasporas/.

Bibliography

Ashraf, A., 'Historical Obstacles to the Formation of a Bourgeoisie in Iran', in M.A. Cook (ed.), *Studies in the Economic History of the Middle East: from the rise of Islam to the Present Day* (London, Oxford University Press, 1970), pp. 308–33.

Aubin, Jean, 'La Propriété foncière en Azerbaydjan', *Le Monde Iranien et L'Islam: Sociétés et Cultures* 4 (1976–1977), pp. 79–132.

Balibar, Etienne, and Immanuel Wallerstein, *Race, Nation, Class: Ambiguous Identities* (London, Verso, 1992).

Bhabha, Homi K., *Nation and Narration* (London and New York, Routledge, 1990).

Bruneau, Michel, *Diasporas et Espaces Transnationaux* (Paris, Anthropos, 2004).

— and Claire Mouradian (eds), *Arméniens et Grecs en diaspora: approches comparatives* (Athènes, École française d'Athènes, 2007).

Chow, Rey, *Writing Diaspora: Tactics of Intervention in Contemporary Cultural Studies* (Bloomington, Indiana University Press, 1993).

Chuh, Kandice, Karen Shimakawa, Russell Leong and Sharon Hom (eds), *Orientations: Mapping Studies in the Asian Diaspora* (Durham, NC, Duke University Press, 2001).

Clogg, Richard, *The Greek Diaspora in the Twentieth Century* (Basingstoke, Palgrave Macmillan, 1999).

Cohen, Abner, 'Cultural Strategies in the Organization of Trading Diaspora', in C. Mesailloux (ed.), *L'Evolution du Commerce en Afrique de L'Ouest* (London, Oxford University Press, 1971).

Cohen, Robin, *Global Diasporas: An Introduction* (Baltimore, University of Washington Press, 1997).

Curtin, P., *Cross Cultural Trade in World History* (Cambridge, Cambridge University Press, 1984).

Dufoix, Stéphane, *Diasporas* (Berkeley, University of California Press, 2008).

Gomez, Michael A., *Reversing Sail: A History of the African Diaspora* (New York, Cambridge University Press, 2004).

Gruen, Erich S., *Diaspora: Jews amidst Greeks and Romans* (Cambridge, Mass., Harvard University Press, 2004).

Harlaftis, Gelina, *Greek Shipowners and Greece 1945-1975: From Separate Development to Mutual Interdependence* (London, Athlone Press, 1994).

—, *A History of Greek-owned Shipping: The Making of an International Tramp Fleet, 1830 to the Present* (London and New York, Routledge, 1996).

Hodder, Rupert, *Merchant Princes of the East: Cultural Delusions, Economic Success and the Overseas Chinese in Southeast Asia* (New York, Wiley, 1996).

Israel, Jonathan I., *European Jewry in the Age of Mercantilism 1550–1750* (Oxford, Littman Library of Jewish Civilization, 1998).

—, *Diasporas Within a Diaspora: Jews, Crypto-Jews, and the World of Maritime Empires 1540–1740* (Boston, Brill Academic Publishers, 2002).

Kardasis, Vassilis, *Diaspora Merchants in the Black Sea* (Lanham, MD, Lexington Books, 2001).

McCabe, Baghdiantz, Ina, 'Merchant Capital and Knowledge: the Financing of Early Armenian Printing Presses by the Eurasian Silk Trade', part of a symposium held in May 1994 at the Pierpont Morgan Library in conjunction with the exhibition, published in *Treasures in Heaven. Armenian Art Religion and Society* (New York, Pierpont Morgan Library, 1998), pp. 58–73.

—, *The Shah's Silk for Europe's Silver: The Eurasian Silk trade of the Julfan Armenians in Safavid Iran and India (1590–1750)* (Atlanta, Scholar's Press, 1999).

—, Gelina Harlaftis and Ioanna Pepelasis Minoglou (eds), *Diaspora Entrepreneurial Networks: Four Centuries of History* (New York, Berg, 2005).

Panossian, Razmik, and Michael J. Dwyer, *The Armenians: From Kings and Priests to Merchants and Commissars* (New York, Columbia University Press, 2006).

Rooks, Noliwe M., *White Money/Black Power: The Surprising History of African American Studies and the Crisis of Race and Higher Education* (Boston, Beacon Press, 2006).

Safran, W., 'Diasporas in Modern Societies: Myths of Homeland and Return', *Diaspora: A Journal of Transnational Studies* 1 (1991), pp. 63–97.

Segal, Ronald, *The Black Diaspora: Five Centuries of the Black Experience Outside Africa* (New York, Farrar, Straus and Giroux, 1996).

Sheffer, Gabriel (ed.), *Modern diasporas in international politics* (New York, St Martin's Press, 1986).

Shukla, Sandya, *India Abroad: Diasporic Cultures of Postwar America and England* (Princeton, Princeton University Press, 2003).

Sifneos, Evridiki, 'The Dark Side of the Moon: Rivalry and Riots for Shelter and Occupation Between the Greek and Jewish Populations in Multi-ethnic Nineteenth-century Odessa', *The Historical Review/Revue Historique* 3 (2006), pp. 189–204.

Subrahmanyam, S. (1992), 'Iranians abroad: Intra Asian Elite Migration and Early Modern State Formation', *The Journal of Asian Studies* LI, no. 2, pp. 340–63.

Tölölyan, Khachig, 'Rethinking Diaspora(s): Stateless Power in the Transnational Moment', *Diaspora: A Journal of Transnational Studies* 5, no. 1 (1996), pp. 3–36.

—, 'Armenian Diaspora', in M. Ember, Carol R. Ember, and I. Skoggard (eds), *Encyclopedia of Diasporas Immigrant and Refugee Cultures Around the World. Vol. I: Overviews and Topics* (New York, Springer Science Media, Inc., 2005), pp. 35–46.

—, 'The Contemporary Discourse of Diaspora Studies', *Comparative Studies of South Asia, Africa and the Middle East* 27, no. 3 (2007), pp. 647–55.

Trivellato, Francesca, *The Familiarity of Strangers: The Sephardic Diaspora, Livorno, and Cross-Cultural Trade in the Early Modern Period* (New Haven, CT, Yale University Press, 2009).

Tziovas, Dimitris, *Greek Diaspora and Migration Since 1700: Society, Politics and Culture* (Surrey, Ashgate, 2009).

Vertovec, Steven, *Transnationalism* (New York, Routledge, 2009).

Vertovec, Steven and Robin Cohen, *Migration, Diasporas and Transnationalism* (Cheltenham, Edward Elgar, 1999).

—, *Conceiving Cosmopolitanism: Theory, Context, and Practice* (New York, Oxford University Press, 2003).

13

Maritime History or the History of *Thalassa*

Gelina Harlaftis

καὶ ἡμᾶς οἰκεῖν … ἐν σμικρῷ τινι μορίῳ,
ὥσπερ περὶ τέλμα μύρμηκας ἢ βατράχους
περὶ τὴν θάλατταν οἰκοῦντας
[We inhabit … a small portion of the earth
living round the sea like ants and frogs round a pond.]
Socrates in Plato, *Phaedo*, 109B

Θάλασσα [*thalassa*] in Greek is the sea, *mare* in Latin is the sea. Maritime history or the history of *thalassa* is the history of mankind's relation to the sea. Maritime history is primarily international and comparative, with a global perspective. It is the history of the people who sail on the sea and live round the sea, that is, of littoral societies, of maritime regions, of seas and oceans, of the effects on land of man's interaction with the sea. Maritime history offers the liberation of a borderless world in a synthesis of history and the social sciences, including economics, sociology, politics, anthropology, linguistics and geography. It 'sails' on the sea-routes opened by Fernand Braudel in his sea history *par excellence*, *The Mediterranean and the Mediterranean World in the Age of Philip II*, the 'total history' of the *Annales* School, which inspired the emergence of maritime history as a new field of history and which stressed an interdisciplinary approach.[1] The history of *thalassa* is a sub-history that subsumes all 'histories'. However, maritime history or the history of *thalassa* means different things to different historians.

Maritime history should be defined as widely as possible wrote Frank Broeze, who, in his seminal article in the *Great Circle*, in 1989, gave the definition that delineated the field of maritime history in his famous six categories of man's relation to the sea.[2] The first category is the use of the resources of the sea and its subsoil; it includes fishing industries, economic and social life of local communities. The second category is the use of the sea for transport; the sea as a means of communication, of carrying people and cargoes, of the development of ports and port cities for the development of the hinterland. This category is usually the largest in maritime history and includes sea-trade, ships, navigation, seamen, island communities, port cities, shipowners/shipping companies and shipping institutions (insurance, banking, international registers, etc.). The third category is the use of the sea for power projection; this focuses on commerce-raiding, corsairing/ piracy, naval power, strategy and technology, government policies. The fourth category is the use of the sea for scientific exploration; this includes oceanography and climatology, and current policies of governments regarding marine science and technology in a historical perspective. The fifth category is the use of the sea for leisure activities; this views, in a historical perspective, the seacoast as a regenerative environment, a place for recreation, swimming, surfing and yachting. And the sixth and last category is the use of the sea as an inspiration in culture and ideology; this includes the role of the sea in visual arts and literature, the sea in the self-vision of a nation.

These are the lines along which maritime history has flourished in the past two decades. Maritime history has been organized internationally under the professional body of the International Association of Maritime Economic History Association (IMEHA), which was formed initially in 1986 as a 'Maritime History Group' and was instituted formally as the IMEHA in 1990. The IMEHA has published the *International Journal of Maritime History* (IJMH) since 1989 and has organized the International Congresses of Maritime History since 1992. One of its principal aims was to espouse an international/comparative dimension, a global perspective. Each historian functions in a national environment and studies the local, the regional, the national. Maritime history gives historians the tools for comparing beyond their own boundaries and with the burgeoning of maritime history publications, opportunities have arisen to compare across the oceans and the seas globally.

As maritime historians have repeatedly noted, historians have too often neglected the sea, they have long suffered from 'thalassophobia', chief symptom of which is a land-based bias.[3] However, over the last decade, the history of the seas has become very much *en vogue* and historians' 'rediscovery' of the sea has produced a large bibliography on the history of the seas. So, we have the History of the Atlantic Ocean, of the Indian Ocean, of the Pacific Ocean, of the Baltic Sea, of the Black Sea, of the Mediterranean Sea, of the Corrupting Sea, of the Unnatural Sea, of the Oceans Past, and so on.[4]

'If Braudel did not invent thalassology in 1949 … he certainly put it spectacularly on the historian's map', wrote Edward Peters, who coined the phrase 'new thalassology' in reviewing the seminal work by Peregrine Horden and Nicholas Purcell, *The Corrupting Sea. A Study of Mediterranean History*.[5] The 'new thalassology' has 'sailed' together with the upsurge of global history in the twenty-first century, carrying the echoes of the abatement of the cultural history of the 1990s.[6] But does the 'new thalassology' relate to maritime history? The first part of this chapter will discuss what is understood by maritime history in relation to the 'new thalassology'. The second part will deal with maritime history 'on board' the IMEHA. The last part of the chapter will present a sample of the 'poetic' of the sea; the inspiration that literature and history of *thalassa* gives.

What's in a name? Maritime history, the 'new thalassology' and global history

'One of the major problems of maritime history is its very name and some very fundamental misconceptions that have arisen from it. Many people, and not only outside the field, believe that maritime history is all about ships and navigation, and about nothing else', wrote Frank Broeze, a Dutchman, in 1989.[7] It seems that this misconception continues to the present day, as is indicated by another Dutchman, Henk Driessen, when he writes, in 2008, about 'the emergence of late of a maritime perspective and a "new thalassology" beyond the narrow specializations of maritime history …'.[8] Driessen sees maritime history as 'narrow' and in so doing he is representative of the line of thinking of a main group of scholars engaged in the wave of 'new thalassology', a group that has ignored maritime history. At the same time, in a book entitled *Maritime History as World History*, Felipe Fernández-Armesto argues that it is through knowledge of the seas, of their winds, currents and tides, along with advancements in sailing ship technology that enabled reliable long distance voyage, that 'global history became a reality. It grew out of maritime history'.[9] How and why can maritime history be defined as 'narrow' and 'global' at the same time? I propose six reasons.

The first reason is that even after so many decades, maritime history is still identified with ships, navigation and naval history. And this has a lot to do with the importance of the maritime tradition and heritage of nations, as shown and highlighted in their national histories, in maritime museums and maritime societies. The 'glory at sea', from antiquity to today, of the Greeks, the Scandinavians, the Dutch, the Spanish, the Portuguese, the Italians, the British and Americans, has concentrated on famous sea-warriors, sea-battles and admirals, and has formed an important part of hero-worship and the national self-image. The immense output of naval history in both the United Kingdom and the United States, not only for the imperial or colonial era but also for the two world wars of the twentieth century, has intensified its identification with maritime history. Harvard University's first Professor in 'Oceanic History and Affairs', in 1948, Robert Greenhalgh Albion, considered as the 'dean of American maritime historians', despite his wide perspective that included 'maritime and naval' history was best known for his work in naval history. And as some of the significant American maritime historians of the second half of the twentieth century continued to excel in naval history, the continuation of this old preconception on the other side of the Atlantic was intensified further.[10] In Britain, naval history has been thriving since the nineteenth century, with the formation of the Navy Records Society in 1893, and of several nautical historical societies subsequently, and it continues to thrive today, at the University of Exeter, at King's College, London, with Andrew Lambert, and, recently, at the University of Oxford with Nicholas Rodger. The last has given to naval historical writing another dimension, elevating it from a history of warships and sea-battles to an outstanding synthesis of sea history, war history and social history, of the people of the Navy on board and on land, in all the world's seas and oceans in the wider context of the expansion of the British Empire.[11] For all its growth, naval history can only be accepted and flourish academically when it regards itself as a sub-field of maritime history and uses the interdisciplinary and comparative historical methods of this field. Because the popularity of the history of the sea has meant the wide involvement of many non-professional historians, in combination with the many nautical museums and 'friends of the museums', extolling the virtues of antiquarianism and of local narratives of port-towns and cities, concentrating on the study of glorious ships, admirals or navigators. This has had a negative effect on the name of maritime history, responsible in part for the prejudice of its parochialism.[12]

The second reason is that despite the fact that maritime history has attempted to accomplish the goal of 'total history', through an interdisciplinary approach, it has developed mainly as an economic and social history focused on communication and exchange, on port-cities, littoral maritime communities, long-distance trade, shipping routes, seamen and maritime enterprise. We can distinguish two periods in the discipline of maritime history in the second half of the twentieth century. The first period, during which the French-speaking world in general and the *Annales* School in particular were pre-eminent, commenced in the mid-1950s and continued into the 1970s. Research was conducted almost exclusively by European scholars and centred on the early modern age, from the fifteenth to the eighteenth centuries.[13]

In the second period, starting in the 1970s, the route of maritime history departed from the *Annales* School, and the centre of gravity shifted to English-speaking historians, mainly based in the UK, Canada and Norway, who still kept the wheel geared towards economic and social history and who focused on the modern age, from the eighteenth century to the present day.[14] The great impetus of this upsurge came from the other side of the Atlantic, which many a time sets the pace by funding grand projects; not least, the Atlantic Canada Shipping Project that ran from 1976–1982 at Memorial University of Newfoundland, which has been a centre of maritime history ever since. The Atlantic Canada Shipping Project combined 'the skills of economists, geographers, maritime historians and regional Canadian historians', who looked at merchant fleets of the North Atlantic, shipowners and economic development, voyage patterns, bulk trades, seafaring labour force, harbours and metropolis, migration, landward and seaward economies, state and regional economic development.[15] Its objectives were to study, document and explain the rise and fall of Atlantic Canadian shipping in the nineteenth and twentieth centuries, through the use of the official documents of the crew lists of the British fleet, which the University of Newfoundland had 'inherited' from the British Public Record Office, today known as the National Archives. The project contributed to the discipline by offering pioneering techniques in the computer-assisted quantitative analysis of large masses of historical material, and attracted the attention of prominent economic historians involved in cliometrics, such as Douglass North and C. Knick Harley, who took part in the conferences held.[16] The studies that came out of this project, however, were not along the lines of new economic history and cliometrics, rather they were consistent with the economic and social history of the Marxist and neo-Marxist tradition, of a 'history from below'; about seamen and their wages, maritime labour movements and labour relations on board, maritime communities.[17] The main contribution of this project to the field of maritime history was the creation of the Maritime History Group, which not only processed the above material but also produced some of the most important maritime historians, among them Lewis R. Fischer, who, as we shall see in the next section, is one of the discipline's leading figures.

Nevertheless, the fact that maritime history developed in the 1970s and 1980s as an economic and social history of the modern age meant that it suffered in popularity in the 1990s, as is indicated clearly in Peter Mathias' chapter in this volume. As its most prominent practitioners were economic and social historians, maritime history was hit hard by the upsurge of post-modernism and cultural studies.

The third reason is that the 'new thalassology' that marked the beginning of the twenty-first century, with Horden and Purcell's *The Corrupting Sea. A Study of Mediterranean History* published in 2000, which provided a highly interesting new account of history *in* the Mediterranean, and history *of* the Mediterranean, covered a period from ancient to early modern times, a period neglected by maritime-history practitioners of the IMEHA.[18] As we have already indicated, maritime history in the last 25 years has focused on early modern and modern history in the seas and oceans other than the Mediterranean, hence Horden and Purcell were right in commenting that in Mediterranean history 'the majority of scholarly writing is conventional, relatively local, political, social, or economic "history in" some Mediterranean country – of no immediate wider significance and with little attention to geography or environment'.[19] Horden and Purcell, although specialized in ancient and medieval times, have transcended time and have taken under consideration some of the bibliography produced by maritime history in the last twenty-five years. But maybe this is because they are based in Europe, a continent with an 'inherent' sense of the diachronic sea. What is remarkable is what has been happening in the 'discovery of the sea' in the other side of the Atlantic, over the past decade.

The history of the seas and oceans of the early modern and the modern age has been 'discovered' to a large extent by geographers, anthropologists and cultural historians mainly from the United States, and these have formed the most important body of scholars involved in the 'new thalassology'. This trend seems to be linked with a crisis in the financing of regional/area studies projects and the promotion (that is the funding by National Resource Centres) of 'globalism', which has triggered a re-thinking of ways in which the world is divided.[20] Within this framework, it seems that the Sea was suddenly discovered, and many cried with joy *Thalatta! Thalatta*! (The Sea! The Sea!), like the Ten Thousand Greeks who sighted the Black Sea after their long march from the interior of Babylon.[21] In this way the sea and maritime connections were brought to the centre of many new projects; the sea, as it was 'discovered', is vast and gives an amazingly different perspective from that of the land.

However, those who have only recently discovered the sea consider maritime history 'narrow' or completely ignore the existence and the work of maritime history in the previous decades. And this is the fourth reason for the neglect of maritime history. It is also the pest of our profession and our times: specialization and lack of communication due to abundance of information. It is actually one of the *raisons d'être* of this book. It is ironic that in the history of the sea, a *par excellence* history of communications, the historians of different periods or different seas, or different histories, or different 'slices' of history, do not communicate with each other. It is telling, to say the least, that in the Forum of the *American History Review* of June 2006, 'Oceans Connect', the organizers seem to have never heard of what has been going on in maritime history just a few hundred (land) miles north, in Canada.[22]

It is true that geography, anthropology and cultural studies have not been at the centre of the interests of maritime history practitioners. Nevertheless, they have not been neglected. In the 1990s, prominent maritime historians such as David J. Starkey and Poul Holm introduced environmental history into maritime history, through the History of Marine Animal Population projects, in a fruitful combination of history and the natural world that produced in 2001 *The Exploited Seas: New Directions for Marine Environmental History* and in 2008 *The Oceans Past.*[23] More maritime interpretations, perceptions, identities and symbols than ever before were presented in the Fifth International Congress of Maritime History, which took place at Greenwich in 2008.[24] There were multiple sessions with papers in which ships were enhanced as places of liberation or freedom, or as a source of fresh identities on board; the various symbols of tattooing in the Victorian Navy were examined; song lyrics were used to analyse tango and sea; film representations of the sea, Victorian myths on Cornish wrecks reminding us of Daphne du Maurier's *Jamaica Inn*, the maritime feasts in Messina, or the womenfolk of seamen as icons, merely indicate the abundance and the inspiration of maritime culture and heritage from archipelagoes, islands and port-towns. Maritime culture was discussed as the image of a nation and its relation to the sea, and maritime museums questioned traditional approaches and presented ways in which new insights and perspectives could be accommodated in maritime history.

The fourth reason lies in maritime history's relation to imperial, colonial history or the history of exploration of the early modern age, otherwise described as overseas or European expansion.[25] This is a history that has a fully maritime perspective; it is all about sea-voyages, sea trade, slave trade, migration, formation of port-cities, corsairing, privateering, development of navigation and scientific exploration with maps and instruments, ship technology, large overseas shipping and trading companies, fishing and maritime communities, seamen. It is all about maritime empires, or sea history in which maritime connections encompass the globe.

Maritime historians have always regarded this kind of history as maritime history; even so, the largest number of the authors on this field did not and do not describe themselves as maritime historians. A prominent example would be J.H. Parry, Professor of Oceanic History and Affairs at Harvard University – a chair that has remained vacant since his death in 1982 – with his books *The Age of Discovery, The Spanish Seaborne Empire, The Discovery of the Sea,* to mention just a few titles.[26] Another one would be Geoffrey V. Scammell of the University of Cambridge, with his works *The World Encompassed: the First European Maritime Empires c. 800–1650, The First Imperial Age: European Overseas Expansion c. 1400–1715, Seafaring, Sailors and Trade 1450–1750: studies in British and European maritime and imperial history.* More examples are Richard Unger with his *Dutch Shipbuilding before 1800: ships and guilds* and *Ships and Shipping in the North Sea and Atlantic, 1400—1800*; Carla Rahn Phillips with her *Life at Sea in the Sixteenth Century: the landlubber's lament of Eugenio de Salazar* and *The Treasure of the San José: Death at Sea in the War of the Spanish Succession*; Felipe Fernández-Armesto, with his *Columbus* and *Pathfinders: a global history of exploration*; Marcus Rediker with his *Between the Devil and the Deep Blue Sea: merchant seamen, pirates, and the Anglo-American maritime world, 1700–1750.*[27]

Ultimately, however, maritime history has profited from historians who consider themselves as working in different historical fields but are involved with their maritime aspects; this was well illustrated at the international congresses of Maritime History, in Corfu (2004) and Greenwich (2008), where scholars in maritime history of the early modern and the modern age finally met. The resurgence of history of the sea and the new wave of 'thalassology' has turned things upside down: early modern imperial history presents itself under the history of sea. As Jack P. Greene and Philip D. Morgan remark, 'Atlantic history is merely imperial history in a more acceptable guise'.[28]

The fifth reason lies in the relation of maritime history to the history of the sea. Horden and Purcell were only partially right when they wrote that 'Sea and Ocean history is more novel than it sounds. It admirably exemplifies a new historiography of large areas'.[29] There have been important studies of seas and oceans by prominent maritime historians. The Indian Ocean, for example, has provided a rich and remarkable historiography, at least since 1985, particularly from Kirti Chaudhuri, Kenneth McPherson, Frank

Broeze and Michael Pearson who has written one of the best books on the history of an ocean.[30] Reflection on large maritime regions has been part of the way of thinking of such outstanding maritime historians as Lewis R. Fischer and Frank Broeze. Fischer's *People of the Northern Seas* was published in 1992,[31] while Frank Broeze had been writing on the Asian seas since the early 1980s.[32] In fact, Frank Broeze suggested that the term 'Asian Seas' should be used instead of 'Indian Ocean', as it is 'a string of closely related regional systems stretching from East Asia around the continent and across the Indian Ocean to East Africa (to which sea space a new generic name, such as the "the Asian Seas", might well be given)'.[33] Broeze had been preparing his book on the Pacific Ocean since the late 1990s, and it was a great loss to maritime history that he left it unfinished in 2001; it would have been a landmark of the convergence of maritime history with the 'new thalassology' that marked the beginning of the twenty-first century.[34] 'The true oceanic history', wrote Broeze, 'is the history in which the sea is not merely the setting but also the main dynamic agent'.[35]

Geoffrey Scammel, who was always concerned with large maritime empires and large maritime regions, started his series 'Seas in History' in the 1990s. It is not accidental that the first book in this series was a translation from the French of Paul Butel's *Histoire de l'Atlantique*; for the French have never ceased dealing with the seas and wide maritime regions, as borne out by Michel Mollat's *Europe and the Sea*, or the 'hidden' work of Michel Fontenay, steadfastly devoted to the whole Mediterranean in the seventeenth and eighteenth centuries.[36]

The sixth reason lies in the relation of maritime history to global history. Global history is the history of contacts and interactions between different civilizations.[37] Maritime history has gained much from its interaction with global history through the re-emergence of ocean/seas studies. Pamela Kyle Crossley supports the view that the history of the oceans has provided a wide new theme, an 'extremely productive sub-genre' of global history 'that will probably only continue to deepen its methodological sophistications and conceptual coherence'.[38] One of the main trends in the current bibliography of global history is the comeback of the periphery/core argument and the 'great divergence', an Asia-centric versus a Euro-centric history.[39] At the centre of the analysis lies the history of the oceans. And the history of the oceans is not Euro-centric. In fact, the study of an ocean or a sea gives the possibility of transforming periphery into core, and forms an exceptionally rich field for comparative study of systems, relations and perceptions. Studies of the seas promote a comparative perspective between, for example, Western Europe, North Africa, West Africa, the Caribbean and

Latin America, the Atlantic and the Mediterranean. The study of the Indian Ocean includes the relations between South and Southeast Asia, the Middle East and East Africa, apart from its relations with Europe.

Maritime historians have always regarded maritime history as global. All globalization is about is global connections and as the sea covers three-quarters of the earth's surface, these are mainly maritime connections.[40] Maritime history is international by nature and global by coverage; it can hardly be written without crossing borders and seas, without dealing constantly with maritime links between different countries, economies and cultures. The titles of a sample of the monographs published by the IMEHA in the series Research in Maritime History suffice to show the importance of the global: in 1998 *Global Markets: The Internationalization of The Sea Transport Industries*,[41] in 2002 *The Globalisation of the Oceans: Containerisation from the 1950s to the Present*, in 2007 *Making Global and Local Connections: Historical Perspectives on Ports* where ship technology becomes a major agent of transformation of port systems and globalization.[42] Nonetheless, the argument that because 'maritime historians deal with a global industry in itself does not make it global', does contain elements of truth.[43] The importance of shipping and sea-trade as an international business has promoted globalization; this has more to do with the importance of multinational business, which shipping has always been, as the shipping sector constitutes the international sector *par excellence* of any economy. But maritime historians do not deal only with a global industry. It is not only through the shipping fleet, shipping businesses or ship technology that maritime history regards itself as global. Although traditionally it has given more weight to port-cities, seamen, shipping, ships, cargoes and long-distance trade, equally important are maritime communities, perceptions, attitudes, beliefs and symbols, violence at sea, or the clash of Islam and Christianity.

What maritime history has done is to provide a methodology for linking the local, the regional, the national, the international, the global, so giving us the possibility of comparing the small and the unimportant, the big and the important, the everyday life, the material culture and the transactions of the most remote places around the world. The view from the sea gives the opportunity to look at maritime regions/seas/oceans that transcend the conventional Euro-centric first/second/third world approaches. Maritime history brings the periphery of world history to the centre of historical research, and this is how it is linked with world and/or global history. What is more, an impressive scaffolding has been built by many a maritime historian, which over the past decades has formed a rich maritime historiography that cannot possibly be ignored by the neophytes of the history of the oceans.

Maritime history on board the IMEHA

The most important international organization involved with maritime history is the International Maritime Economic History Association (IMEHA), which was formed in 1990 and essentially continued the tradition of the French *histoire maritime*. Maritime History emerged almost simultaneously in France and England in the 1950s, but it was only natural that it was organized first in France, under the *Commission Internationale Maritime*, which was set up in the early 1960s and prospered under the roof of the International Commission for Historical Sciences (that changed its title from French to English), which held conferences every five years.

'The uniquely international character of the European maritime economy undoubtedly reflects the production and circulation of goods of the world economy',[44] wrote the first President of the International Commission of Maritime History, Michel Mollat du Jourdin of the University of Paris in 1962.[45] 'Maritime history is a key to general history', wrote Jean Meuvret, Head of the École Pratique des Hautes Études, at the same period.[46] On the other side of the Channel, England, on a lower key, followed the same path as France, opening the way for maritime history through the booming of economic and social history in the London School of Economics and Cambridge University. The development of history in France and in Britain followed parallel paths. In this way, the *Annales*, the University of Paris and the French *Histoire Economique et Sociale* kept up an open dialogue with the British Economic and Social History. The move of Michael Postan, a man with wide knowledge and a cosmopolitan spirit, from the London School of Economics to the Chair of Economic History at Cambridge, was, according to Eric Hobsbawm, pivotal for tightening the relations of the French School of *Annales* with the English Economic and Social History.[47]

In the English-speaking world, the 1970s were decisive. In London, Robin Craig was appointed at University College to teach economic and social history, and became the mentor for maritime history to a whole generation of up-and-coming scholars. He also became the editor of the first *Journal of Maritime History*, which ran for a few years, an academic journal focused exclusively on the economic and social history of merchant shipping – a radical departure from traditional naval history. And last but not least, Robin Craig not only 'discovered' but also helped to save a voluminous collection of crew lists of the British fleet from the Public Record Office, that were rescued and deposited at Memorial University in St John's, Newfoundland in 1971; this move set its seal on the development of maritime history and the IMEHA.

Another centre of maritime history other than London emerged in the shape of the so-called Liverpool School. There, Peter Davies, a former student of, and successor to, Francis Hyde, continued the line of research on maritime business history. The 'boom' in maritime history prompted other universities (Essex, Glasgow and Leicester) to follow the lead of University College, London and the University of Liverpool. At the University of Leicester, for example, Ralph Davis and David Williams must be considered two of the founding fathers of Britain's 'new' maritime history.[48]

In Canada, the Maritime Archive of the Memorial University of Newfoundland became the centre for the 'production' of some of the leading maritime historians of the following decades. The protagonist responsible for the international organization and development of maritime history from this group of historians in Canada is Professor Lewis R. Fischer, one of the founders of the IMEHA and of the *International Journal of Maritime History* (*IJMH*).[49]

The other two 'production' centres in maritime history were the Netherlands and the Scandinavian countries, particularly Norway. Leiden University's Jaap Bruijn is not only the author of a large number of publications on the maritime history of the Netherlands, and a dynamic member of all international maritime and economic history commissions, French or English, but also the mentor to more than 50 maritime historians, including the late Frank Broeze. Norway, one of the most dynamic maritime nations of the twentieth century, could not be left out. Its contribution is due in large part to Helge Nordvik, one of the founders of the IMEHA and co-editor of *IJMH* with Lewis R. Fischer.

In 1986, at the Ninth International Economic History Congress in Bern, the new Maritime History Group was formed, with the aim of creating a new international network of maritime history led by Lewis R. Fischer from Canada, Helge Nordvik from Norway, Peter Davies from Britain and Keiichiro Nakagawa from Japan. In 1990, at the Tenth International Economic History Congress in Leuven, Belgium, the IMEHA was formed. That same year, Frank Broeze was elected as President of the Commission Internationale d'Histoire Maritime/International Commission for Maritime History, for the period 1990–1995. A distinguished maritime historian of the IMEHA group, Broeze also became Vice-President of the IMEHA. The first volume of the *International Journal of Maritime History* was published in 1989, with editors Lewis R. Fischer and Helge Nordvik, and an editorial board of 24 academics from 15 countries in four continents.

What the IMEHA and the *International Journal of Maritime History* have achieved over the last two decades is a steady-growing output of quality writing in maritime history, along the lines of the definition proposed by Broeze. From 1989 to 2008, the IMEHA produced 40 volumes of the *International Journal of Maritime History* or 15,000 pages, and 35 volumes of *Research in Maritime History* or about 10,000 pages, a formidable contribution to scholarship in the field. In the 40 volumes of the *IJMH* there are also scholarly reviews of some 2,500 books. Apart from the *IJMH,* the academic dialogue was kept alive and thriving through the international congresses, which were launched in 1992 and continue, ever bigger, every four years. So, if at the First International Congress of Maritime History, in Liverpool in 1992, there were about 40 participants, at the Third Congress, in Esbjerg (Denmark) in 2000, there were about 80, at the Fourth Congress, in Corfu in 2004, there were about 160 scholars from 23 countries, and at the Fifth International Congress of Maritime History, in Greenwich in 2008, there were 315 participants from 30 countries.

A major achievement of the last – and largest – the Fifth ICMH was that it attracted a large number of historians who would not describe themselves as maritime historians but who write maritime history. Under the IMEHA, maritime history has profited from the wide definition it adopted and from the emerging interest in the history of the seas and global history. Thus, it is no coincidence that the Sixth ICMH is scheduled to take place in 2012 at the University of Ghent, where maritime history will 'sail' along with global history.

A long-standing strategy of the IMEHA, from its inception, has been to embrace the whole world and to promote the periphery versus the domination of northern European and North American scholars. Indicative of these efforts is the fact that for the period 2008–2012, the elected Executive Committee comprises Jesús M. Valdaliso from Spain (President), Amelia Polonia from Portugal (Vice-President), Malcolm Tull from Australia (Vice-President), Berit Eide Johnsen from Norway (Secretary) and Ayodeji Olukoju from Nigeria (Treasurer). The composition of the Editorial Board of the Journal is likewise indicative of the efforts to achieve a wide representation of scholars from all over the world.

Existing associations of various seas, such as the Association for the History of the Northern Seas, organized by scholars from the Scandinavian countries, are affiliated to the IMEHA. One handicap of the IMEHA was that until the beginning of the twenty-first century there was a conspicuous under-representation of scholars from main European countries, such as France, Italy, Spain, and from the Mediterranean. It seemed as if the IMEHA had taken Maritime History out to the big oceans but had isolated the Mediterranean, whose *lingua franca* was still largely French. It was only at the Third International Maritime History Congress, in Ejsberg in 2000, that historians specialized in Mediterranean maritime history attended, six in all. From their meeting and discussions the Mediterranean Maritime History Network was born, which had its first Conference in Malta in 2002, and in many respects opened the way for a larger representation of Mediterranean Maritime History at the Fourth ICMH, in Corfu in 2004, where French was introduced as a second official language of the Congress. A large number of Italian maritime historians took part in the Corfu congress, and also in the Second Mediterranean Maritime History Conference, held in Messina in May 2006; this was a successful and fruitful gathering of about 80 scholars from Turkey, Greece, Italy, France, Spain, Malta, Tunis, Cyprus, Israel, Britain, United States and Ukraine. The next conference is scheduled to take place in Smyrna in 2010.

Another effect of the IMEHA was the re-organization of French maritime history. In 2007, at the University of Bretagne-Sud, a conference was organized with the title 'La Recherche Internationale en Histoire Maritime. Essai d´Evaluation', with the participation not only of scholars from 9 countries, but also of 33 French researchers and professors from 13 French universities and research institutions. As Professor Bouedec pointed out in his introductory address, 'the organization of this colloquium was born in 2004 from a sentiment of fragility as one saw the marginalization of French research at an international level and the need to restructure research and place it within an international perspective'. 'The beneficial shock', he writes, 'was given by the International Maritime Economic History Congress in Corfu in June 2004 … where I discovered the power of the international maritime history network'. So, in 2005 French maritime historians formed the 'French Scientific Interest Group of Maritime History', in which 23 French universities and research centres, and 70 maritime historians and 30 PhD students participated. Since 2004 they have undertaken the publication of the *Revue d' Histoire Maritime* with the Professor Jean Pierre Poussou of University of Paris IV-Sorbonne as the editor of the journal.

The IMEHA is formed worldwide by a group of people who regard themselves as maritime historians, who follow an interdisciplinary path by offering considerable insights over a wider historical field and who publish in both maritime and non-maritime academic journals. However, maritime history as a new field of history has been institutionalized in higher education and is taught at undergraduate and/or post-graduate level mainly in European universities: in Britain at the Maritime Historical Studies Centre of the University of Hull, at the Centre of Maritime History of the University of Exeter, at the University of Swansea and at the Greenwich

Maritime Institute of the University of Greenwich; in Norway at Bergen University and the University of Oslo; in Denmark at the University of Southern Denmark; in the Netherlands at the University of Leiden; in Germany at Bremen University; in Greece at the University of Piraeus, the Aegean University and the Ionian University. Beyond Europe, it is taught mainly in Canada, at the Memorial University of Newfoundland, and in Western Australia, at Murdoch University. Furthermore, aspects of maritime history are taught in courses on colonial/imperial histories of the early modern age in many other European, Australian, American and Asian universities. With the wave of 'new thalassology' there are also hopes that interest in maritime history will be boosted in the United States.

Back in 1989, Frank Broeze wrote that the 'maritime element has until now remained underdeveloped and isolated; our challenge then is to push forward with maritime history and to bring it from the periphery to the mainstream'. So, has maritime history come from the periphery to the centre of historical studies? This is what every discipline that is not considered 'mainstream' wonders. One can find in many chapters of this book authors evaluating *ubi sumus*. But this is the job of the historians, to question and re-write history from many angles.

At Greenwich in the June 2008 the President of the IMEHA announced that, after a voyage of 20 years, the 'crew' of the IMEHA have brought Maritime History from the periphery to the centre, as a collective act of many historians:[50] 'Historians have come on board and manned the fleet of Maritime History, as international crew sailing under various flags, in harmonious collaboration, at conferences, seminars, workshops, colloquiums, lectures, committees. The quality of human relations in any restricted community is set when there are sentiments of camaraderie, co-operation, 'synagonism' and not antagonism, friendliness, respect of seniority, creation of opportunities and the 'opening of doors' to the younger generation'. And the IMEHA has been for many a maritime historian suffocating in the micro-politics of national waters, the academic utopia of heterotopia.

The 'poetic' of the sea and history

The sea and the ship have been an inspiration to many. Michel Foucault, writing on heterotopia, meaning a space with several places, explained the concept by using the metaphor of a ship. The ship, 'a piece of floating space' is a place without a place that moves to many places, is the epitome of heterotopia.[51] There is the 'new thalassology', which draws more from postmodernism, and the 'linguistic turn', which discusses the relation of the man with the sea from perceptions, attitudes, beliefs and symbols. And it is mainly human geographers who have used the concept of 'place' in their analysis of the social, political cultural aspects of this world.[52]

The 'linguistic turn' has given maritime history the freedom to use some of the 'poetic' of the sea, for a more popular approach. The sea is a source of inspiration for historians. In the words of Felipe Fernández-Armesto:

> The sea can shape island civilizations either by confining them or by linking them to other lands. Either way, proximity to the sea is such a powerful feature of any environment which includes it that it dwarfs all the others. Whatever the nature of the soil or temperature, the relief or biota, if the sea is at hand it has a shaping force. Nearness to the shore moulds one's outlook and affects the way one thinks. The sea is awesome because it is intractable, untrappable; it changes everything it touches without being easily changed in turn. It makes coral bones and pearls of eyes. It reshapes shorelines, erodes coasts, gulps swards and cities, chews continents. At us land-creatures it flings weather systems which, after all millennia of civilization, symbolize the continuing feebleness of our power over the environment. The sea has no appointed limits, except in the pious cravings of the prayerful. It is part of chaos that survived creation. It makes us feel small.[53]

It is the journey that gives magic to the writing of history and it is true that history has a lot to gain from literature. As Karen van Dyck observes, '... what makes literature important to the historian is not only the way it can be mined for historical details and descriptions of times and places we no longer inhabit and philosophical and political insights we no longer remember, but also for the manner in which it presents its messages'. One of her examples is the Greek writer Giannis Psycharis, who starts his book *Journey* with a chapter entitled 'The Secret Passion'. The passion, it turns out, is the Greek sea and its ability to bring him home after many years in exile in Paris:

> I saw the beautiful view before me, above me the sky with its brilliance, beside me the hills and green, and suddenly, further below, if I raised my eyes, the endless sea with the purple waves, the laughing sea, decorated in white foam. Ah! the sea, why did I have to see her? Why couldn't the plane trees, the willows, and the other trees that grow out of the French earth conceal her? As soon as I saw the sea my fantasy

took me in a new direction. I remembered my homeland! It was to this homeland that the sea could take me.[54]

In some of the American 'new thalassology' it seems to me that *thalassa* (apart from the fact that Americans almost never say '*thalassa*/sea' but 'ocean') is nobody's homeland. A lot of writing is about the history of the sea, without the sea. It is as if the sea has been lost; it seems that the people who write about it have never had a true feeling of it; they have just imagined it. They remind me of the verses of the Greek seaman and poet Nikos Kavadias, who in his poem *Mal de Depart* talks of 'an ideal but unworthy lover of the endless voyages and blue oceans', who sits 'in an office bent over some nautical maps making calculations in ledger books', while 'Proudly as always, the ship will set sail/For Madras, Algeria and Singapore'.[55] And I suppose if someone wants to 'deconstruct' my writing in this paragraph, he may say that because I am a maritime historian I cannot believe that one can write the history of the sea, of man's relationship with the sea, without understanding sea voyages, without trying to get a feeling of how it must have been to struggle with the waves, to get some sense of 'the men who get wet' on board a vessel.[56]

I will finish this chapter, there where the Mediterranean Sea meets the Atlantic Ocean, in the Portuguese novel that superbly blends land and sea, José Saramago's *A jangada de pedra* (*A Stone Raft*, 1986), a novel inspired by older Portuguese myths about Portuguese explorers and Vasco de Gama. There, the Iberian peninsula becomes a land that suddenly drifts apart from the European continent and becomes an island, a stone raft, that sails around the world, the land like a ship, a place in no place. 'As a raft-island it does not anchor in any port but, on the contrary, opens itself to all exchanges and communications because its border is the sea.'[57] The sea that embraces the globe and history.

Notes

1 See also Harlaftis, Gelina, 'Storia maritima e storia dei porti', *Memoria e Ricerca* 11 (2002), pp. 5–22 and eadem, 'Maritime History since Braudel', in Gelina Harlaftis and Carmel Vassalo (eds), *New Directions in Mediterranean Maritime History*, RMH no. 28 (St John's, Newfoundland, 2004).

2 Broeze, Frank, 'From the Periphery to the Mainstream: The Challenge of Australia's Maritime History', *The Great Circle* 11/1 (1989), pp. 1–14.

3 Pearson, Michael, *The Indian Ocean* (London, 2003), p. 3; Driessen, Henk, 'Seascapes and Mediterranean crossings', *Journal of Global History* 3 (2008), pp. 445–9.

4 Just to give some titles, Butel, Paul, *The Atlantic* (New York, 1999); Matvejević, Predrag, *Mediterranean: A Cultural Landscape* (Berkeley, 1999); Horden, Peregrine and Nicholas Purcell, *The Corrupting Sea. A Study of Mediterranean History* (Oxford, 2000); Kirby, David and Merja-Liisa Hinkkanen, *The Baltic and the North Seas* (London and New York, 2000); Pearson, Michael, *The Indian Ocean* (London and New York, 2003); King, Charles, *The Black Sea: a History* (Oxford and New York, 2004); Roberts, Callum, *The Unnatural History of the Sea* (Washington, DC, 2007); Starkey, David J., Poul Holm and Michaela Barnard (eds), *Oceans Past: Management Insights From The History of Marine Animal Populations* (London, 2008).

5 Peters, Edward, 'Quid nobis cum pelage? The New Thalassology and the Economic History of Europe', *Journal of Interdisciplinary History* xxxiv/I (summer 2003), pp. 49–61. Horden and Purcell, *The Corrupting Sea.*

6 Driessen, 'Seascapes and Mediterranean Crossings', pp. 445–9.

7 Broeze, Frank, 'From the Periphery to the Mainstream: the Challenge of Australia's Maritime History', *The Great Circle* 11/1 (1989), pp. 1–14.

8 Driessen, 'Seascapes and Mediterranean Crossings'.

9 Finamore, Daniel (ed.), *Maritime History as World History* (Gainsville, 2004), p. 2.

10 Hattendorf, John B. (ed.), *Ubi Sumus? The State of Naval and Maritime History* (Newport, RI, 1994); Labaree, Benjamin W., 'The State of American Maritime History in the 1990s', in Hattendorf, *Ubi Sumus.*

11 Rodger, N.A.M., *The Command of the Ocean: A Naval History Of Britain, 1649–1815* (London, 2004); *The Safeguard of the Sea: A Naval History of Britain, 660–1649* (London, 2004).

12 See Broeze, Frank, 'Maritime History at the Crossroads: A Critical Review of Recent Historiography', in Frank Broeze, *Maritime History at the Crossroads: A Critical Review of Recent Historiography*, RMH no. 9 (St John's, Newfoundland, 1995); Bruijn, Jaap, 'Recent Developments in the Historiography of Maritime History in the Netherlands', in Broeze, *Maritime History at the Crossroads,* pp. 193–212; Valdaliso, Jesùs, 'The Progress of Maritime History in Spain since 1975', in Broeze, *Maritime History,* pp. 229–48; Harlaftis, Gelina, 'The Maritime Historiography of Greece in Recent Decades', in Broeze, *Maritime History at the Crossroads*, pp. 135–50; D'Angelo, Michela and Elisabetta Tonizzi, 'Recent Maritime Historiography on Italy', in Harlaftis and Vassalo (eds), *New Directions in Mediterranean Maritime History.*

13 See also Harlaftis, 'Storia maritima' and 'Maritime History since Braudel', in Harlaftis and Vassalo (eds), *New Directions in Mediterranean Maritime History.*

14 Ibid.

15 Fischer, Lewis R. and Eric W. Sager (eds), *Merchant Shipping and Economic Development in Atlantic Canada*, Proceedings of the Fifth Conference of the Atlantic Canada Shipping Project, Maritime History Group (St John's, Newfoundland, 1982).

16 Fischer, Lewis R. and Eric W. Sager, 'An Approach to the Quantitative Analysis of British Shipping Records', *Business History* XXII/2 (July 1980), pp. 135–51;

Fischer, Lewis R., 'Maritime History in Canada', in Broeze, *Maritime History at the Crossroads*, pp. 31–52.

17 Sager, Eric, *Seafaring Labour: the Merchant Marine of Atlantic Canada, 1820–1914* (Kingston, ON, 1989); Sager, Eric W. with Gerald E. Panting, *Maritime capital: the shipping industry in Atlantic Canada, 1820–1914* (Montreal and Buffalo, 1990).

18 Horden and Purcell, *The Corrupting Sea.*

19 Horden and Purcell, 'The Mediterranean and "the New Thalassology"', Forum, *American Historical Review* (June 2006), pp. 722–40.

20 Lewis, Martin W. and Kären Wigen, 'A Maritime Response to the Crisis in Area Studies', *The Geographical Review* 89/2 (April 1999), pp. 161–8.

21 Written by Xenophon in his *Anabasis*; this is a popular saying among modern Greeks as it is included in all Greek high-school ancient history books. For translation in English see *The Anabasis of Cyrus*, transl. by Wayne Ambler (Ithaca, 2008).

22 *The International Journal of Maritime History* is published in the Memorial University of Newfoundland, St John's, Canada. See also the Editor's note, the *International Journal of Maritime History* XVIII/2 (December 2006), pp. xiii–xiv. It is worth mentioning here that this particular volume of the *IJMH* runs to 654 pages of articles, research notes, source essays, forums, roundtables and reviews of 97 books on maritime history of all periods and themes.

23 Holm, Poul, Tim D. Smith, and David Starkey (eds), *The Exploited Seas: New Directions for Marine Environmental History*, No. 21 (St John's, Newfoundland, 2001); Starkey, Holm and Barnard (eds), *Oceans Past: Management Insights from the History of Marine Animal Population.*

24 http://web-dev-csc.gre.ac.uk/conference/conf34/index.php.

25 For example, the National Maritime Museum of the United Kingdom has its Centre for Imperial and Maritime Studies. See also Cannadine, David (ed.), *Empire, the Sea and Global History: Britain's Maritime World, c. 1760–c. 1840* (London, 2007).

26 Parry, John Horace, *The Spanish Seaborne Empire* (London, 1966); idem, *The Discovery of the Sea* (Berkeley, 1981); Scammell, Geoffrey V., *The World Encompassed: The First European Maritime Empires c. 800–1650* (London, 1981); idem, *The First Imperial Age: European Overseas Expansion c. 1400–1715* (London, 1992); idem, *Seafaring, Sailors and Trade, 1450–1750: studies in British and European maritime and imperial history* (Aldershot, AshgateVariorum, 2003).

27 Unger, Richard W., *Dutch Shipbuilding before 1800: Ships and Guilds* (Assen, 1978); idem, *The Ship in the Medieval Economy, 600–1600* (London and Montreal, 1980); idem, *Ships and shipping in the North Sea and Atlantic, 1400–1800* (Aldershot and Brookfield, 1997); Phillips, William D. Jr and Carla Rahn Phillips, *The Worlds of Christopher Columbus* (Cambridge and New York, 1992); Rahn Philips, Carla, *Life at Sea in the Sixteenth Century: The Landlubber's Lament of Eugenio de Salazar* (Minneapolis, 1987); eadem, *The Treasure of the San José: Death at Sea in the War of the Spanish Succession* (Baltimore, 2007); Fernández-Armesto, Felipe, *Columbus* (Oxford and New York, 1991); idem, *Pathfinders: A Global History of*

Exploration (New York, 2006); Rediker, Marcus, *Between the Devil and the Deep Blue Sea: Merchant Seamen, Pirates, and the Anglo-American Maritime World, 1700–1750* (Cambridge, 1987).

28 Greene, Jack P. and Philip D. Morgan (eds), *Atlantic History. A Critical Appraisal* (Oxford, 2009), p. 6. See also Games, Alison, 'Atlantic History: Definitions, Challenges, and Opportunities', Forum, *American Historical Review* (June 2006), pp. 741–57.

29 Horden and Purcell, 'The Mediterranean and "the New Thalassology"'.

30 For an insightful overview see Vink, Markus P.M., 'Indian Ocean Studies and the "New Thalassology"', *Journal of Global History* 2 (2007), pp. 41–62.

31 Fischer, Lewis R. and Walter Minchinton (eds), *People of the Northern Seas*, RMH no. 3 (St John's, Newfoundland, 1992).

32 Broeze, Frank, 'Underdevelopment and Dependency: Maritime India during the Raj', *Modern Asian Studies* 18 (1984), pp. 429–57; idem, 'From Imperialism to Independence: The Decline and Re-emergence of Asian Shipping', *The Great Circle* 9 (1987); idem, 'The Ports and Port System of the Asian Seas: An Overview with Historical Perspective from c. 1750', *The Great Circle* 18/2 (1996), pp. 73–96; idem, *Gateways of Asia. Port Cities of Asia in the 13th–20th Centuries* (New York, 1997).

33 Broeze, Frank, *Brides of the Sea: Port Cities of Asia from the 16th–20th Centuries* (Sydney, 1989), pp. 3, 21.

34 Frank Broeze died in 2001, and his last seminar at the end of March of that year was on his book on the Pacific Ocean – a book that he never finished. See also my 'Tribute to Professor Frank Broeze', in Ina McCabe Baghdiantz, Gelina Harlaftis and Ioanna Pepelasis Minoglou (eds), *Diaspora Entrepreneurial Networks: Five Centuries of History* (Oxford, 2005), pp. xv–xvii.

35 Broeze, Frank, 'Notes on Paul Butel', Roundtable, *International Journal of Maritime History* XII/1 (June 2000), pp. 261–70.

36 Butel, Paul, *The Atlantic* (New York, 1999); Mollat, Michel, *Europe and the Sea* (Oxford, 1993); Fontenay, Michel, 'The Mediterranean World, 1500–1800: Social and Economic Perspectives', in Victor Mallia-Milanes (ed.), *Hospitaller Malta, 1530–1798. Studies on Early Modern Malta and the Order of Saint John of Jerusalem* (Msida, 1993).

37 Osterhammel, Jürgen and Niels P. Petersson, *Globalization. A Short History* (Princeton and Oxford, 2005), p. 19.

38 Kyle Crossley, Pamela, *What is Global History?* (Cambridge, 2008), p. 117.

39 Pomeranz, Kenneth, *The Great Divergence: China, Europe, and the making of the modern world economy* (Princeton and Oxford, 2000).

40 Johnman, Lewis and Hugh Murphy, 'Maritime and Business History in Britain' *International Journal of Maritime History* XIX/1 (June 2007), pp. 238–70.

41 Starkey, David J. and Gelina Harlaftis (eds), *Global Markets: The Internationalization of the Sea Transport Industries Since 1850*, RMH no. 14 (St John's, Newfoundland, 1998).

42 Broeze, Frank, *The Globalisation of the Oceans: Containerisation from the 1950s to the Present*, RMH no. 23 (St John's, Newfoundland, 2002); Bergholm, Tapio, Lewis R. Fischer, and M. Elisabetta Tonizzi (eds), *Making Global and Local Connections: Historical Perspectives on Ports*, RMH no. 35 (St John's, Newfoundland, 2007).

43 Grafe, Regina, 'Why maritime history has yet to become global history', in session H6, 'Maritime history as global history' of the World Economic History Congress, Utrecht 2009.

44 Mollat, Michel, *Les Sources de l'Histoire Maritime en Europe, du Moyen Age au XVIII siècle*, Actes du Quatrième Colloque International d'Histoire Maritime, 20–23 May 1959 (Paris, 1962).

45 Michele Mollat remained the only President of the International Commission of Maritime History for the next 25 years.

46 Mollat, *Les Sources de l'Histoire* Annexe I, p. X.

47 Hobsbawm, Eric, *On History* (London, 1997), p. 179.

48 Davis, Ralph, *The Rise of the English Shipping Industry in the Seventeenth and the Eighteenth Centuries* (London 1962). Williams, David, 'Bulk Passenger Shipping, 1750–1870', in Lewis R. Fischer and Helge W. Nordvik (eds), *Shipping and Trade, 1750–1950: Essays in International Maritime Economic History* (Yorkshire, 1990); Ville, Simon and David M. Williams (eds), *Management, Finance and Industrial Relations in Maritime Industries: Essays in International Maritime and Business History*, RMH no. 6 (St John's, Newfoundland, 1994); Jackson, Gordon and David M. Williams, *Shipping, Technology and Imperialism* (Aldershot, 1996).

49 Fischer, Lewis R. and Walter Minchinton (eds), *People of the Northern Seas* (St John's, Newfoundland, IMEHA in conjunction with the Association for the History of the Northern Seas, 1992); Fischer, Lewis R. et al. (eds), *The North Sea: Twelve Essays on Social History of Maritime Labour* (Stavanger, Norway, 1992); *The Market for Seamen in the Age of Sail*, RMH no. 7 (St John's, Newfoundland, 1994); Fischer, Lewis R. and Andrian Jarvis, *Harbours and Havens: Essays in Port History in Honour of Gordon Jackson* (St John's, Newfoundland, 1999); Bergholm, Tapio, Lewis R. Fisher and M. Elisabetta Tonizzi (eds), *Making Global and Local Connections: historical perspectives on ports*, RMH no. 35 (St John's, Newfoundland, 2007).

50 Speech of the 4th President of IMEHA, Gelina Harlaftis, 'Reaching the centre', 5th IMHC, Thursday 26 June.

51 'Le navire, c'est l'hétérotopie par excellence', in Michel Foucault, 'Dits et écrits', *Des espaces autres* (conférence au Cercle d'études architecturales, 14 mars 1967), in *Architecture, Mouvement, Continuité* 5 (October 1984), pp. 46–9.

52 Bentley, Jerry H., Bridenthal, Renate and Wigen, Kären (eds), *Seascapes: maritime histories, littoral cultures, and transoceanic exchanges* (Honolulu, 2007).

53 Fernández-Armesto, Felipe, *Civilizations* (Basingstoke, 2000), p. 327.

54 Van Dyck, Karen, 'Greek Literature, the Diaspora and the Sea', in Maria Christina Chatziioannou and Gelina Harlaftis (eds), *Following the Nereids. Sea Routes and Maritime Business, 16th–20th Centuries* (Athens, 2006), pp. 233–44.

55 'Mal de depart', *The Collected Poems of Nikos Kavadias*, transl. Gail Holst-Warhaft (Amsterdam, 1987).

56 After the title of the volume by Ommer, Rosemary and Gerald Panting (eds), *Working Men Who Got Wet*, Proceedings of the Fourth Conference of the Atlantic Canada Shipping Project (St John's, Newfoundland, 1980).

57 Wiltshire de Oliveira, Maria Lúcia, 'The Sea Seen, between Rafts of Rock and Wooden Caravels: The Sea as Past, Future and Destiny in the Portuguese Literature', in Gelina Harlaftis (ed.), *Proceedings, 4th International Congress of Maritime History*, CD, International Maritime Economic History Association, Corfu, 21–27 June 2004.

Bibliography

Bentley, Jerry H., Bridenthal, Renate and Wigen, Kären (eds), *Seascapes: maritime histories, littoral cultures, and transoceanic exchanges* (Honolulu, University of Hawai'i Press, 2007).

Bergholm, Tapio, Lewis R., Fisher, M. and Elisabetta Tonizzi (eds), *Making Global and Local Connections: historical perspectives on ports*, RMH no. 35 (St John's, Newfoundland, IMEHA, 2007).

Broeze, Frank, 'Underdevelopment and Dependency: Maritime India during the Raj', *Modern Asian Studies* 18 (1984), pp. 429–57.

—, 'From Imperialism to Independence: The Decline and Re-emergence of Asian Shipping', *The Great Circle* 9 (1987).

—, *Brides of the Sea: port cities of Asia from the 16th–20th centuries* (Sydney, New South Wales University Press, 1989), pp. 3, 21.

—, 'From the Periphery to the Mainstream: The Challenge of Australia's Maritime History', *The Great Circle* 11/1 (1989), pp. 1–14.

—, 'Maritime History at the Crossroads: A Critical Review of Recent Historiography', in Frank Broeze, *Maritime History at the Crossroads: a critical review of recent historiography*, RMH no. 9 (St John's, Newfoundland, IMEHA, 1995).

—, 'The Ports and Port System of the Asian Seas: An Overview with Historical Perspective from c. 1750', *The Great Circle* 18/2 (1996), pp. 73–96.

—, *Gateways of Asia. Port Cities of Asia in the 13th–20th Centuries* (New York, Kegan Paul International, 1997).

—, 'Notes on Paul Butel', Roundtable, *International Journal of Maritime History* XII/1 (June 2000), pp. 261–70.

—, *The Globalisation of the Oceans: containerisation from the 1950s to the present*, RMH, No. 23 (St John's, Newfoundland, IMEHA, 2002).

Bruijn, Jaap, 'Recent Developments in the Historiography of Maritime History in the Netherlands', in Frank Broeze, *Maritime History at the*

Crossroads: a critical review of recent historiography, RMH no. 9 (St John's, Newfoundland, IMEHA, 1995), pp. 193–212.

Butel, Paul, *The Atlantic* (New York, Routledge, 1999).

Cannadine, David (ed.), *Empire, the Sea and Global History: Britain's maritime world, c. 1760–c. 1840* (London, Palgrave Macmillan, 2007).

D'Angelo, Michela and Elisabetta Tonizzi, 'Recent Maritime Historiography on Italy', in Gelina Harlaftis and Carmel Vassalo (eds), *New Directions in Mediterranean Maritime History*, RMH no. 28 (St John's, Newfoundland, IMEHA, 2004).

Davis, Ralph, *The Rise of the English Shipping Industry in the Seventeenth and the Eighteenth Centuries* (London, St Martin's Press, 1962).

Driessen, Henk, 'Seascapes and Mediterranean Crossings', *Journal of Global History* 3 (2008), pp. 445–9.

Fernández-Armesto, Felipe, *Columbus* (Oxford and New York, Oxford University Press, 1991).

—, *Civilizations* (Basingstoke, Macmillan, 2000).

—, *Pathfinders: a global history of exploration* (New York, W.W. Norton, 2006).

Finamore, Daniel (ed.), *Maritime History as World History* (Gainsville, University Press of Florida, 2004).

Fischer, Lewis R. and Eric W. Sager, 'An Approach to the Quantitative Analysis of British Shipping Records', *Business History* 22/2 (July 1980), pp. 135–51.

Fischer, Lewis R. and Eric W. Sager (eds), *Merchant Shipping and Economic Development in Atlantic Canada*, Proceedings of the Fifth Conference of the Atlantic Canada Shipping Project, Maritime History Group (St John's, Newfoundland, Memorial University of Newfoundland, 1982).

Fischer, Lewis R. and Walter Minchinton (eds), *People of the Northern Seas* (St John's, Newfoundland, IMEHA in conjunction with the Association for the History of the Northern Seas, 1992).

Fischer, Lewis R. (ed.), *The Market for Seamen in the Age of Sail*, RMH no. 7 (St John's, Newfoundland, IMEHA, 1994).

— (ed.), 'Maritime History in Canada', in Frank Broeze, *Maritime History at the Crossroads: a critical review of recent historiography*, RMH no. 9 (St John's, Newfoundland, IMEHA, 1995), pp. 31–52.

— and Adrian Jarvis (eds), *Harbours and Havens: essays in port history in honour of Gordon Jackson* (St John's, Newfoundland, IMEHA, 1999).

— et al. (eds), *The North Sea: twelve essays on social history of maritime labour* (Stavanger, Norway, Stavanger Maritime Museum/Association of North Sea Societies, 1992).

Fontenay, Michel, 'The Mediterranean World, 1500–1800: social and economic perspectives', in Victor Mallia-Milanes (ed.), *Hospitaller Malta, 1530–1798. Studies on early modern Malta and the Order of Saint John of Jerusalem* (Msida, Malte, 1993).

Foucault, Michel, 'Dits et écrits', *Des espaces autres* (conférence au Cercle d'études architecturales, 14 mars 1967), in *Architecture, Mouvement, Continuité* 5 (October 1984), pp. 46–9.

Games, Alison, 'Atlantic History: definitions, challenges, and opportunities', Forum, *American Historical Review* (June 2006), pp. 741–57.

Greene, Jack P. and Philip D. Morgan (eds), *Atlantic History. A critical appraisal* (Oxford, Oxford University Press, 2009).

Grafe, Regina, 'Why Maritime History has yet to become Global History', in session H6, 'Maritime History as Global History', World Economic History Congress, Utrecht 2009.

Harlaftis, Gelina, 'The Maritime Historiography of Greece in Recent Decades', in Frank Broeze, *Maritime History at the Crossroads: a critical review of recent historiography*, RMH no. 9 (St John's, Newfoundland, IMEHA, 1995), pp. 135–50.

—, 'Storia maritima e storia dei porti', *Memoria e Ricerca* 11 (2002), pp. 5–22.

—, 'Maritime History since Braudel', in Gelina Harlaftis and Carmel Vassalo (eds), *New Directions in Mediterranean Maritime History*, RMH no. 28 (St. John's, Newfoundland, IMEHA, 2004).

—, 'Tribute to Professor Frank Broeze', in Ina McCabe Baghdiantz, Gelina Harlaftis and Ioanna Pepelasis Minoglou (eds), *Diaspora Entrepreneurial Networks: Five Centuries of History* (Oxford, Berg, 2005), pp. xv–xvii.

Hattendorf, John B. (ed.), *Ubi Sumus? The State of Naval and Maritime History* (Newport, RI, 1994).

Hobsbawm, Eric, *On History* (London, Weidenfeld and Nicolson, 1997).

Holm, Poul, Tim D. Smith and David Starkey (eds), *The Exploited Seas: new directions for marine environmental history*, No. 21 (St John's, Newfoundland, IMEHA, 2001).

Horden, Peregrine and Nicholas Purcell, *The Corrupting Sea. A study of Mediterranean history* (Oxford, Blackwell Publishing, 2000).

—, 'The Mediterranean and "the New Thalassology"', Forum, *American Historical Review* (June 2006), pp. 722–40.

Jackson, Gordon and David M. Williams, *Shipping, Technology and Imperialism* (Aldershot, IMEHA, 1996).

Johnman, Lewis and Hugh Murphy, 'Maritime and Business History in Britain' *International Journal of Maritime History* 19/1 (June 2007), pp. 238–70.

Kavadias, Nikos, *The Collected Poems of Nikos Kavadias*, transl. Gail Holst-Warhaft (Amsterdam, Adolf m. Hakkert, 1987).

King, Charles, *The Black Sea: a history* (Oxford and New York, Oxford University Press, 2004).

Kirby, David and Merja-Liisa Hinkkanen, *The Baltic and the North Seas* (London and New York, Routledge, 2000).

Kyle Crossley, Pamela, *What is Global History?* (Cambridge, Polity, 2008).

Labaree, Benjamin W., 'The State of American Maritime History in the 1990s', in John B. Hattendorf (ed.), *Ubi Sumus? The state of naval and maritime History* (Newport, RI, Naval War College Press, 1994).

Lewis, Martin W. and Kären Wigen, 'A Maritime Response to the Crisis in Area Studies', *The Geographical Review* 89/2 (April 1999), pp. 161–8.

Matvejević, Predrag, *Mediterranean: a cultural landscape* (Berkeley, University of California Press, 1999).

Mollat, Michel, *Les Sources de l'histoire maritime en Europe, du Moyen Âge au XVIII siècle*, Actes du Quatrième Colloque International d'Histoire Maritime, 20–23 May 1959 (Paris, 1962).

—, *Europe and the Sea* (Oxford, Blackwell 1993).

Ommer, Rosemary and Gerald Panting (eds), *Working Men Who Got Wet*, Proceedings of the Fourth Conference of the Atlantic Canada Shipping Project (St John's, Newfoundland, 1980).

Osterhammel, Jürgen and Niels P. Petersson, *Globalization. A short history* (Princeton and Oxford, Princeton University Press, 2005).

Parry, John Horace, *The Spanish Seaborne Empire* (London, Hutchinson, 1966).

—, *The Discovery of the Sea* (Berkeley, University of California Press, 1981).

Pearson, Michael, *The Indian Ocean* (London and New York, Routledge, 2003).

Peters, Edward, 'Quid nobis cum pelage? The New Thalassology and the Economic History of Europe', *Journal of Interdisciplinary History* xxxiv/I (summer 2003), pp. 49–61.

Phillips, William D. Jr and Carla Rahn Phillips, *The Worlds of Christopher Columbus* (Cambridge and New York, Cambridge University Press, 1992).

Pomeranz, Kenneth, *The Great Divergence: China, Europe, and the making of the modern world economy* (Princeton and Oxford, Princeton University Press, 2000).

Rahn Philips, Carla, *Life at Sea in the Sixteenth Century: the landlubber's lament of Eugenio de Salazar* (Minneapolis, Associates of the James Ford Bell Library, University of Minnesota, 1987).

—, *The Treasure of the San José: death at sea in the War of the Spanish Succession* (Baltimore, Johns Hopkins University Press, 2007).

Rediker, Marcus, *Between the Devil and the Deep Blue Sea: merchant seamen, pirates, and the Anglo-American maritime world, 1700–1750* (Cambridge, Cambridge University Press 1987).

Roberts, Callum, *The Unnatural History of the Sea* (Washington, DC, Island Press/Shearwater Books, 2007).

Rodger, N.A.M., *The Safeguard of the Sea: a naval history of Britain, 660–1649* (London, HarperCollins Publishers in association with the National Maritime Museum 1997).

Rodger, N.A.M., *The Command of the Ocean: a naval history of Britain, 1649–1815* (London, Allen Lane in association with the National Maritime Museum, 2004).

Sager, Eric, *Seafaring Labour: the Merchant Marine of Atlantic Canada, 1820–1914* (Kingston, ON, McGill-Queen's University Press, 1989).

— with Gerald E. Panting, *Maritime capital: the shipping industry in Atlantic Canada, 1820–1914* (Montreal and Buffalo, McGill-Queen's University Press, 1990).

Scammell, Geoffrey V., *The World Encompassed: the first European maritime empires c. 800–1650* (London, Methuen, 1981).

—, *The First Imperial Age: European overseas expansion c. 1400–1715* (London, Routledge, 1992).

—, *Seafaring, Sailors and Trade, 1450–1750: studies in British and European maritime and imperial history* (Aldershot, AshgateVariorum, 2003).

Starkey, David J. and Gelina Harlaftis (eds), *Global Markets: the internationalization of the sea transport industries since 1850*, RMH no. 14 (St John's, Newfoundland, IMEHA, 1998).

Starkey, David J., Poul Holm and Michaela Barnard (eds), *Oceans Past: management insights from the history of marine animal populations* (London, Earthscan, 2008).

Unger, Richard W., *Dutch Shipbuilding before 1800: ships and guilds* (Assen, Van Gorcum, 1978).

—, *The Ship in the Medieval Economy, 600–1600* (London and Montreal, Croom Helm and McGill-Queen's University Press, 1980).

—, *Ships and Shipping in the North Sea and Atlantic, 1400–1800* (Aldershot and Brookfield, Ashgate/Variorum, 1997).

Valdaliso, Jesùs, 'The Progress of Maritime History in Spain since 1975', in Frank Broeze, *Maritime History at the Crossroads: a critical review of recent historiography*, RMH no. 9 (St John's, Newfoundland, IMEHA, 1995), pp. 229–48.

Van Dyck, Karen, 'Greek Literature, the Diaspora and the Sea', in Maria Christina Chatziioannou and Gelina Harlaftis (eds), *Following the Nereids.*

Sea routes and maritime business, 16th–20th centuries (Athens, Kerkyra Publications, 2006), pp. 233–44.

Ville, Simon and David M. Williams (eds), *Management, Finance and Industrial Relations in Maritime Industries: Essays in international maritime and business history*, RMH no. 6 (St John's, Newfoundland, IMEHA, 1994).

Vink, Markus P.M., 'Indian Ocean Studies and the "New Thalassology"', *Journal of Global History* 2 (2007), pp. 41–62.

Williams, David, 'Bulk Passenger Shipping, 1750–1870', in Lewis R. Fischer and Helge W. Nordvik (eds), *Shipping and Trade, 1750–1950: Essays in International Maritime Economic History* (Yorkshire, Lofthouse Publications, 1990).

Wiltshire de Oliveira, Maria Lúcia, 'The Sea Seen, between Rafts of Rock and Wooden Caravels: the sea as past, future and destiny in the Portuguese literature', in Gelina Harlaftis (ed.), *Proceedings, 4th International Congress of Maritime History*, CD, International Maritime Economic History Association, Corfu, 21–27 June 2004.

14

What is the Role of the Historian in an Increasingly Presentist World?

François Hartog

Anxieties about the present have always coloured the writing of history. In different ways, the present and history have always joined forces, and it is this which enables us to trace the past, whether we choose to confirm or denounce it. However, in defining, and indeed questioning, what is meant by a presentist era, I am referring to something different. As has frequently been claimed, the conditions within which historians work have changed over the last 30 years. Indeed, they continue to change before our eyes. To explain this, we have taken hasty refuge in the somewhat convenient buzzword, 'crisis', as numerous articles and books attest.

What new questions, then, does the historian face? What role is he demanded to play or to avoid? What is the place and function of what the nineteenth century – a time when history was thought of in terms of discipline and 'desired' knowledge as a science – defined as the wise mediator between the past and the present, dealing with the specific, if not unique, subject of the Nation and the State, in a world which now privileges the importance of the present, of the present alone, and which sees itself as globalized and possibly even post-national? A presentist world is one in which the present has become the most all-encompassing and explanatory category, and memory, for the last 20 years at least, has been considered not only as a contemporary concept but as one which creates the contemporary.

What is the task, or rather the duty, of the historian if not to use his knowledge to enlighten his contemporaries? And yet, proposing a critical perspective presupposes the scrutiny and acknowledgement of the conditions of historiographical practice, in order to assess the effects on the existing and possible attitudes of the historian. Among such conditions, I want to focus primarily on time. If the relationship with time is, for everyone, a fundamental part of the way we experience ourselves and the world around us, it is doubly so for the historian. Firstly, time constitutes the dimension within which a historian lives and works, but is it also 'his' period, the period *on* which he works. Thus time, 'the fugitive', or rather times and the differences between the two – not only the distance but also the ways in which they differ – are at the heart of his work, if not his very *raison d'être*. François Bédarida describes the historian as 'Time's director'.[1]

'It is often the case that, influenced by strong and rich traditions, an entire generation can go by without engaging in intellectual revolution.' This warning, once articulated by Fernand Braudel, serves as a useful reminder, because, as we know, we are faced constantly with the monotony of discipline, the routine of academic establishments and the weight of institutions. Responsible as he is of the past, the historian must also be the present's sentinel. As a historian, I want to move away from the (shared) diagnosis that emphasizes the strength and fertility of the present (to use the title of Zaki Laïdi's work, *Le sacre du présent*) and formulate a new hypothesis. I intend to employ presentism to describe the contemporary nature of our experience of time and I suggest that we use a heuristic approach to carry out this inquiry, considering primarily the idea of a regime of historicity. To what end? The aim will be to interrogate the various experiences of time, or rather its crisis. These moments, described by Hannah Arendt as 'breaches', that is, moments when the evidence that time is passing becomes blurred, and when, more precisely, one begins to lose any sense of how to define and to differentiate between the past, the present and the future. Using regimes of historicity as my tool, I aim to compare the crises of time in the past and the present, in order to identify better their specificity: does our contemporary present differ and, if so, how, from other presents of the past? Will risking the hypothesis of a new regime of historicity improve the intelligibility of the contemporary experience of time? This was the approach I adopted in my book *Régimes d'historicité*.[2] Thus, one of the ways in which a historian can become a contemporary of the contemporary is to start by questioning the overwhelming proof he has of its existence. This is quite the opposite to the constant broadcasting and availability of current events, or to following contemporary trends. As the philosopher Marcel Gauchet notes, 'the individual has to want to belong to their period in order to belong, and he has to work hard to get there'.

What is the current situation of the historian's craft and position?

The rapid rise and dominance of the 'contemporary' and the 'present' is the first point I shall consider. This rise has certainly taken place in history. It is also the case in anthropology, where the shift from the remote and tradition to the contemporary and to what is happening right now, with particular focus on all that pertains to modernity, has been even more remarkable. Sociology is not exempt from this either, even though its principal project has been to explore contemporary society. It is possible to comprehend the present, or indeed some of its characteristics, through the vocabulary that bears witness to it. Although grand narratives no longer exist, we do have certain key terms that are so inescapable that that they have become part of our everyday vocabulary. 'Present', 'memory', 'commemoration', 'heritage', 'identity', 'crimes against humanity', 'witness', 'globalization' are but a few of the most frequently used.

The contemporary is an imperative. Social sciences are under significant pressure to focus more on the contemporary and to respond more effectively and quickly to 'social requirement', to the urgency of certain situations, emotions and problems, and to be able to convey these in figures and writing. Experts are called upon to carry this out, and the historian in particular is sought as an expert.[3] He is called upon by various *ad hoc* commissions to provide the facts, and nothing but the facts, just like the witness in a trial.

However, the field of the contemporary, to which the historian is somewhat of a latecomer, is already occupied. Journalists, for example, already hold sway. So, where does that leave us? Since we live in a media world where current events are immediately, even daily, historicized, how can the historian be quickest off the mark and also produce 'live history', providing the analytical perspective of hindsight on the day of the event?

The witness

This focus on the contemporary and the present is parallel to an increase in the public use of the past; to quote Jurgen Habermas' phrase, coined during the much-publicized debate in 1986 among German historians over the place of Nazism in German history, a debate that was turned into a public scandal by leading German newspapers of the time. How is the past useful? How can it be used positively? And, importantly, what do we mean by the past? It is the recent past that is primarily referred to here: that which 'has not yet passed', or what in France is called the 'history of the present'. Among the different protagonists on stage, witnesses in particular played an increasingly important role – to the extent that the historian Annette

Wieviorka described this period as 'the time of the witness'.[4] Today, a witness is principally conceived of as the face and voice of a victim, as a survivor who is made to recount his/her story, whom we listen to, record and film. The most significant recent project of this nature has been set up by the Spielberg Foundation. It aims to gather the testimonies of all the survivors of Nazi camps. Is the witness then a 'source' or a 'voice' that should be heard 'live' (or rather online) without the 'mediation' of a historian?

This trend for commemoration can be seen in the 60th-anniversary celebrations of the Normandy Landings, in 2004. According such importance to veterans is not only a means of showing respect, but also turns them into media-friendly material for television. They become both spectators and actors, occupying the past and the present. In 2005, leaders of 45 countries gathered amongst thousands of survivors and witnesses at Auschwitz-Birkenau, to mark the 60 years since the concentration camps were liberated. These celebrations have come to punctuate public life, combining memories (whether forgotten, re-remembered or newly-triggered) with political and social agendas to create a 'collective memory', broadcast television and radio programmes, and provide moral lessons. A European Parliament resolution refers to 'the lessons of the Holocaust'. Although historians are by no means in charge of the public calendar or even necessarily the questions and terms of debate surrounding it, nevertheless, the commemorations do have some influence over the direction of research, publications, media attention and, therefore, the perception of the historian in the public domain. Has this figure become an authoritative commentator to be summoned in such circumstances?

The legislator

Over the last few years, lawmakers' involvement in history and memory has intensified. Influenced by the Gayssot Law of 13 July 1990, which had 'the intention of punishing any racist, xenophobic or anti-Semitic act', in 2001, the French Parliament voted for two successive 'remembrance laws'. The first, which referred to the 1915 Armenian genocide, contained this unique article: 'our country and other democracies have a heightened duty towards remembrance. It must not be limited to the history of each individual nation, but must be extended to include the memory of every human being tragically affected by genocide in the twentieth century'. Through the logic of this clause, the 'duty of remembrance' has taken us from the particular to the universal, from remembering Armenians to the whole of humanity. In this case, the legislator does not consider himself so much a historian but as a guardian and spokesperson of memory. The second law, which 'recognized trafficking and slavery as crimes against humanity', was passed in May 2001. It asked France to 'consider the memory of all those who were victims of such crimes'. This also appeals to our duty to remember. The symptomatic value of these texts lies in the way the legislator understands, employs and even (in a repetant laic manner) applies to himself this 'duty towards remembrance'. This is by no means an isolated act. UNESCO declared 2004 to be 'the international year of commemoration for the struggle against slavery and its abolition'.

The final manifestation of this in France (for now at least) can be seen in article 4 of the law passed in February 2005, suggesting that the school curriculum should recognize 'the positive effects' of colonialism. Thankfully, this was repealed. Here we have moved from the duty of remembering to dictating history. In reaction to that, the late René Rémond set up an association of historians called 'Freedom for History'.

Crimes against humanity

The duty to remember applies first and foremost, and rightly so, to crimes against humanity. Having been defined by lawmakers, these crimes are presented to the judge before the historian of the present has had a chance to address their unique relationship to time. For, in the case of such crimes, time does not pass. As we know, since the Charter of the Nuremberg Trials, everyone has the inalienable right to bring to trial a crime against humanity, which is exempt from the statute of limitations. This right was recognized by the French Penal Code in 1994 and was later recognized by most countries (following a decision to create an International Criminal Court, ratified by France in 2000). The inalienability of the right means that here the usual writing off of a crime, foreseen by the law after a period of time has passed, does not apply. As the academic lawyer, Yan Thomas, suggests, 'the opposite of permanence, is not time that passes, but that which is finite'; both of these are constructed.[5]

The intrinsic relationship between the public domain and crimes against humanity, creating their permanence, also means that the criminal will remain a contemporary of his crime until his death, just as we are all contemporaries of the actions judged as crimes against humanity. The inherent permanence of such crimes thus creates a sort of 'legal atemporality', causing the criminal to be locked in the same timeframe as his crime. This could also be seen as a means by which the past asserts itself in the present, as a sort of present-past; or rather, it could represent the ongoing nature of the present (and by present I mean the moment of the trial). Under French law, the only way a historian can figure in a trial and enter into this legal atemporality is as witness required to make an oral statement. In general, we are able to ascertain shifts (or mixtures) between the time of the law (juridical time), which has its own temporalities, and social time, and indeed exchanges between them, which are made through responsibility. The reign of permanence in the public domain is one of the symptoms of its increasing judiciarization, which is, indeed, another defining characteristic of our time.

The judge

The historian will encounter, whether directly or indirectly, actually or metaphorically, another figure of authority in the contemporary field: that of the judge. The encounter is not necessarily initiated by judges themselves, but is rather an inevitable consequence of the increasing judiciarization, just referred to, of the public domain. Judges have to be unfailingly decisive in almost all matters and to 'heal' public, private, past, present and even future problems. We even use the term legal 'therapy'. In history, this has led us to look again at the question of 'the judge and the historian', and the relationship between the legal and the historical.[6] Even though the idea of a history tribunal is outdated, questions are once again being asked about the relationship between the judge and the historian, about the figure whose role it is to pass sentence, or rather to prepare a case for judgement. Taking these thoughts as a pretext and questions about proof and the idea of context, little has been said about historical judgement: indeed, does this even exist? And if so, how would it differ from legal judgement?

New quasi-formal and official commissions of historians have also been established. The independent Committee of Swiss Experts, for example, was created in 1996 in response to a decision made by the Swiss Confederation and Government. Its aim is to investigate the question of 'Jewish wealth and Nazi gold'.[7] The Truth and Reconciliation Commission in South Africa is another, although rather different, such example. It was more than just a committee of historians assigned to interrogate the facts. Through its court hearings, this committee began to recognize and distinguish between various different types of truth. Allowing a victim to state publicly what he or she has suffered was considered a 'healing truth', for example.[8] Chilean, Argentinean and Moroccan committees have also been set up. Furthermore, a number of trials, namely for crimes against humanity, have taken place. Here, memory was privileged as victims had to be given the chance to give their accounts, be listened to and receive some sort of compensation. Yet, such trials were primarily conceived of as 'historical documents', as is demonstrated by the decision to film them.[9] These trials raised the question – which has also sparked debate – of whether the historian is a sort of witness.

The media and our emotions

In the current climate, our daily experiences take place in a world which gives priority to that which is direct, interactive, real time, live, online, immediate and without distance (such as the compassionate humanity of politicians, the practice of instant remorse and 24-hour mourning); a world which can conceive more easily of the 'past', as a rather vague category, than of history, which stresses the importance of commemoration and its ceremonies, and of the 'presentification' rather than explanation of events; a world which values the affective and compassionate over detached analysis, appealing always to witnesses, feeding on memory, and which pays homage to memorial sites. In such a climate, the duty of remembering translates as the individual's right to his own memory. Cultural heritage is currently sustained by a host of associations that are trying to find ways of truly inhabiting the present. There are numerous strategies and claims in place for finding, or providing each one of us with, 'our own history', to clarify who we are and, more precisely, who I am right now. I can discover who I am in this very memory and it is this memory which, in turn, expresses who I am. Our quest for identity has become the driving force!

The role of a historian

Over the nineteenth and twentieth centuries, the historian has held four major different roles. Michelet conceived of him as a prophet, the 'vates' of the people; Monod and Lavisse saw him as an indispensable pedagogue and teacher, arguing that he instructs the Republic by bridging the gap between an old and a new France. Some scholars, such as Fustel de Coulanges, claimed oblivion (lethe) as precondition of the present, in order to devote themselves to knowledge only of the past. Others stressed the need for one to hold both ends of the chain: the past and the present (such as the founders of the *Annales*). For Marc Bloch, history, defined as 'understanding men through time', has 'a constant need to unite the study of the dead with the living'.[10] The conclusion to the 1867 *Report on Historical Studies* in France contained this powerful statement: 'the history of a period can only be conceived of when that period is entirely over. The past is thus the domain of history; the present is that of politics and the future belongs to God'.[11] In fact, the compiler of the report presented himself to the government minister as a 'faithful' (that is, to the letter) 'judicial secretary'. Today, to be accepted in the public domain and recognized in civil society, does the historian have to 'presentify' himself by promoting himself as an expert about the present and a sort of ferryman whose job it is to convey us from the present to the present?

Contemporary and ultra-contemporary historians, who are often high-profile public personalities, place great emphasis on their position as vehicles for the present. We can see this in the very rhetoric they employ. Pierre Nora's comments, such as 'the present has become the category through which we understand ourselves' and it is up to the historian to 'explain the present to the present', express this perfectly. Likewise, the journal *Vingtième siècle*, founded in 1984, stated that its aim was to 'be responsible for the identity of the present'. This is precisely the approach of the author of the *Lieux de mémoire*. This work explicitly privileges the present, which here also includes the past as it is constructed within the present, and a type of national history that is neither teleological nor futurist, neither epic nor grandiose. In *Lieux de mémoire*, the first volume of which was published in 1984, Nora argues that the past's very existence lies in the fact that it resurfaces in the present, and it does so under a historian's control.

If we follow Nora's argument, the historian as a vehicle is unquestionably but solely operating within the present, caught between 'confused questions and an enlightened response, between public pressure and the solitary patience of private research, between what he feels and what he knows'. Modest as he may be, he has become the historian of the present by right and by craft. In this way, whether the history studied is of the present or of another period, it still has to be considered as history *in* the present. The argument behind the *Lieux de mémoire* asks us to consider the historian, in the very practice of his craft, as a place of memory (which gave rise to Nora's *Ego-histoire*). And yet, modern historians insist on the necessary separation of the past and the present. They argue that history is a science, a pure science, of the past, and its servant an exact decoder of documents housed in silent archives. Indeed, according to Fernand Braudel, the historian considers himself (albeit implicitly) to be endowed with a somewhat detached critical eye.

The future: contingency and crisis

The future arrived in 1989. This was epitomized by 9 November, when the Berlin Wall fell and an ideology that was thought to be the apex of modernity came to an end. This was by no means the end of history, not even in the sense meant by Francis Fukuyama (who described 'end' not as cessation but as *telos* or destination), but rather a pause or a caesura in the sequence of time (in Europe first and then, little by little, all over the world).[12] If the trend for commemoration began before 1989, it is since then that we have become aware of time as disoriented. This is the same as when, two centuries earlier, in about 1789, the former order of time fell apart with the very regime of historicity that had structured it. The experience of the contemporaries was the experience of the acceleration of time, hitherto inconceivable, while with progress the future was transformed into a motive force. Along with progress, the future was understood as being the driving force. However, the principal difference is that now, the future is increasingly far away from us: more and more do we consider it closed off. Indeed, I have just referred to its crisis. The collapse of the Berlin Wall did not free the future! The future is still there, but despite our huge advances in knowledge (as information has been revolutionized), it has become more impenetrable than ever. Perhaps, in some respect, we have just given up on it: projects, prospects and futurology have been put aside. We are completely focused on responding to the immediate and on reacting in real time. Or maybe the future is simply too predictable, if indeed it has not already occurred (such a catastrophe is already there). The prevalence of fear and precaution in today's society attests to this predictability.

In dispelling the future's tyranny over the past, we have also managed to return the past to obscurity and, to a certain extent, have made the past equally impenetrable. This past that we now seek to save from such obscurity, which is neither linear nor univocal, needs to be seen as a dimension in which passed pasts have been, once, possible futures. In some respects it has already begun to be, in others it has been prevented. Philosophers, such as Paul Ricoeur, have emphasized this necessity and historians have championed its cause with renewed vigour, and rightly so, as it can benefit our general knowledge and understanding.[13] It is important that ethics are neither already established nor available for the historian to adopt.

The relationship between memory and cultural heritage

In France, *Lieux de mémoire* led us both to acknowledge that the 'national' existed and that it had changed. It also identified a new approach to remembering the past, appealing more to the representation of the past than to the comprehension of it: it was more an archivist's past than a historian's. In short, what was once a messianic nation is now heritage-centred, partaking in a shared culture. But who shares this culture? It manages to create a sense of national identity without encouraging nationalism, that is both active and yet pacified in a France which still needs to cultivate its collective memory as one would cultivate a garden, as if having taken early retirement from history.

The ever topical nation-state, according to a shared opinion, no longer needs to impose its values, but must instead protect what, in the present moment, immediately or even urgently, is thought of as 'heritage' by various social agents.[14] Historical monuments are often replaced by memorials.

These are not so much monuments as places of memory, where people try to revive or resuscitate one particular memory or several different memories. History, however, tends to melt into the past. It is seen as 'an entity, located closer to sensation than narrative, demanding emotional participation rather than expecting analysis'. In this respect, it is not so much history that the historian tries to make felt, using all the techniques of 'presentification', as an 'affective past'.[15] He can achieve this by employing the past in an explicitly presentist manner.

Over the last 20 years, more than 2,000 organizations have been established (in France at least) specifically for cultural heritage and environment. This refers mainly to local heritage. By associating memory and territory, these projects aim firstly to render more tangible and to produce a sense of continuity where people live, especially since often people have not lived there long. 'The organisations that focus on cultural heritage construct a memory which is not given but not lost. They create a more symbolic world. Furthermore, heritage should not be viewed from the perspective of the past, but rather of the present. It is an active component of the present which relates to the present.'[16] Moreover, heritage, which has become one of the main components of the leisure industry, has important economic implications. Tourist guides and package holidays have firmly established the place of the leisure business in globalization. As a business, it fits right into the rhythm and speed of today's market economy, or at least, is affected by it. This large sector has thus achieved its autonomy, with its own ways of working, constraints, objectives and figures.

After the catastrophes of the twentieth century, the numerous conflicts and so manifest a speeding up of the way we experience time, the increasing importance placed on memory or on cultural heritage should not have surprised or should not surprise us in the end. On the contrary, what distinguishes the upsurge in contemporary cultural heritage is the speed of its growth, its numerous guises and its overwhelmingly presentist nature –, and all this at the very time when the present has also asserted its place and grown (it is now in its seventies!). I have identified several manifestations of this: the memorial, which is preferred to a monument (or the latter comes back in the guise of a memorial); the past, which is more attractive than history; the way the past is made present, by giving emotion and evocation precedence over distance and mediation; the increasing importance placed on what is local, which goes hand in hand with an emphasis on one's personal history and, finally, cultural heritage, which is also effected by the speed of today's world. It has to move quickly before it is too late, and before nightfall and the day has utterly disappeared.

Whether in the form of a question, duty or right, memory acts both as a response to presentism and as a symptom of it. This is also the case for heritage. Here, however, the perspective of experience and the order of time figure more prominently. Making the environment part of cultural heritage, which was given international importance by the UNESCO Convention in 1972, demonstrates the most significant and novel application of this idea. It suggests new implications for the future and new elements of the relationship between the present and future, since the environment is a threatened collective good that member-states must endeavour to protect. Yet, this future is no longer a promise or 'full of hope', rather it is seen as full of threat. Such is the extent of the turn around in attitudes. The future represents a threat that is in fact our responsibility; now, if we have not already done so, we must acknowledge our role. The future is no longer a promising goal towards which we hasten with excitement, but rather a shadow we have invited to loom over us while we tramp around in the present and contemplate a past that will not pass.

A critical perspective

Having shed some light on the conjuncture, looking at it from some key words and from the various positions occupied by the historians yesterday and today, my provisional conclusion will be more of a suggestion: to move from the period of time in question to considering time as a question. How can we do this? By employing the idea of a regime of historicity in a heuristic manner is one possible option. My meditation as a historian is part of the present, so that I look at it as a perspective, with the aim of confronting it better prepared. I consider the historian to be a traveller who comes and goes between the past and the present: his journey is made up of a constant pattern of leaving and returning. In and through this action, he creates a perspective that is continuously repeated and never-ending. He seeks the moments of doubt and, as may be the case, when the very relation to time turns out to be riddled with uncertainty.

What I mean by regimes of historicity, to make it clear once again, are the different means available to us for articulating the categories of the past, the present and the future. The very nature of time varies according to whether we focus on the past, the future or the present. The idea of a regime of historicity is not something tangible as such, but rather a tool to aid our understanding.

Currently, the pre-eminent category is that of the present. It is as if all our means of comprehension come almost exclusively from it. In this respect (and only in this respect), there is no past, nor future, nor historical time, if it is true, as Reinhart Koselleck argues, that the modern historical period is caught between the tension created by the field of experience and the horizon of expectation. Whether this situation is transitory or permanent, no one can tell. We do know, however, that this present is a period of memory and of debt, of daily amnesia, uncertainty, endless polls and more and more sophisticated predictions. Should we infer a new regime of historicity from this? A regime which includes local, fragmentary and even disciplinary formulations, but perhaps not yet a general or unified expression? Is it expedient even to recognize one, if we consider the widespread nature and multiplicity of different temporal regimes to be an essential and distinctive part of our present? In other words, does this new regime refer to (and this is the question) a sort of default presentism, something that is transitory, temporary and waiting for something else, such as the reactivation of some modern regime of historicity? Or does it refer to an all-encompassing presentism, to an almost entirely new situation in which the present becomes the dominant category, a present produced by our societies of immediacy, with their technologies, the dominance of market, the media-based economy, with their histories and their mass-murders, with the present of memory, heritage and debt?

Notes

1 Bédarida, François, *Histoire, critique et responsabilité* (Bruxelles, 2003), pp. 305–29.

2 Hartog, François, *Régimes d'historicité, Présentisme et expériences du temps* (Paris, 2003).

3 Dumoulin, Olivier, *Le rôle social de l'historien, De la chaire au prétoire* (Paris, Albin Michel, 2003).

4 Wieviorka, Annette, *L'ère du témoin* (Paris, Plon, 1998); Hartog, François, 'Le témoin et l'historien', *Evidence de l'histoire, Ce que voient les historiens* (Paris, 2005), pp. 191–214.

5 Thomas, Yan, 'La vérité, le temps, le juge et l'historien', *Le Débat* 102 (1998), p. 27.

6 See, in *Le Débat*, 'Vérité judiciaire, vérité historique '; ibidem, pp. 4–51; Ginzburg, Carlo, *Le juge et l'historien,Considérations en marge du procès Sofri*, trad. fr. Lagrasse (Verdier, 1997). For further detail on this see the forthcoming thesis by Cédric Terzi, 'Qu'avez-vous fait de l'argent des Juifs?' (EHESS, 2006).

7 For further detail on this see the forthcoming thesis by Cédric Terzi, 'Qu'avez-vous fait de l'argent des Juifs?' (EHESS, 2006).

8 *Amnistier l'Apartheid, Travaux de la commission Vérité et Réconciliation*, Desmond Tutu (Paris, 2004).

9 Footage from the trials of Klaus Barbie and of Maurice Papon was broadcast by the History Channel in autumn 2000 and in 2005 respectively.

10 Bloch, Marc, *Apologie pour l'histoire ou Métier d'historien* (Paris, 1997), p. 65.

11 *Rapport sur les études historiques* (Paris, 1868), p. 356.

12 Fukuyama, Francis, *La fin de l'histoire et le dernier homme*, trad. fr. (Paris, 1992).

13 Ricœur, Paul, *Temps et récit III* (Paris, Seuil, 1985), p. 313 ; Lepetit, Bernard, 'Le présent de l'histoire', in *Les formes de l'expérience, Une autre histoire sociale* (Paris, 1995), pp. 295–8.

14 Glevarec, Hervé et Guy Saez, *Le patrimoine saisi par les associations* (Paris, 2002), p. 129. The number of listed buildings in France increased from 24,000 in 1960 to 44,709 in 1996.

15 Fabre, Daniel, 'L'histoire a changé de lieux', *Une histoire à soi*, sous la direction de A. Bensa et D. Fabre (Paris, 2001), pp. 32, 33.

16 Glevarec et Saez, *Le patrimoine*, p. 263.

Bibliography

Amnistier l'Apartheid, Travaux de la commission Vérité et Réconciliation, édition établie par Philippe-Joseph Salazar (Paris, Seuil, 2004).

Bédarida, François, *Histoire, critique et responsabilité* (Bruxelles, Complexe, 2003).

Bloch, Marc, *Apologie pour l'histoire ou Métier d'historien* (Paris, Armand Colin, 1997).

Dumoulin, Olivier, *Le rôle social de l'historien, De la chaire au prétoire* (Paris, Albin Michel, 2003).

Fabre, Daniel, 'L'histoire a changé de lieux', *Une histoire à soi*, sous la direction de A. Bensa et D. Fabre (Paris, Éditions de la Maison des Sciences de l'Homme, 2001).

Fukuyama, Francis, *La fin de l'histoire et le dernier homme*, trad. fr. (Paris, Flammarion, 1992).

Ginzburg, Carlo, *Le juge et l'historien. Considérations en marge du procès Sofri*, trad. fr. Lagrasse (Paris, Verdier, 1997).

Glevarec, Hervé et Guy Saez, *Le patrimoine saisi par les associations* (Paris, La Documentation française, 2002).

Hartog, François, *Régimes d'historicité, Présentisme et expériences du temps* (Paris, Seuil, 2003).

—, 'Le témoin et l'historien', *Evidence de l'histoire, Ce que voient les historiens* (Paris, Editions de l'EHESS, 2005), pp. 191–214.

Lepetit, Bernard. 'Le présent de l'histoire', in *Les formes de l'expérience, Une autre histoire sociale* (Paris, Albin Michel, 1995), pp. 295–8.

Ricœur, Paul, *Temps et récit III* (Paris, Seuil, 1985).

Terzi, Cédric, 'Qu'avez-vous fait de l'argent des Juifs?' (EHESS, 2006). (forthcoming dissertation).

Thomas, Yan, 'La vérité, le temps, le juge et l'historien', *Le Débat* 102 (1998), pp. 17–36.

'Vérité judiciaire, vérité historique', *Le Débat* 102 (1998), pp. 4–51.

Wieviorka, Annette, *L'ère du témoin* (Paris, Plon, 1998).

Notes on Contributors

Benjamin Arbel is Professor of Early Modern History and Incumbent of the Chair for the History and Culture of the Jews of Salonica and Greece, School of History, Tel Aviv University. His main publications are: *Trading Nations. Jews and Venetians in the Early Modern Eastern Mediterranean* (Leiden and New York, 1995); *Cyprus, the Franks and Venice* (Aldershot, 2000); *The Italian Renaissance: The Growth of a Secular Culture* (Tel Aviv, 2000); *Venetian Letters from the Archives of the Bank of Cyprus Cultural Foundation and Other Cypriot Collections* (Nicosia, 2007). As editor, his publications include (with D. Jacoby and B. Hamilton) *Latins and Greeks in the Eastern Mediterranean after 1204* (London, 1989); *Intercultural Contacts in the Medieval Mediterranean. Studies in Honour of David Jacoby* (London, 1995); and (with J. Terkel and S. Menache) *Human Beings and other Animals in Historical Perspective* (Jerusalem, 2007).

Ina Baghdiantz McCabe is Professor at the Department of History at Tufts University, USA. She has degrees from the Sorbonne and Columbia and holds an endowed chair in Armenian History. Her publications include: *The Shah's Silk for Europe's Silver: The Eurasian Silk trade of the Julfan Armenians in Safavid Iran and India (1590–1750)* (Philadelphia, 1999), *Orientalism in Early Modern France. Eurasian Trade, Exoticism, and the Ancien Régime* (Oxford, 2008), co-author of *Slaves of the Shah: New Elites of Seventeenth Century Safavid Isfahan* (London, 2003), editor of *Du bon usage du thé et des épices en Asie Réponses à Monsieur Cabart de Villarmont* by Jean Chardin (Paris, 2002) and co-editor of *Diaspora Entrepreneurial Networks. Five Centuries of History* (Oxford, 2005).

John Bintliff is Professor of Classical Archaeology at the University of Leiden, Netherlands. He received his PhD from Cambridge University. Among his many publications are: *The Future of Surface Artefact Survey in Europe* (London, 2000), Bintliff, J. (ed.) *The Blackwell Companion to Archaeology* (London and New York, 2003), with Anthony Snodgrass, *Testing the Hinterland* (Cambridge, 2008).

Penelope J. Corfield is Professor of History at Royal Holloway, University of London. She has been a Visiting Fellow at Nuffield College, Oxford, and at All Souls College, Oxford. She teaches and writes on modern British social, cultural and urban history, as well as on the concepts and theories that underpin history as a field of study. Her latest book is *Time and the Shape of History* (New Haven, 2007).

Walter A. Friedman is Research Fellow at Harvard Business School and a visiting lecturer in Harvard's History Department. He is co-editor of *Business History Review* and a former Trustee of the Business History Conference. He is author of *Birth of a Salesman: The Transformation of Selling in America* (Cambridge, 2004). Currently he is writing a history of the economic forecasting industry and has published 'The Harvard Economic Service and the Problems of Forecasting', *History of Political Economy* 41/1 (2009), pp. 57–88. Along with Geoff Jones he edits the monograph series, Harvard Studies in Business History, published by Harvard University Press.

Gelina Harlaftis is Associate Professor in Maritime History at the Department of History, Ionian University. She has studied at the universities of Athens, Cambridge (MPhil) and Oxford (DPhil). She has been President of the International Maritime Economic History Association (2004–2008), an Alfred D. Chandler Jr International Visiting Scholar at Harvard Business School (2008) and a Visiting Fellow at All Souls, Oxford (2009). Among her publications in English are *Greek Shipowners and Greece, 1945–1975* (London, 1993), *A History of Greek-Owned Shipping* (London, 1996); she has co-authored *Leadership in World Shipping: Greek Family Firms in International Business* (Basingstoke, 2009); she has co-edited, *Global Markets: The Internationalization of Sea Transport Industries since 1850s* (IMEHA, 1998), *Diaspora Entrepreneurial Networks. Five Centuries of History* (Oxford, 2005).

François Hartog is Professor at the École des Hautes Études, Directeur d'études (EHESS), France. He is a specialist in historiography. His major publications include: *Le Miroir d'Hérodote* (Paris, 1980); *Mémoire d'Ulysse* (Paris, 1996); *Régimes d'historicité* (Paris, 2003); *Anciens, modernes, sauvages* (Paris, 2005); *Évidence de l'histoire. Ce que voient les historiens* (Paris, 2005).

Anita Guerreau-Jalabert is Director of Research at CNRS, Honorary Director of the École Nationale des Chartes, France. She is a specialist in western medieval history. Among her publications are: *Index des motifs narratifs dans les romans arthuriens français en vers (XIIe–XIIIe siècle)* (Geneva, 1992); with J.P. Boudet and Michel Sot (eds), *Histoire culturelle de la France, 1, Le Moyen Âge*

(Paris, 1997); 'Nutritus/oblatus: parenté et circulation d'enfants au Moyen Âge', in M. Corbier (sous la direction de), *Adoption et fosterage* (Paris, 2000).

Nikolaos Karapidakis is Professor at the Department of History, Ionian University where he teaches medieval history. He studied at Strasbourg University (1977), at the École Nationale des Chartes (1982) and in the École Pratique des Hautes Études (IVe section) and received his 'Docteur en Histoire' from the University of Paris I Sorbonne. He served as Director of the General State Archives in Greece (1989–1993). He has been Visiting Professor at the University of Montpellier, University of Milan, École Nationale des Chartes, and the École Pratique des Hautes Études. He collaborated with Spyros Asdrachas in the book *Greek Economic History (15th–19th Century)* (Athens, 2003), and is author of a large number of articles and books on the history of institutions, social groups, historiography and Venetian colonial history.

Paschalis Kitromilides is Professor of Political Sciences at the University of Athens; PhD, Harvard University. He is currently Director of the Institute for Neohellenic Research at the National Research Foundation. Among his books in English are *The Enlightenment as Social Criticism* (Princeton, 1992), *Enlightenment, Nationalism, Orthodoxy* (Aldershot, 1994) and *An Orthodox Commonwealth* (Aldershot, 2007).

Peter Mathias is former Chichele Professor of Economic History at Oxford and Master of Downing College (Cambridge), now Emeritus Professor at Cambridge University. He is Honorary President of the International Economic History Association and a Vice-President of the Economic History Society (UK). Among his works are *English Trade Tokens* (London, 1962), *Science and Society* (Cambridge, 1972), *The First Industrial Nation: an Economic History of Britain 1700–1914* (London, 1983), *L'Idea di Europa* (Naples, 2009). He has also edited, with M.M. Postan, *The Cambridge Economic History of Europe (1966–1989)* (Cambridge, 1978), and with J.A. Davis, *The First Industrial Revolutions* (Oxford, 1980). He is General Editor of vol. VI, *The History of Humanity* (Paris, 2008).

Cécile Morrisson is Director of Research (Emeritus) at the CNRS and Advisor for Byzantine Numismatics at Dumbarton Oaks. She is a corresponding member of the Académie des Inscriptions et Belles-Lettres (Paris) and the Academy of Athens. She has written extensively on Byzantine coins and monetary history, notably in the *Economic History of Byzantium* (Washington, 2002), *Oikonomike istoria tou Byzantiou: apo ton 7o eos ton 15o aiona* (Athens, 2007) and coauthored with Angeliki Laiou *The Byzantine Economy* (Cambridge,

2007). She also directed and participated in the three volume series, *Le Monde Byzantin I. L'Empire Romain d'Orient (330–641)* (Paris, 2004) and *II. L'Empire Byzantin (641–1204)* (Paris, 2006) (J.-Cl. Cheynet, éd.) (*O Byzantinos Kosmos, I. H Anatolikè Romaikè Autokratoria (330–641)* (Athens, 2007)).

Robin Osborne is Professor of Ancient History at the University of Cambridge and a Fellow of King's College. His many publications include *Demos: The Discovery of Classical Attika* (Cambridge, 1985), *Classical Landscape with Figures. The Ancient Greek City and its Countryside* (London, 1987), *Greece in the Making 1200–479 BC* (London, 1996), *Archaic and Classical Greek Art* (Oxford, 1998) and seven edited or co-edited collections.

Donald Quataert is Distinguished Professor at Binghamton University at the State University of New York, where he has been teaching since 1987. He is the author of six monographs and the editor or co-editor of a further 10 books dealing with various aspects of Middle East and Ottoman history. His most recent book publication is *Coal Miners and the State in the Ottoman Empire: the Zonguldak Coalfield, 1822–1920* (New York, 2006). He is the holder of grants from the Social Science Research Council, the National Endowment for the Humanities and the John Simon Guggenheim Memorial Foundation. He currently is researching a book on the social history of the late Ottoman Empire.

Kostas Sbonias is Assistant Professor at the Department of History, Ionian University. He has graduated from the University of Athens and has completed his graduate studies in the University of Heidelberg (PhD) and in the Universities of Cambridge and Durham (post-doctoral). He has taught in the Universities of Crete, Thrace and the Open University. He participates in research projects of archaelogical excavations and the study of landscape in Boetia, Crete and the Ionian Islands. He is the author of many studies among which are *Frükretische Siegel: Ansätze für eine Interpretation der sozial-politischen Entwicklung auf Kreta während der Frühbronzezeit* (Oxford, 1995) and *Reconstructing Past Population Trends in Mediterranean* (Oxford, 2000) (ed. with J. Bintliff).

Vaios Vaiopoulos is Assistant Professor at the Department of History, Ionian University. He studied at the University Athens where he carried out his undergraduate and postgraduate studies. His main research interests are in Latin literature during the Augustan period and also on the translation of the Classics in Latin during the Medieval and Renaissance periods on which he has written a significant number of articles and books. His last book is *Plague of the Orientalis Type* (in Greek) (Athens, 2005, with Dimitrios Anogiatis Pelé).

Index